INDIA IN SOVIET GLOBAL STRATEGY

INDIA IN SOVIET GLOBAL STRATEGY

A CONCEPTUAL STUDY

JYOTIRMOY BANERJEE

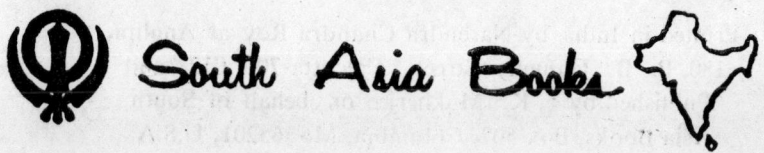

SOUTH ASIA BOOKS
Box—502 : Columbia, Mo. 65201, U.S.A.
In arrangement with
Minerva Associates (Publications) Pvt. Ltd.
7-B, Lake Place, Calcutta-700 029
INDIA

Copyright : J. Banerjee, 1977
First Published : June 1977
ISBN : 0-88386-908-X

Printed in India by Narendra Chandra Roy at Anulipi, 180, B. B. Ganguly Street, Calcutta-700 012, and Published by T. K. Mukherjee on behalf of South Asia Books, Box 502, Columbia, Mo. 65201, U.S.A.

To

MA, DIDI AND SHYAMALI

PREFACE

THIS BOOK responds primarily to two needs. First, it attempts to fuse theory-building efforts in International Relations with traditional area-studies approach. This is partly in response to relatively recent invitation of attention by scholars in that direction.[1] And second, it tries to study the impact of post-Stalin Soviet ideology upon Soviet policy towards India. Indeed, it recedes one more step and posits the question : why do the Russians view India today as they in fact happen to do ? This is not a diplomatic history of Indo- Soviet relations. Its thrust lies in the direction of creating a conceptual framework of Soviet global outlook and policy and examining ideology and policy towards India in that broader context. The chief concern of this approach is how to reorganize published data better so as to generate fresh insights. Hence, this book is as much sensitive to the methodology of organizing knowledge as to substantive issues lying within its purview.

There is fortunately no dearth of Soviet publications on India, and these have been liberally used. The *Soviet Review*, the official bulletin of the Soviet embassy in India, has turned out to be a veritable mine of information of the specifics of Indo-Soviet relations. It frequently carries articles and interviews of high-level officials and Ministers on either side. It has, therefore, been widely used in the penultimate chapter covering economic and trade relations. Quite typically, however, it has nothing to offer on Indo-Soviet military relations.

Before turning to acknowledgements, mention should be made of the influence of systems analysis on the author's thinking. This is reflected in his choice of a number of concepts (e.g., step-function, feedback, etc.) in describing his framework of Soviet foreign policy. They have been used in the same

---

1. See, for example, Frederic J. Fleron, Jr., "Soviet Area Studies and the Social Sciences : Some Methodological Problems in Communist Studies", in his *Communist Studies and the Social Sciences* : *Essays on Methodology and Empirical Theory*, Chicago, Rand McNally, 1969.

sense as Morton Kaplan originally used them in his *System and Process in International Politics* (see bibliography).

The author wishes to acknowledge his debt to the Goethe Institut (Munich) and its Calcutta affiliate, the Max Mueller Bhavan, for his ability to use the original German classics of Marxist thought. His four years of formal study of the German language in Max Mueller Bhavan was rewarded by the Goethe Institut in 1968 with a scholarship to West Germany for studying the language at an advanced level. He is also grateful to the Ramakrishna Mission Institute of Culture (Calcutta) for his working knowledge of Russian which he acquired there during a two-year study programme.

The United States Educational Foundation in India (USEFI) has helped sharpen the author's methodological awareness by placing him in the live environment of the U.S. academia. He studied methodological problems and Soviet affairs at the University of Pennsylvania (Philadelphia) as a Fulbright Scholar during 1974-75 and was exposed to a number of stimulating intra-mural and extra-mural ideas. He is also thankful to the USEFI for a generous book grant which enabled him to procure some valuable materials on Soviet affairs while in the U.S.A. Some of these find their place in this dissertation.

Further, gratitude should also be expressed to the UGC for extending financial support to the research project, as well as to various journals like *Problems of Communism* (Washington, D.C.), *Institute for Defence Studies and Analyses Journal* (New Delhi), *China Report* (Delhi), etc., for encouraging his academic interests by publishing a number of articles by the author on communist affairs.

Last, but not least, the author wishes to record his gratitude to St. Xavier's College (Calcutta) for instilling in him keen interest in International Relations and to the Department of International Relations, Jadavpur University (Calcutta) for numerous instances of encouragement towards developing that interest. Not least among the latter is his present faculty position of a Lecturer there.

Several mentors kept alive, and have given further direction to the author's academic pursuits. Prominent among them are

Fr. J. W. Schneider, S. J. (formerly of St. Xavier's College), Fr. A. Huart, S. J. (Now Vice-Principal, St. Xavier's College), Dr Georg Lechner (former Director, Max Mueller Bhavan, Calcutta), and Dr Jayantanuja Bandyopadhyaya (Professor, Department of International Relations, Jadavpur University). Without Professor Bandyopadhyaya's stimulating guidance this book probably would not have approached anywhere near completion.

P. S. : This book was in the press when in March 1977 the Janata Party assumed power in New Delhi. Hence, most references to the Government of independent India (including the Ministers) are to be construed as those made in the context of Indira Gandhi's Government. Only a brief reference to Gromyko's meeting with the Janata Government has been added in the concluding chapter.

J. B.

Calcutta
June 1977.

CONTENTS

Preface		vii
Chapter I :	Post-Stalin Soviet Foreign Policy : A Theoretical Framework	1
Chapter II :	The Central Dynamics	14
Chapter III :	The Nodal Restraint as Reflected in the Soviet Military and Doctrinal Posture	55
Chapter IV :	The Non-Capitalist Path and India	92
Chapter V :	India's Formative Sector in Soviet Ideology	114
Chapter VI :	Trade, Economic Aid and Collaboration with India	131
Chapter VII :	Conclusion : The Underlying Issues	164
Bibliography		175
Index		200

CHAPTER I

POST-STALIN SOVIET FOREIGN POLICY : A THEORETICAL FRAMEWORK

IN THE PRESENT era of transformation of the structure of international relations,[1] in which the third world in particular stands at a crossroads with uncertainty and apprehension of its future course of development, the multiplying ties between the Soviet Union, a superpower, and India, a front-rank nation of the third world, represent a significant object of study for the student of international relations. This hardly needs much elaboration. Time and again the Czars had eyed the Indian subcontinent interestedly and even for a while had considered reviving the original course of the Oxus to facilitate trade with it.[2] Also, much of the nebulous character of the status of Tibet under international law prior to its occupation by China had grown out of the threat posed by the expanding Russian colossus at the turn of this century as perceived from British India. These considerations, however, receded to the background as a new paradigm of diplomacy and foreign policy was introduced into the international system following the Bolshevik revolution in Russia. Marxist Russia weathered many a storm over the subsequent decades, albeit at a high cost, and pioneered the way, directly and indirectly, for a third of mankind to proclaim Marxism-Leninism as their official creed. The resources and politico-military power mobilized by the U.S.S.R. in the wake of the Second World War placed her on a level comparable to the leading capitalist states of the world. The colossal leader of the socialist bloc has revealed a more or less steady interest in building multi-structured relationships with the second-most populous state in the world over the past two decades. Given the superpower competition for global influence and power and the place of the third world in it, the importance and relevance of the current study can hardly be overestimated.

The standard explanations offered for the development of Indo-Soviet relations in the post-Stalin period are that it was initiated in response to the U.S. befriending of Pakistan and that it has been sustained through the subsequent years right to the present by the additional factor of China's drive toward a prominent power position in the third world generally and in Asia in particular. These monocausal explanations, although correct to a substantial degree, are inadequate in throwing light upon certain fundamental dynamics of Soviet foreign policy. While it is true that the U.S. politico-military backing of Pakistan as well as the elevation of China to the rank of a major Asian power have added momentum to those dynamics, the latter themselves did not result from them. A central concern of this book will be to lay bare the aforementioned nodal dynamics of Soviet foreign policy, only in the light of which Soviet third-world policy, especially that relating to India, can be adequately grasped.

This line of argument perhaps already sets the tone of this book and reflects its orientation. While the importance of empirical referents in any scientific study worth the name is beyond question, an in-depth comprehension of the object of study may sometimes be better achieved with a set of theoretical formulations. In the present case, for instance, the two empirically valid data mentioned above do explain, albeit inadequately, the cementing forces of Indo-Soviet relations. However, to keep the focus of analysis confined to such juxtaposed cause-and-effect sequences would be to opt for a rather simplistic method ; it would barely scratch the surface of the material under study, given its nature. Instead of constricting the focus on piecemeal empirical referents, this study will endeavour to organize a set of central premises of Soviet foreign policy, to explain how they relate to India, and to use empirical referents as props, not as nodal structures.

Traditionally, single-factor analyses have dominated Soviet studies, prominently featuring among them the power vs. ideology approaches. Among the more recent approaches a major work in the field by Jan Triska and David Finley has spelt out a changed paradigm in terms of a multivariegated analysis of the making of Soviet foreign policy.[3] Since the present study is not concerned with the decision-making processes of Soviet foreign policy, there is no need to follow its imaginative but grossly detailed institutional model of the Soviet foreign policy decision-making apparatus. To classify and assimilate data in terms of these institutions would mean a shift of the analytical focus from the central dynamics of Soviet foreign policy—a major concern here—and getting involved in its complicated organizational evolution, reliable data for which is hard to come by in any case. That is not the aim of this book. Consequently, this study does not tread the new path opened up by Triska and Finley.

This does not imply, however, that the analysis is fully tradition-bound either. It "dialectically" transcends the power vs. ideology approaches in adopting its method of inquiry. The central hypothesis on which the latter is based affords a proper perspective of interaction between the phenomena of power and ideology. To be sure, the major material on which a study such as the present one has to be based remains the spate of the carefully "doctored" printed matter emanating from the Soviet Union. There is also a whole spectrum of emphases in the non-communist world on the degree of its acceptability. Scholars like Hans J. Morgenthau, Robert V. Daniels and Samuel L. Sharp, for instance, reject the idea of doctrinal motivation behind Soviet foreign policy.[4] Marxist doctrine for them merely serves as an ex-post facto rationalization. A large number of scholars, on the other hand, do not reject the role of doctrinal belief systems in the essential sweep of Soviet foreign policy, although they are by no means unanimous regarding the degree of their effectiveness. Zbigniew K. Brzezinski, Richard Lowenthal, R. N. Carew Hunt, Bertram D. Wolfe and Herbert Marcuse, among others, take the universe of Marxist-Leninist doctrine more seriously.[5] The first three scholars point out individually that certain Soviet foreign policy moves such as the massive socio-economic transformation of eastern Europe in the wake of the Second World War cannot be sufficiently explained in total isolation from doctrinal variables. Lowenthal also imputes ideological conditioning to the Soviet interpretation of the Yalta agreements, and Marshall D. Shulman traces some of the roots of the cold war back the same.[6] While Adam B. Ulam[7] and Brzezinski have maintained that the role of doctrine in the domestic context is becoming increasingly irrelevant, others have pointed to the likely continuation of Marxism-Leninism in the Soviet Union as a factor legitimizing continued rule by the CPSU.[8] Whether hard core Marxist-Leninist tenets are about to "erode" or are likely to continue to mould Soviet perceptions may be a debatable point. The fact remains, however, that a large body of scholarly opinion is in favour of allotting weight to doctrinal factors affecting Soviet foreign policy. Coupled with this remains the problem of the lack of other primary sources of research, which leaves, as already mentioned, only the way to official and semi-official publications open. This is illustrated by the fact that even more recent approaches to the study of Soviet foreign policy (e.g., the interest-group approach, content analysis and the technique of DSQ-analysis constructed by Triska and Finley, etc.) rely heavily on the printed word from the U.S.S.R.[9]

For the purposes of this study ideology is seen as a meaningful vocabulary, flexing its form and transforming its content in response to the dynamics of reality. It may, at times, reinforce Soviet power and be itself reinforced by the latter. Soviet "ideology", in the sense Brzezinski imputed to it,[10] is not something immutable. The central tenets of Marxism-Leninism which are, in fact, largely immutable (e.g., the tenet of class-struggle) are called "theory" by Brzezinski for the purpose of distinguishing them from a large number of derivative intellectual constructs which are together called "ideology". Ideology, in this narrower, more specific sense, stands, as it were, like a bridge between "theory" and the ever-evolving reality. Its purpose is to reflect and explain more specific segments of reality in the light of theory. Changes in ideological formulations of the Soviet Union have been noticed not infrequently, and they have caused confusion among many observers. Doubts have been raised regarding the doctrinal conviction of the Soviet decision-makers. However, ideology seen in the light of Brzezinski's typology serves to give a powerful insight into the Soviet decision-makers' interpretation of reality, which, in its turn, can give useful clues to an understanding of Soviet perceptions and values. William Zimmerman's study of the impact of the international system upon Soviet perceptions parallels this approach. Similarly, R. Barry Farrell stresses the hypotheses that ideological factors are given great emphasis in closed societies and that they colour the perceptions of their decision-makers.[11] In short, if ideology is seen as a different language, sensitive and responsive to changing reality while always making its rearrangements in terms of the immutable grammar called theory, then its validity as a tool for analysis of Soviet foreign policy remains.

Soviet publications on international affairs abound as much as stereotype expressions in them flourish, and these do not make reading particularly stimulating. However, if it is assumed that the concepts expressed are but a different way of intellectual structuring and reproducing reality, are "constructs" in Kerlinger's sense,[12] which become intelligible in the light of core doctrinal tenets and shifting empirical reality, then their analysis could yield at least a modest amount of reward. Charles Gati, however, would raise a well-taken contrapoint at this juncture.[13] Discussing the usefulness of the concept of the DSQ of Triska and Finley as a means of content analyzing Soviet texts, he grants the possibility that there can be link between political vocabulary and thought patterns. But he then goes on to question the assumption that there is a necessary linkage between the latter and action. It is true that what one preaches one may not practice. In the specific instance of Soviet foreign policy, however, there is sufficient evidence of a correlation between publicized conceptualizations and foreign policy operation. Exceptions do not necessarily invalidate it.

The analytical method of this study rests largely upon the aforementioned conclusion and borrows freely, though not exclusively, of Herbert Marcuse's "immanent critique".[14] The latter assumes that ideological pronouncements emanating from the Soviet Union are to be taken seriously, and that any critical investigation should start by accepting their theoretical premises and examining the soundness of logic binding the manifold extrapolations. In other words, an immanent critique of Soviet Marxism limits itself to testing its inner coherence and logicality. It, therefore, allows for dealing with the Marxist paradigm *in its own terms* and avoids superfluous criticism from outside Marxist premises. This method would thus seem to be a rigorous and sophisticated intellectual apparatus, especially when its results are tested against empirical reality.

There is no dearth of literature on the theme at hand, a fact which is quite commensurate with its international significance. Volumes have been written, especially in India, covering, as far as possible, every nook and corner of the evolution of Indo-Soviet relations. Among the number of books published in India, almost all have been diachronic-idiographic studies cataloguing notable events. While a few of these works have had the same specific focus as the present study—namely, Soviet policy towards India—the majority of them have been concerned with Indo-Soviet relations, i.e., with a tangential, and broader, theme. Among these diachronic-idiographic studies produced in India, a considerable proportion is of the "bhai-bhai" type.[15] They make no attempt at maintaining scholarly detachment and objectivity and tend to portray Indo-Soviet relations as an immutable phenomenon in a milieu of fluctuating international relations. Tending to generally gloss over the embarassing phases of Indo-Soviet relations (e.g., during Stalin's rule or in the 1960's following the partial swing of Soviet foreign policy towards Pakistan), these works serve as little more than propaganda platforms and surplus relay systems for ideas emanating from Moscow.

The less profuse number of works on Indo-Soviet relations which have appeared in Europe and the U.S.A. are generally written with greater competence and objectivity.[16] The analyses of Arthur Stein, Charles B. McLane, Dietmar Rothermund and Robert H. Donaldson, for instance, stand out for their parsimony in juxtaposing data and cogent argumentation. Nevertheless, they have one central element in common with their Indian counterparts, viz., their diachronic-idiographic arrangement. None of the works perused for the preparation of this study has been able to create any theoretical insights into the subject. All of them have meticulously chronicled events and have commented upon them piecemeal. While Donaldson's work focuses upon Soviet ideological writings on India, it also does not offer any theoretical treatment. Although there has been no lack of intelligent guesses, no attempt has been made to integrate the processes of Soviet foreign policy in the light of a broad theoretical framework. It is this lack of a theoretical integration of the present topic that provides the raison d'etre for this study. Hitherto all that has been available has been a rehash of the same diplomatic history.

The material and the method of this study stand in a mutually reinforcing and interacting relationship. A theoretical framework is but a convenient structure designed to arrest data and logical relationships which might otherwise escape the researcher's attention. It helps generate questions and problems which can normally remain buried under an ever-multiplying volume of empirical data, given today's information explosion. At the same time the data chosen through a given framework may demand further sophistication and structural adjustment of the latter so as to lend themselves more satisfactorily to analysis. Method and object of study, hence, should ideally be as compatible as possible.

This is not the place to introduce elaborate arguments in favour of studies in theory. Suffice it to say that the modern accent of international relations lies distinctly on the latter. Conventional chronicling of diplomatic events is considered today useful but inadequate. The structure of the present study reflects, what Johann Galtung has called, the "nomothetic" type.[17] In his essay entitled "The Social Sciences. An Essay on Polarization and Integration", he makes a distinction between "idiographic" and "nomothetic" studies. The following diagrams are reproduced from the essay to clarify the distinctiveness of the two approaches.[18]

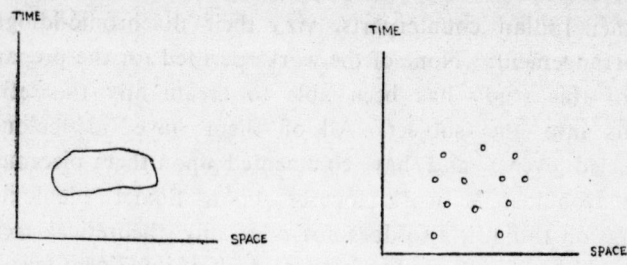

The Idiographic Approach   The Nomothetic Approach

According to Galtung :

> In the idiographic approach a contiguous Space-Time region is selected and the investigator proceeds according to the classical rules of drama, preserving the unity of action, Time and Space.... The goal in the idiographic approach is to bring in everything that is relevant, to enrich the presentation with much detail, to fill in gaps in Time and Space by collecting more data within the region delimited.[19]

While detailed substantiation of generalizations is unavoidable in this dissertation, its overall framework reflects the nomothetic pattern, which, according the Galtung :

> ...is also based on the collection of data from Space-Time points or even regions—but those points or regions are no longer contiguous, but scattered. The nomothetic approach is based on a higher level of abstraction and has a quite different target : some problem is formulated according to which a universe of Space-Time points or regions is defined as relevant for the testing of the hypothesis.[20]

The present study, therefore, attempts to fill the gap left open by the existing idiographic studies on Soviet policy toward India. Consequently, the main emphasis of this dissertation is not on discovery of new facts but rather upon revealing new implications of and relationships between the facts already available in the oft-repeated chronology of events. The thrust is in the direction of arranging the material of this study around a set of concept-oriented questions and problems in order to generate greater insights and higher levels of generalizations than have been offered hitherto. First, an attempt is made to reveal the "central dynamics" of Soviet foreign policy, a concept which relates to the Soviet proclivity to change the world in accordance with Marxist tenets. Next comes an analysis of the major environmental influence on the "central dynamics" called here the "nodal restraint". The latter is a fundamental restraint imposed upon Soviet foreign policy by the present nuclear age which makes any Soviet confrontation with the West anywhere in the world highly risky. It, therefore, tends to weaken the impulse behind the central dynamics of Soviet foreign policy.

From the counterposing of the two antithetic concepts sketched above, a synthetic scenario of the operation of the post-Stalinist Soviet foreign policy is drawn. When Soviet ideas on and policy towards India are studied in the light of such synthetic scenario they become far more intelligible than when studied without that context. It is hoped that the framework schematically offered in the following page would afford a better grasp of the subject.

The theoretical framework sketched so far is of a general character. The two major components constituting it, as has been shown, are the constructs "central dynamics" and "nodal restraint", and it has been maintained that the Soviet foreign policy towards India can be better understood in the light of the interaction between them. In a study such as this, which is restricted in time and space, the introduction of certain other idiographic variables into the broad framework becomes unavoidable for arresting the tendency of its frame of reference from becoming, what Oran Young has called, a "logical closure",[21] and for endowing it with adequate empirical content which it deserves. Hence, a balance has to be struck at some point between theorizing in pure abstraction and concentrating solely on the universe of empirical referents. A study of the Soviet foreign policy towards India,

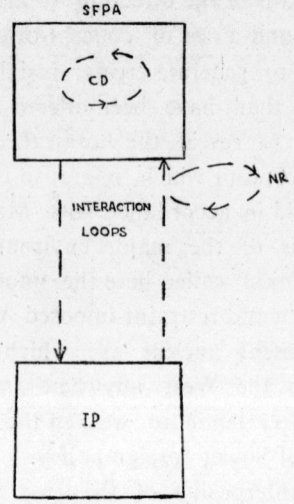

SFPA—Soviet Foreign Policy Apparatus
CD   —Central Dynamics
NR   —Nodal Restraint
IP   —Indian Polity

by virtue of its specificity, has to take into account a number of important variables characterizing the South Asia political environment and affecting such policy. However, it is the contention here that such variables (e.g., China's policy towards South Asia) can be reasonably accommodated and absorbed by the general frame-work proposed; they do not, therefore, provide empirical contradiction of the latter but rather supplement it.

A purely power-political frame of reference would have simplified problems confronted by this study. It can be shown, a la journalism, that the Soviet policy towards India has been motivated by such considerations of power as containing China, elimination of Western influence, and extension of the Soviet influence to the South Asia subcontinent. A sufficient number of newspaper reports and editorials, arranged and dressed up in accordance with Hans Morgenthau's "political realism", would do an admirable job. However, such an analysis, which hardly makes any distinction, for example, between the foreign policies of the communist states on the one hand and those of the West on the other, and posits the power-maximizing motivation of foreign policy without further reference to aims, values and other longer-term considerations, would surely be inadequate. Morgenthau's "realism", although it reveals an important characteristic of the foreign policies of a number of states (with as many notable exceptions), has long been rejected on grounds of inadequate explanatory power. An expretation must go for a deeper probe into the subject searching out relatively more enduring underlying trends, if any.[22] Since the degree of the explanatory power of a theory is reflected in the inverse ratio between its explanans and explananda, the current framework with its basic two-component structure should be judged in this light as to its plausibility.

The next two chapters concentrate on a detailed exposition of the twin concepts of central dynamics and nodal restraint, respectively, and attempt at their substantiation. The remaining chapters are, in a theoretical sense, extrapolations from this basic framework. The data covered in them can be perceived to be organically linked with the latter.

REFERENCES

1. For an illuminating discussion on this theme, see Marshall D. Shulman, *Beyond the Cold War*, Yale University Press, New Haven and London, 1966, Chapter 2.

2. For rather Quixotic Czarist designs on India, see H. Sutherland Edwards, *Russian Projects against India. From the Czar Peter to General Skobeleff*, Remington & Co. Publishers, London, 1885.

3. Jan F. Triska and David D. Finley, *Soviet Foreign Policy*, Macmillan, Toronto, 1969.

4. Hans J. Morgenthau, *Politics among Nations* (Indian ed.), Scientific Book Agency, Calcutta, 1966.

Samuel L. Sharp, "National Interest : Key to Soviet Politics", in Erik P. Hoffmann and Frederic J. Fleron, Jr. (eds), *The Conduct of Soviet Foreign Policy*, Aldine, Chicago, 1971, pp. 108-117.

Robert V. Daniels, "Doctrine and Foreign Policy", in Hoffmann and Fleron, *op. cit.*, pp. 154-164.

5. Z. K. Brzezinski, *Ideology and Power in Soviet Politics*, Praeger, New York, 1962, Introduction and Part II.

Richard Lowenthal, "The Logic of One-Party Rule" and "A Difference in Kind", in Hoffmann and Fleron, *op. cit.*, pp. 117-130, and pp. 134-135, respectively.

R. N. Carew Hunt, "Importance of Doctrine", in Hoffmann and Fleron, *op. cit.*, pp. 101-108.

Bertram D. Wolfe, "Communist Ideology and Soviet Foreign Policy", *Foreign Affairs*, New York, Vol. 41, No. 1 (Oct. 1962), pp, 152-170.

Herbert Marcuse, *Soviet Marxism. A Critical Analysis*, Pelican, London, 1971.

6. Lowenthal, "The Logic of One-Party Rule", *op. cit.*, pp. 123-124. Shulman, *op. cit.*, Chapter I.

7. Adam B. Ulam, "Soviet Ideology and Soviet Foreign Policy", in Hoffmann and Fleron, *op. cit.*, pp. 136-153.

8. See, for instance, Wolfe, *op. cit.*, pp. 169-170.

9. For one of the insightful new approaches to the study of Soviet foreign policy, see "Techniques of Analysis : What Soviet Politics Looks and Sounds Like", Sidney I. Ploss (ed.), *The Soviet Political Process. Aims, Techniques, and Examples of Analysis*, Gim & Co., Massachusetts, 1971, introductory article, Part II.

10. Brzezinski, *op. cit.*

11. William Zimmerman, *Soviet Perspectives on International Relations. 1956-1967*, Princeton, New Jersey, 1969.

R. Barry Farrell, "Foreign Policies of Open and Closed Political Societies", from R. Barry Farrell (ed.), *Approaches to Comparative and International Politics*, Northwestern University Press, Evanston, 1966.

12. Fred N. Kerlinger, *Foundations of Behavioral Research*, New York, 1964, p. 4n, quoted in Stephen L. Wasby, *Political Science. The Discipline and Its Dimensions* (Indian ed.), Scientific Book Agency, Calcutta, 1970, p. 64.

13. Charles Gati, "History, Social Science, and the Study of Foreign Policy", Hoffmann and Fleron, *op. cit.*, pp. 11-17.

14. Marcuse, *op. cit.*, see Introduction.

15. See, for example, Devendra Kaushik, *Soviet Relations with India and Pakistan*, Vikas, Delhi, 1971.

Jagdish Bibhakar, *A Model Relationship. 25 Years of Indo-Soviet Diplomatic Ties*, Punjabi Publishers, New Delhi, 1972.

Litto Ghosh and Kartar Singh (eds.), *Unity in Diversity. 50 Glorious Years of Union of Soviet Socialist Republics*, Indo-Soviet Cultural Society, New Delhi.

Trevor Drieberg, Harji Malik and D. K. Joshi, *Towards Close Indo-Soviet Coopeartion*, Vikas, Delhi, 1974.

16. Reference is to the following works :

Arthur Stein, *India and the Soviet Union. The Nehru Era*, University of Chicago Press, Chicago and London, 1969.

Charles B. McLane, *Soviet-Asian Relations*, Vol. II of *Soviet-Third World Relations*, London, Central Asian Research Centre, 1973.

Dietmar Rothermund, *Indien und die Sowjetunion*, Arbeitsgemeinschaft fuer Osteuropaforschung, Boehlau Verlag, Tuebingen, 1968.

Robert H. Donaldson, *Soviet Policy Toward India : Ideology and Strategy*, Harvard University Press, Cambridge, Massachusetts, 1974.

Harish Kapur's work, although published from London, forms an exception here in its triteness. See his *The Soviet Union and the Emerging Nations. A Case Study of Soviet Policy Towards India*, Michael Joseph Ltd, London, 1972.

17. Johan Galtung, "The Social Sciences. An Essay on Polarization and Integration", in Klaus Knorr and James N. Rosenau (eds.), *Contending Approaches to International Politics*, Princeton, New Jersey, Princeton University Press, 1969.

18. Galtung, *op. cit.*, p. 251.

19. Galtung, *op. cit.*, pp. 251-252.

20. Galtung, *op. cit.*, p. 252.

21. Oran R. Young, "The Perils of Odysseus : On Constructing Theories of International Relations", in Raymond Tanter and Richard H. Ullman (eds.), *Theory and Policy in International Relations*. Princeton. University Press, Princeton, 1972.

22. Expretation involves "a *deeper analysis*, one often involving a reference to levels of reality (usually deeper) other than the level to which the explanandum belongs." See Mario Bunge, *Scientific Research II*, Springer Verlag, New York, 1967, p. 29.

Chapter II

THE CENTRAL DYNAMICS

THE CENTRAL DYNAMICS of the Soviet foreign policy is the perennial obsession with transforming the structure and processes of the international system. The term dynamics here connotes, to borrow the concept of Talcott Parsons, a "mechanism" which influences the functioning of a system[1].

To be sure, there have been moments of ebb in the Russian Marxist urge to that transformation,[2] moments dictated by such situational determinants as obtaining during the signing of the Treaty of Brest-Litovsk, the Molotov-Ribbentrop Pact, etc. However, the fact remains beyond dispute that during more opportune time-frames the Bolshevik revolutionaries and their successors have not relented in their endeavour to recast the world in terms of their "theory" in its special sense.[3] The post-Stalin era has witnessed a *fundamental change* in the over all *mode*, but not the *essential content*, of that dynamics. This is a notable distinction that characterizes the anti-status quo nature of the Soviet foreign policy and sets it apart from that of, for instance, Tsarist foreign policy.

This chapter makes an exposition of the central dynamics and illustrates it in a historical perspective in the Indian context. It then goes on to examine three major variables affecting its operation—the U.S. foreign policy and the Soviet domestic economic necessities blunting its edge while rivalry with China acting as a reinforcing agent. An important factor generating this distinctive feature of Soviet foreign policy is the domestic milieu of the U.S.S.R. and the complex system of beliefs and values that adds cohesion to it. Marxists have long considered foreign policy to be an extension of the domestic compendium of interests and values, and recently Western International Relations specialists have increasingly been concentrating their academic endeavour on "linkages" existing between them.[4] When it is argued that the central dynamics of Soviet foreign policy remains the steady commitment to global transformation, this need not conjure up the vision of a kind of neo-Tsarist ambition on a global scale. Indeed, the intervening variable in this case would be the Soviet domestic scene which radically differs from any prior domestic milieux in Russia under Tsardom. Marxist-Leninist categories of thought, concepts and values orient the Soviet foreign policy to categories of reality at significant variance with those familiar to the noncommunist states. An appreciation of this is essential to a proper grasp of the central dynamic.

As Henry A. Kissinger explains :

> The essence of Marxism-Leninism—and the reason that normal diplomacy with Communist states is so difficult—is the view that "objective" factors such as the societal structure, the economic process, and, above all, the class struggle are more important than the personal convictions of statesmen.[5]

Further :

> The reliance on objective factors has complicated negotiations between the West and the Communist countries. Communist negotiators find it difficult to admit that they could be swayed by the arguments of men who have, by definition, an inferior grasp of the laws of historical development. No matter what is said, they think that they understand their Western counterpart better than he understands himself. Concessions are possible, but they are made to "reality", not to individuals or to a bargaining process. Diplomacy becomes difficult when one of the parties considers the key element to negotiation—the give-and-take of the process of bargaining—as but a superstructure for factors not part of the negotiation itself.[6]

The above characterization of the nature of the Soviet diplomacy is more cogent and subtle than the oversimplified postulates of the "realist" school. The decline of the classical diplomacy in the aftermath of the Second World War, which is lamented by the latter,⁷ is not least due to a whole array of doctrinal factors feeding the central dynamics of the Soviet foreign policy. It is precisely these factors that may yet obstruct a full revival of classical diplomacy informed by political prudence and enlightened national interest, as recommended by the "realist" school. Brzezinski points out, for instance, that "the Soviet Communist ideology has made an important contribution toward the transformation of international politics from a 'game' with certain commonly accepted rules into a profoundly intense conflict."⁸ Whether the present "era of negotiations" is but a prelude to such revival remains to be seen.

This is not to deny, however, the hard core of power calculations involved in the central dynamics of the Soviet foreign policy. Soviet politicians are also, after all, politicians who are faced with the daily task of surmounting obstacles and overwhelming—within limits—recalcitrant circumstances in trying to give material content to their transformationist urge. Hence, the Soviet ideology as an action programme can hardly operate outside the realm of power. In Brzezinski's words :

> ...When the movement [with a history of acute ideological ferment]* is built around an ideology that combines both an overt statement of normative ends and a set of intellectual categories for analyzing changes in the existing reality with specific guides to action, then considerations of ideology and power become so enmeshed in the performance of a particular political act that to isolate one from the other is to deny that which is precisely most characteristic of the movement—the blending of ideology with power.⁹

Brzezinski goes on to argue that while in its short-term aspects Soviet foreign policy is concerned with issues like national security, frontiers, national power, etc.—issues which normally engage attention of all states—these are not considered to be ends in themselves. They are viewed in terms of certain long-range perspectives :

> ...While the concept of "national interest" may not be irrelevant to an understanding of Communist foreign policy, to be useful it must be linked to the ultimate ideological objective.[10]

A dovetailing of national and international interests, hence, become part of ideology itself.

The central dynamics of Soviet foreign policy, which is generated by thought categories and concepts moulded by ideology in the light of theory, influences and creates in its turn further concepts and constructs. The net result of such interaction is seen in the traditional Soviet perception of hostility in the noncommunist environment, particularly in the advance capitalist world. It has been well-nigh impossible for the Soviet leaders for the past half-a-century to view the capitalist states in a light other than that of antagonistic contradiction. Two years after the Bolshevik revolution Lenin noted with satisfaction :

> The bourgeoisie are terror-stricken at the growing workers' revolutionary movement. This is understandable if we take into account that the development of events since the imperialist war invevitably favours the workers' revolutionary movement, and that the world revolution is beginning and growing in intensity everywhere.[11]

Three decades later, Stalin in his last political tract stated :

> It should be observed that the USA, and Great Britain and France, themselves contributed—without themselves desiring it, of course—to the formation and consolidation of the new, parallel world market. They imposed an economic blockade on the USSR, China and the European people"s democracies, which did not join the "Marshall plan" system, thinking thereby to strangle them. The effect, however, was not to strangle, but to strengthen the new world market.[12]

During his India-sojourn in 1973, Brezhnev struck a familiar note :

> It is surely appropriate to recall......the words of Karl Marx who likened progress under capitalism to a cruel deity that would drink nectar only from the skulls of those it had slain.[13]

A standard and stereotype image is common to all three statements selected at random from different contextual and time dimensions. All three Soviet leaders perceive capitalist hostility, even though they are separated from each other by different time zones. Such perceived hostility stimulates suspicions and confirms fears, and Soviet foreign policy makes shifts and adjustments accordingly in order to meet the open or insidious "capitalist threat". This process sets off a corresponding reaction in the West. A spiral of interstimulating suspicion, fear and hostility thus develops a momentum of its own. In fact, scholars like Robert North, Ole Holsti, Richard Brody, Dina Zinnes, etc. have improved upon the simplistic stimulus-response model for the study of international relations by introducing perception (stimulus-perception-response) as a crucial factor.[14] Brzezinski notes, for example, that :

> Soviet insistence (derived from the conceptual elements of ideology......and from their general impact on Soviet foreign policy) that ultimate peace depends on the total victory of a particular social system led by a particular political party injects into international affairs an element of a fundamental struggle for survival not conducive to conflict resolution.[15]

Shulman in his analysis of the cold war strikes a similar chord :

> The whole notion of the Soviet revolution as a first episode in worldwide proletarian overturning of other governments, however unrelated to reality, predisposed the Soviet leaders to perceive hostility and inevitable conflict in its foreign relations, and provoked a fear abroad against the promise of "the worldwide triumph of Communist revolution"—a fear which reciprocally confirmed Soviet suspicions and nourished its expectations.[16]

Finally, Kissinger voices the same opinion :

>......Communist ideology is, in part, responsible for international tensions. This is less because of specific Marxist tactical prescriptions—with respect to which Communists have shown a high degree of flexibility—than because of the basic Marxist-Leninist categories for interpreting reality.[17]

A Diachronic Perspective :
The Central Dynamics and India, 1917-1949

There are a number of works available on the subject of the varying analyses of the Indian scene by the Comintern and the CPSU over the several decades that marked the rule of Lenin and Stalin in Russia.[18] The purpose of this survey is not to provide primarily the history of Soviet policy toward India under Lenin and Stalin but rather to illustrate the operation of the central dynamics component of Soviet foreign policy as related to India. The spate of analyses, formulation and reformulation of intellectual constructs, and the often doctrinaire outlook which become evident from this survey highlight that component suitably. The passion for changing the world—and, hence, India too—blends inextricably with security and other considerations of the interests of the Soviet state. The resulting fluctuations in the conceptualization of India and the corresponding adjustments in foreign policy provide a good example of the central dynamics.

The point may be raised here whether the Comintern and Soviet policies can be considered identical. According to all available evidences, however, the difference between the two—if ever there was any—existed only in the first few years. The fact that Bolshevik Russia was the only Marxist state in the world effectively established in power at the time of the founding of the Comintern and that it was hosting the organization (despite intentions of shifting it later to Germany) led to the dominant role of the Russians within it. According to Nollau, since the latter were required to assume "the burden of the work" of the Comintern right from the beginning, "they took over not only the work of the International but also the power".[19] Further, the Russians turned out to be the most powerful group within the Executive Committee of the Comintern (ECCI). Since the Second Comintern Congress they had the right to send five delegates while the other parties were allowed one each.[20] They also had effective control over representatives of youth and trade union representatives, while Radek, officially representing Poland, was no less in the service of the Russians.[21] Lenin's intentions notwithstanding, Russian influence dominated the Comintern and virtually turned its sections and sub-sections into channels for the Soviet foreign policy operations under Stalin's regime.[22] The Soviet Military Intelligence Service, for instance, was utilizing the Comintern's foreign contacts for its own purposes at the turn of the 1930's, while the OGPU got busy penetrating into the internal organs of the organization.[23] The dissolution of the latter in May, 1943 was the result of the decision taken by Stalin to assuage the feelings of his wartime allies and not in consequence of a ECCI resolution, as claimed at the time. In fact, the ECCI was not even technically competent to dissolve the organization.[24]

Hence, for the purposes of the present analysis, it would not be perhaps far-fetched to consider both the Comintern and other Soviet writings and debates on India under the common rubric of the central dynamics of Soviet foreign policy.

A distinctive feature of the intellectual history of Marxism-Leninism has been the transformationist attention paid to those regions of the world which are now collectively called the third world. Marx had written about how the global function of capital was generating a process of drastic socio-economic restructuring of the colonial areas. In the *Communist Manifesto*, he observed that the opening up of new market areas such as eastern India gave trade, shipping and industry of Europe a tremendous boost as well as hastened the process of the decay of feudalism.[25] From the 1850's on, Marx became interested in India and prepared notes on her history, devoting over two-thirds of it to events under British rule.[26] In 1853, he wrote a series of articles on India for the American newspaper, *New-York Herald Tribune*.[27] He noted in one of them the impact of the forces of transformation which had been set in motion by the British. "British steam and science uprooted, over the whole surface of Hindustan, the union between agricultural and manufacturing industry."[28] He concluded from his observations that "...whatever may have been the crimes of England she was the unconsious tool of history in bringing about that revolution."[29]

Marx, however, was preoccupied in the main with problems nearer home. Lenin, the organizer and practitioner of politics, initiated the Soviet tradition of assessing trends in the then colonial areas of the world within the Marxist conceptual framework. The history of the Soviet analyses of colonial problems and socio-economic trends reveals considerable fluctuation and variety which are partly attributable to particular diplomatic and contextual dimensions which the Soviet state had to accept as given from time to time. The Soviet ideological line vis-a-vis India, for instance, tended to be sensitive to oscillations in Anglo-Soviet relations. The proclivity, however, to theorize, to reshape or form socio-economic concepts relating to India and other colonial and backward areas remained a more or less perennial feature reflecting the interplay of the power and ideological components of the Soviet foreign policy. An overview of the Soviet ideological concern with India, especially in its special manifest form of the Communist International, will serve to illustrate this.

As early as October 31, 1917 a communist agency called League for the Liberation of the East put out a call for the overthrow of imperialism in the orient. On November 24, the same year, the newly installed Council of People's Commissars in Russia called out to India and the Middle East to shake off Western tyranny.[30] In the following spring, the Bolshevik government made public a Blue Book containing secret documents on relations between Czarist Russia and British India. Its editor, K.M. Troyanovsky, indicated the Bolshevik assessment of India's conditions at the time. Criticizing the British rule in and economic exploitation of India, he visualized Indians as yearning for liberation. Hence, he concluded, India would be a natural ally for Bolshevik Russia.[31]

In May, 1918 it was announced by Bolshevik Russia that

communist propaganda would be disseminated in India. In March, the following year, the First Comintern Congress noted that the recently concluded World War had been fought with the help of the colonies, prominent among which was India. It was further perceived that the revolutionary ferment in India had not been absent for a single day.[32] During July-August, 1920 the Second Comintern Congress was held. In consequence, a Central Asiatic Bureau (also called the Turk-Bureau) was set up to propagate communism in a number of directions including India, and an agreement was reached on holding a congress in Baku of the peoples of the Near, Middle and Far East. The congress was held in September. Zinoviev, the Comintern President, stressed at the congress that the entire East ought to follow the example of the Bolshevik revolution, while Karl Radek insisted on similar revolutionary activities in the East along with violent Anglophobia. He declared that there could be no permanent peace "between the countries of labour and the countries of exploitation".[33]

In the same fall, the Politburo of the Russian Communist Party and the Council of People's Commissars approved M. N. Roy's plan of liberating India with the help of the Red Army, the Afghans and the expected indigenous uprisings in India. The Central Asiatic Bureau, of which Roy was a prominent member, had been instrumental in liberating the Khanate of Bukhara, and this might have added to the credibility of Roy's ambitious project. The latter, however, fell through.

The Second Comintern Congress also featured the Lenin-Roy controversy over the role of the bourgeoisie in the colonies. While Lenin perceived that the bourgeoisie in the colonies had a revolutionary role to play and, hence, required the Comintern to cooperate with it, M. N. Roy was more pessimistic in his assessment and required the leading revolutionary role in the colonies to be assigned to proletarian parties. The subsequent compromise marked Lenin's victory, albeit in a modified form.

During June-July 1921 the Third Comintern Congress was held. It laid emphasis upon the need to organize communist parties in the East in view of the perceived close ties of the bourgeoisie there with foreign capital. It also emphasized that henceforth the communist parties in the imperialist countries were to take greater responsibility in propagating aud organizing communism in the respective colonies.[36] Following the Congress, the Tashkent school and the Central Asiatic Bureau were abolished to assuage British feelings. It was decided, however, to set up a University of the Toilers of the East in Moscow.[37]

On October 27, 1921 the Comintern's labour wing, the Red International of Labour Unions, invited the AITUC to join it in the solidarity movement of international labour.[38] Two months later, an appeal was sent in the name of the Indian Communist Party to the Ahmedabad meeting of the Indian National Congress to lead India's revolution[39] reflecting Moscow's interest in India's non-cooperation movement. M. N. Roy's articles appearing in *Advance Guard* during the following year reflected the Comintern's policy of encouraging a communist takeover of the INC leadership.[40] The same year, the inaugural issue of *Novyi Vostok* revealed again the Soviet interest in India's nationalist movement.[41] An article on Gandhi appearing in the May 1922 issue of *Mezhdunarodnaya Zhizn* was only mildly critical; he was called a "petty landowner" and his ideas were branded "utopian", but he was also credited with uniting India and rousing her consciousness.[42]

During the Fourth Comintern Congress held that year, its chairman, Zinoviev, professed optimism about the results of the Comintern's policy towards India. Karl Radek, however, was more cautious; while congratulating Roy on his good work, he pointed out that the trade union movement or strikes in India had not yet been organized by the communists.[43] The congress adopted theses on colonial questions extending ideological support to a large number of Asian colonies and semi-colonies, although, admittedly, the bourgeoisie of India, Egypt, China, etc. were about to compromise with their foreign rulers. The congress observed in its "Theses on the Eastern Question" that whereas agrarian problems were of primary importance for countries like India, the national bourgeoisie of these countries were not living up to their historic mission of speeding up the decay of feudalism. "It is precisely this lack of resolution that hinders the organisation of the toiling masses as is proved by the bankruptcy of the tactics of non-cooperation in India."[44] Such renewed interest of the Fourth Congress in colonial problems must have been partly caused by the receding prospects of a proletarian upheaval in the advanced capitalist states of Europe.

The Cawnpore Conspiracy Trial the following year reflected again the link between the central dynamics of Soviet foreign policy and India. The ECCI drew appropriate conclusions from the trial and recommended that India's national liberation movement be restored on a revolutionary basis, abandoned as it had been by the big bourgeoisie ; that a mass party of petty bourgeoisie, small clerks and pauperized intellectuals be formed ; and that a truly proletarian party also be formed. The latter should then capture the trade union movement and reorganize it on class lines.[45]

Meanwhile, early that year, Stalin in his Sverdlov University speech declared that India constituted the weakest link in the chain of imperialism. He perceived the national liberation movement there as struggling along with a young and militant proletariat against imperialism.[46] The success of communism in India in the early 1920's was overestimated by Moscow at the time reflecting the distorting effects of ideology.

In June, the same year, a Pan-Pacific Labour Conference was held in Canton under the auspices of the Red International of Labour Unions. The conference decided on establishing a labour bureau in China with representations inter alia from India. It also put forth the thesis that control over trade unions, especially transport unions, was vital for the success of revolution in the East.[47]

The Fifth Comintern Congress, held in mid-1924, again downgraded consideration of colonial problems. Soon after the congress was held, the Communist Party of Great Britain (CPGB) set up a Colonial Department to exercise leadership of the communist movements in the British colonies, particularly in India. During 1924-25, new communist leaders like S. V.

Ghate et al. were emerging in India to fill in the vacuum created by the Cawnpore trials. They founded the Labour Swaraj Party of the Indian National Congress on November 1, 1925 in Calcutta ; the addition of the INC to the nomenclature of their new party reflected the communist aim of infiltrating the INC proper.[48] During the same period, M. N. Roy's influence declined in India while the CPGB took over the tasks of organizing cammunism there.[49]

In March, 1925 the Fifth Plenum of the ECCI was held. It instructed the Indian communists that they should continue working within the INC and the left-wing of the Swaraj Party. Further, all nationalist organisations were to be formed into a mass revolutionary party.[50] When strikes broke out in India that year under communist inspiration, the All-Russian Textile Union financially supported the Indian textile workers striking work.[51] In May, 1927 the Indian communists drew up a declaration formally acknowledging the need of the Communist Party of India to be guided and directed by the Comintern.[52] In December, in the course of the Fifteenth CPSU Congress Stalin set the ideological line for the next Comintern congress by declaring that the period of peaceful coexistence was making way for a period of renewed imperialist interventions against the U. S. S. R.

Bukharin, his ally at the time, struck a critical note on the policy of supporting the national bourgeoisie in India.

In 1928, workers struck work in various parts of India, again under communist inspiration. Druhe observes in this connection :

> In addition to winning over a number of impressionable educated Indian youths to Communism, the ideology of Communism made a profound impression upon a number of great Indian intellectuals who had nothing whatever to do with the clandestine Communist Party of India or its workers' and peasants' parties.[53]

Meanwhile disaster struck the communists in China who had been cooperating with Wang Chin-wei's left-wing KMT faction under the Comintern's guidance. In 1927, the two rival KMT factions joined hands and turned against the communists. Whether it was the meekness of the latter towards the KMT or their belated counter-offensive, they virtually ceased to exist as an organized force in China.⁵⁴ The debacle in China was reflected in the Sixth Comintern Congress deliberations in July, 1928, the orientation of the latter having already been set by Stalin, as seen earlier. Arguments tended to gravitate on the theory of "decolonization" associated with M. N. Roy. Its central thesis was that the growing manufacturing bourgeoisie in India was extracting concessions from the British under the trreat of siding with the masses if they were not granted. Hence, British imperialism was being forced to "decolonize" in exchange for the Indian bourgeoisie's cooperation in dampening the revolutionary ardour of the masses. Thus contradictions within Indian society were assuming greater importance than the nationalist struggle.⁵⁵ Bukharin stressed in the course of the congress that the INC had lost its revolutionary potential. Otto Kuusinen, who delivered the main report on the colonies, attacked the INC for its reformist nature. The WPP (Workers' and Peasants' Party created in India by the communists) had already been criticized as a mere left-wing appendage to the INC by the ECCI,⁵⁶ and Kuusinen only repeated the criticism in his report.⁵⁷ As Overstreet and Windmiller point out, elimination of the WPP at the time would mean the removal of the most effective instrument of communist propaganda in India.⁵⁸ This was also yet another example of ideology leading the communists to a cul d' sac. Zafar Imam's contention that the new ultra-leftist Comintern line was designed to strengthen the U.S.S.R. vis-a-vis Britain⁵⁹ appears unconvincing. Abandoning the WPP and steering clear of the INC could only weaken, not strengthen, the communists in India, as indeed it turned out to be. By early 1929, the WPP was abandoned by the communists. In April, that year, the Public Safety Act was proclaimed as law by the British authorities in India which reduced the scope of communist activities, particularly in organizing strikes.⁶⁰ The central dynamics from Moscow alienated the CPI from the INC as well as from the Independence for India League of J. Nehru and S. Bose (the latter being opposed to Gandhi's approach to independence) and contributed, as Druhe points out, to its ineffectiveness.[61] Soon its members were rounded up and their prolonged trial begun in Meerut from May. In the Tenth ECCI Plenum of July, 1929 Kuusinen and Molotov reiterated the ultra-left line for India.[62] From 1928 through May, 1932, the Soviet stand on the Indian nationalist movement was characterized by great hostility. Gandhi and his civil disobedience movement, Jawaharlal Nehru, Subhas Bose, and the INC—all came in for scathing attacks. An accompanying theme was the need for the formation of a strong and illegal communist party.

The Soviet ideological mood was reflected also in an *Izvestia* article of February 9, 1930 which recommended correct guidance by the communists to the petty bourgeois terrorist youths in India.[64] Even after the Meerut disaster, which hurt communism in India badly, the Comintern kept up its ultra-radical line. A "Draft Platform of Action of the Communist Party of India" published in *Inprecor* (December 18, 1930) set the CPI's goals as attainment of complete independence of India by violent means, the establishment of a Soviet government and the creation of a workers' and peasants' Soviet republic, confiscation of all lands, forests and other property of the wealthy classes, etc. The declaration also announced that the CPI considered itself as a section of the Comintern.[65]

On May 9, 1931 a *Pravda* article gave incitement to the CPI to organize "revolutionary disturbance" and to carry out violent activities against the British authorities in India. This article is stated to have led to an official British enquiry of Moscow whether the latter had definite designs of India.[66] Not surprisingly, Soviet criticism was extended to the Gandhi-Irwin Pact of 1931 signalling the end of civil disobedience as well to the communists in India for failure to isolate the INC.[67]

In June, 1932 an "Open Letter to the Indian Communists" from the Comintern noted that while the working class movement was growing in an unprecedented fashion, the CPI was still an inchoate force and often isolated from the masses. The Indian bourgeoisie, on the other hand, had succeeded in influencing the latter. The CPI was encouraged to mobilize the revolutionary strata of the petty bourgeoisie as well as the peasantry, to seize the initiative from the INC and to explore the latter along with its left wing.⁶⁸

In November, a year later, another Open Leter of the Comintern stressed the need for a better organized CPI and that of applying the united front tactic from below involving workers, peasants and the urban petty bourgeoisie, The response of the British authorities in India did not take long to come ; in July, 1934 the CPI was banned.⁷⁰

During July-August, 1935 the Comintern line achieved another volte face. Its Seventh Congress at that time featured prominently Wang Ming, the delegate from China. The latter took his Indian comrades to task for in effect having faithfully followed the hitherto existent Comintern line and branded their activities as left sectarian. He proceeded to set the new line of establishing united anti-imperialist fronts both within and outside the INC.⁷¹ This united front tactic was now introduced in view of the growing fascist danger in Europe and Japan. Consequently, the CPI was required to play up in its programmes not only the interests of the peasants and workers but also those of the middle classes. Dimitrov in his message stressed the importance of forming a socially broad-based anti-imperialist front. In his "Report on the United Front", he stated that "In India the communits have to support, extend and participate in all anti-imperialist activities, not excluding those which are under national-reformist leadership".⁷²

As a result of the new orientation, the CPI merged with the Congress Socialist Party under the Lucknow Agreement of May, 1936 and was able to keep up its united front tactics-vis-a-vis the CSP till 1940.⁷³ During 1936-39, the CPI was formally all praises for the INC policies in both domestic and external spheres. For instance, the Haripura plenary session of the INC held in February 1938 was assessed by the CPI as anti-fascist. The CPGB sent its greetings to both the Haripura session and the Tripuri session (March, 1939) of the INC, and Jawaharlal Nehru was rediscovered as a man who had after all proved his mettle.[74]

The Comintern was now no longer inciting the CPI to stage armed insurrections and found a Soviet republic in India. Instead, it started stressing the importance of freedom of speech, press, etc. and the repeal of repressive laws in India.[75] The impact of the Soviet central dynamics upon Indian communism is seen in an interesting situation in February 1937 when the CPI politburo found itself stressing that the anti-imperialist front must count in not only the INC, the CSP and the CPI itself but also organisations of Indian merchants and industrialists. The CSP now had the privilege of opposing the CPI's suddenly acquired liberal outlook and calling it "revisionist".[76]

In the late 1930's, there was a marked decrease in the Soviet interest in Indian affairs in view of the gathering storm of World War II and the purges within the U.S.S.R.[77] The Nazi-Soviet Pact of August 23, 1939 was followed by the outbreak of World War II. It was branded by Soviet ideology as an "imperialist war" and the CPI became active in organizing demonstrations against India's participation in it. The CPI, therefore, had to face British repression again. It should be added at this juncture that the CPI was not consistently subservient to the Comintern; at times it tended to exceed the mandate of the latter.[78] However, on the whole the impact of the Soviet central dynamics on the CPI's policies was undeniable. This is again borne out by the occasion of Hitler's attack on Russia in June, 1941, which upset the neatly formulated tenet of "imperialist war". The CPGB declared that "the path to Indian Independence lies through the victory of the Soviet Union and its allies over Fascism."[79] The war was now characterized as "people's war". No wonder that the British authorities in India turned out to be magnanimous in allowing incarcerated communists to receive communications from the CPGB containing the new policy orientation.[80] In the fall of 1941, the "Deoli Thesis", after a detention camp for the communists, reflected the acceptance

tion of the "people's war" line by the CPI's top leadership, then serving prison sentences.[81] In consequence, the party was legalized in July, 1942, an occasion reflecting British appreciation of the new Soviet ideological line. Paradoxically, the CPI now found itself moving in the same direction as the Hindu Mahasabha and the Muslim League in opposing the "Quit India" resolution of August, 1942 taken by Gandhi and Nehru. This alienated the CPI from the mainstream of India's nationalist sentiment which had by then geared itself to achieving India's freedom, war or no war.[82]

During 1941-45, Soviet attention to India remained at a low level since during most of this period the very existence of the Soviet state was in danger. Emerging victorious from the war, the U.S.S.R. began to renew her interest in the Indian situation. The Comintern meanwhile had gone out of existence in 1943. Soviet publicists like Boris Izakov and Dyakov generally took a critical attitude towards the end-phase of the British policies in India. Izakov struck a critical note on the Cabinet Mission Plan in his *Pravda* article (July 15, 1946). V. V. Balabushevich also revealed the prevalent Soviet mood in an article in *World Economy and World Politics* (September, 1946) where he stressed that the Cabinet Mission Plan was a mere eyewash and that the British were going to retain the levers of power in India.[83] Dyakov revealed his disapproval of India's Interim Government in *Pravda* (October 21, 1946) as an imperialist manoeuvre.[84]

In June, 1947 prominent Soviet ideologues like Dyakov, Balabushevich and Zhukov struck a critical chord on the role of the Indian bourgeoisie and the INC in a conference held in Moscow.[85] In September, Andrei Zhdanov, a top-ranking CPSU-member, while addressing the first session of the Cominform in Poland, propounded his thesis of global bipolarity. It reflected the cold war environment of the time. The world, for him, had come to be split into "democratic" and "imperialist" camps. He further alleged that the bourgeoisie everywhere (therefore including India) belonged to the "imperialist" camp. For the CPI, this was a signal to reassert itself against the Nehru government.[86]

In early 1948, the CPI decided to launch a programme of violent struggle aimed at the creation of a "people's democracy" and against the bourgeois, feudal and foreign reactionary forces. This took the CPI back to its course of action of the early 1930's. The ultra-leftist swing of the CPI during 1948-49 turned out to be largely fruitless. The Cominform advised the CPI in January, 1950 in effect to oppose only the big bourgeoisie but not its lesser strata and to count on the aid of all forces opposed to Anglo-American policies.[87]

The next decade brought about a major paradigm-shift in Soviet idelogy and foreign policy with the demise of Stalin and with Khrushchev's doctrinal "revisions". This shift has lasted into the present decade and is likely to continue in its overall pattern. It also constitutes a large part of the subject of this dissertation and need not be repeated or anticipated here.

What is remarkable about the foregoing discussion of Soviet central dynamics and India is the analytical obsession of Soviet Union. It is not the accuracy of such analyses that holds interest—for ideology also served to mislead the Marxists —but the way in which a state, for the first time in history, was manipulating with all earnestness sociological categories and concepts of supposed universal validity, and shaping its foreign policy in accordance with such manipulations.

The survey of the Soviet policy towards the colonies, especially India, reveals, to be sure, vacillations, mistaken assumptions and often rigid doctrinaire stands. For instance, the Comintern document entitled "Draft Platform of Action of the Communist Party of India", which called for the establishment of a Soviet government in India and was widely circulated among Indian communists in December, 1930, was out of touch with reality.[88] It is also evident that the U.S.S.R. played little direct role in the achievement of the independence of India and other Asian states following closely upon the end of the Second World War. Nevertheless, the fact remains that the U.S.S.R. right from her inception took up the case for decolonization energetically — albeit in a subsidiary vein, since her chief preoccupation was, in accordance with strict Marxist tenets and her own security considerations, with the industrially advanced West. The overt Soviet concern with the question or the colonies and the numerous propaganda moves on the theme served to *sensitize* the issue. It no longer remained the exclusive privilege of the metropolitan states to deal with their respective colonies on the basis of a mutual and tacit recognition of the right to exploitation. The U.S.S.R. in the 1920's and 1930's was the only state which, at least theoretically, vowed to combat imperialism and colonialism. The internationalization of this issue brought the colonies and other backward areas to the limelight and helped project an image of the U.S.S.R. as a basically well-intentioned state in the minds of the nationalists fighting for independence. Michael Edwardes in his biography of Nehru observes, for instance :

> Nehru never lost his view of the Russia of the inter-war years, embattled and revolutionary, and its post-war imperialism was always somehow less offensive to him than the pre-war imperialism of the west.[89]

Brzezinski addresses himself to the Soviet attention to areas and concludes :

> ...given the fact that modernization, particularly industrialization, has produced a world-wide awakening of the political consciousness of the masses, the Communist ideology, even while serving to intensify conflicts, underscored the necessity to base international conduct less and less on legal and diplomatic devices and more and more on political-sociological insights that cut across state frontiers. The Communist realization, even though often not successfully exploited in policy, that the key to the future of our era lies in the transformation of the colonial and underdeveloped parts of the world preceded similar recognition on the parts of Western chancelleries by several decades. The focusing on certain long-range social-economic and political trends, a matter increasingly accepted in the West since

World War II, has doubtless contributed to a more sophisticated appreciation of certain international issues....[90]

In the foregoing section, an attempt has been made to characterize the central dynamics of the Soviet foreign policy and to cast it in a historical perspective, particularly with reference to India. In the following section, three significant parameters, which have a bearing on the Soviet foreign policy towards India, are to be examined.

The U.S. Response to the Soviet Central Dynamics

In Europe, as the tide of the Second World War gradually turned against the Axis powers the only common basis for the Grand Alliance started crumbling. During the final years of the war as well as several years following its end in 1945, the establishment of socialist governments in the East European states, the division of Germany which showed every sign of perpetuation, and the general atmosphere of mutual suspicion and even hostility between the Western Allies and the U.S.S.R. helped launch the cold war. Already in 1947 the Truman Doctrine had revolutionized U.S. foreign policy by arresting the isolationist trends in the U.S.A. following immediately upon the successful conclusion of the war. Insurgency in Greece and Turkey, widely held to be aided and encouraged by the U.S.S.R. by proxy, had been countered. The spectre of a communist tide sweeping across the whole of western Europe — weakened as the latter was by the war — was dispelled gradually by a two-pronged U.S. attack on the problem. The creation of the NATO symbolized the collective will of the U.S. and western European community of states to stop a Soviet military advance; the Marshall Plan lent economic substance to that will which successfully revised western Europe as a stable region. The central dynamics of the Soviet foreign policy was thus held up there as a result of its restabilization and reinvigoration under U.S. sponsorship.

In Asia, however, reality presented a different picture. It is in this vast and highly complex threatre that the same U.S. panacea, which was successful in Europe, failed. A sizable and most populous chunk of territory—China—was lost to the newly augmented socialist camp. Shortly thereafter followed the North Korean attack on South Korea. The U.S.A. immediately intervened under the U.N. banner. With China becoming involved following the crossing of the 38th. parallel by the U.S. troops, the war became protracted. The highly unsettling effects which the end of the Second World War had brought in its wake in the inner crescent regions of the massive Eurasian landmass helped conjure up the vision of Sir Halford MacKinder's mysterious and omnipotent heartland taking full advantage of them. In order to counter heartland pressure, a number of bilateral defence treaties were concluded by the U.S.A. as well as a number of regional security organs established in the 1950's along the sprawling Eurasian periphery. The idea of containment was thus given material content also in Asia. Mahan and MacKinder, as it were, stood face to face in a protracted battle of nerves.

However, while containment in Europe worked well it connoted staticity and negativism in Asia which lay at the throes of great social, political and economic ferment. The Asian regimes which welcomed close alliance with the U.S.A. generally turned out to be pro-status quo internally, incapable of coping with the great number of socio-economic problems, and even corrupt. The U.S. definition of a "free world", in Asian context, could hardly become attractive since it gave license even to the most corrupt dictators lacking in popular support and legitimacy.

There was no quick Machiavellian response on the part of the U.S.S.R. to curry favour with Asian nations irrespective of their domestic composition and creed. The Soviet leaders did not enter into an immediate competition with the U.S.A. in instituting military alliances in Asia with non-communist states. Instead, between 1947 and 1952, the Soviet ideology took an extreme leftist direction which only served to forfeit for the time a large amount of sympathy for the U.S.S.R. that was to be found with many a newly born nation. It is timely to remember at this juncture why a purely power-political approach to the study of the Soviet foreign policy may be inadequate. As Donald Zagoria observes in another context, to believe that the Soviet leaders "are 'realists' like their Western opposites and do not take their revolutionary ideology very seriously" is to misappreciate communism.[91]

While the U.S. military alliances and various strategic postures served on the whole to discourage any Soviet or Chinese designs for overt, frontal attack on the Eurasian periphery, the basic problem of modernization of the Afro-Asian states and the attendant problems of overcoming cultural, ethnic, religious, racial and other barriers remained. The preconditions to the Western institution of free enterprise—so vital to the Western concept of democracy—were generally absent. Hence, efficient organizational drive could only be undertaken either by the armed forces or by communist or communist-type elements through the extensive use of state power, both cases offering the prospect of a radicalization of politics. Hindered in the Afro-Asian scene by the lack of coherent ideology because of her inherent liberal philosophy, the U.S.A. could not trap some of the indigenous socio-economic dynamism which the communists were often able to do. As John H. Badgley observes :

> The difficulty we in the United States must face up to......is to recognize that, despite our enormous power, the application of military force and selected economic assistance is generally tangential to the processes that are shaping Asia's future...... The myth fostered since World War II, that the will of the American people would be decisive in Asian politics, has been shattered.[92]

Too much of U.S. efforts in keeping the third world "free" has been influenced by the Department of Defense, which gave the U.S. power-projection abroad a conspicuous military inflection.[93] Jules Davids, writing U.S. diplomatic history, notes in the Vietnam context :

> During the winter of 1964-65, Washington officials found that the twin pillars upon which American policy had been based—the creation of a reason-

ably stable government in Saigon and the ability of South Vietnamese forces to cope with and eventually destroy the Viet Cong—were not tenable without more vigorous American military support[94]

It is these factors of the U.S. policy in Southern Asia that explain the American political defeat in Indochina. The protracted war in Vietnam symbolized, as it were, the clash between the long-term trends of the nationalist communist politics and the U.S. policy in a telescoped and concentrated form. It is inconceivable that without mass support a Viet Cong-type guerrilla warfare could be waged. Again, it is that same factor which explains why despite the capital-intensive warfare waged against a backward area of the world—in the course of which, till 1971, 6.3 million tons of air ordance was dropped by the U·S. Air Force[96]—the political objectives of the most highly advanced state of the world remained as elusive as ever.

For a proper understanding of the central dynamics of Soviet foreign policy, the contrasting background of the main trends of U.S. policy in the third world, especially Afro-Asia, becomes helpful. Henry Kissinger categorizes the U.S. leadership as the "bureaucratic-pragmatic" type ; his characterization of its functioning is worth quoting at length :

> Problems are segmented (by such leadership)* into constituent elements, each of which is dealt with by experts in the special difficulty it involves. There is little emphasis or concern for their interrelationship. Technical issues enjoy more careful attention, and receive more sophisticated treatment, than political onces. ...(Pragmatism)* compounds the already powerful tendencies within American society to identify foreign policy with the solution of immediate issues. ...Problems are dealt with as they arise. ... When a problem is recognized, it is dealt with by a mobilization of all resources to overcome the immediate symptoms. This often involves the risk of slight-

* Author's note.

ing longer-term issues which may not yet have assumed crisis proportions and over-whelming, perhaps even undermining, the structure of the area concerned by a flood of American technical experts proposing remedies on an American scale.

Further:

The *ad hoc* tendency of our decision-makers and the reliance on adversary proceeding cause issues to be stated in black-and-white terms. This suppresses a feeling for nuance and makes it difficult to recognize the relationship between seemingly discrete events. ... The same quality also produces a relatively low valuation of historical factors. Nations are treated as similar phenomena, and those states presenting similar immediate problems are treated similarly.[96]

The premises and assumptions of U.S. foreign policy, moulded as they have been in the postwar period by cold war perceptions, are now being increasingly questioned by U.S. domestic opinion. The overwhelming military response to perceived central pressure from the Eurasian heartland ignored important local factors which tended to generate anti-Western and leftist orientations. As Shulman reflects:

The slowness of the West to become sensitive to local political realities has been due in large measure to the fact that the West, and the United States in particular, has approached the problems of the under-developed areas primarily as a sector of the fight aginst Communism.[97]

The relative irrelevance of and the limits to the U.S. military power-projection in Southern Asia received dramatic official recognition in the shape of Nixon's Guam doctrine and recognition of communist China at the turn of the present decade. Following Nixon's modification of the structure of U. S. foreign policy towards Southern Asia, which had remained quite rigid from Truman to Johnson, the question of the future shape of events arose involving relations among the superpowers, China and Japan. While intellectual projections are increasing regarding the future of Asia in the context of its fluid situation and the evolving relations among the powers mentioned above, it is well-nigh impossible to venture as yet out of the realm of conjecture.[98] Nevertheless, a tentative conclusion can be reached regarding the foreseeable future of global affairs with a particular eye to the central dynamics of the Soviet foreign policy. There has been a marked improvement in relations between the Soviet bloc and China on the one hand and the West and Japan on the other. The SALT agreements—which incidentally put an end to the U. S. strategic aspiration of superiority—the increased trade and other forms of cooperational flows, the U. S.-Soviet joint space programmes, the dramatic 35-nation European security conference, the normalization of east-west tension in Germany, and a whole variety of related factors have helped partially brighten the prospects of peace. On the other hand, this partial stabilization of relations fails to cover for a large part the third world, particularly Asia, where conditions continue to become increasingly unstable, not least due to the fact of the growing economic gap between the "have" and the "have-not" countries.[99] It is the third world where a large residue of anti-Western ideological relevance remains, varying in scope and nature over time and space, and it is this crucial factor which will tend to attract the transformation-oriented foreign policies of the U.S.S.R. and China. It is to be noted in this connection that a section of American analysts still tend to think of the problems of the third world in terms of policing the status quo and international order. For them, it is a question of how far the burdens on the U.S.A. of maintaining stability, e. g., in eastern Asia, should be shared in future by others, notably Japan.[100] More sensitive analysts, however, gear their thought to more constructive channels. They consider questions like how the future U.S. foreign policy could become more responsive to local needs without being obtrusive.[101] George Liska, in his review of the Nixon doctrine and its implications for the third world, upholds the "need to integrate a bothersome but indispensable third world into a 'new' American global policy before the void created by the 'liquidation' of the Vjetnam war has evolved into a dangerous vacuum of purpose..."[102]

Some of the arguments presented above find resonance in Brzezinski's writings. He notes that "in the present epoch non-democratic forces enjoy a definite advantage over the democratic countries in being able to export their political structure to the newly liberated peoples not only through conspiratorial action, but also through the dynamics of the situation given the economic and political aspirations of these peoples."[103] Arguing that efforts at rapid modernization generate institutions and processes that tend to gravitate towards the communist orbit, Brzezinski recommends that the U.S.A. should concentrate more on trade with the third world than aid—the latter being suspect of neo-colonialism—and should give up "illusory structures" like the SEATO.[104] Elsewhere, he concludes rightly that whereas a great deal of *functional* co-operation may be expected between the U.S.A. and U.S.S.R. in future, this would not provide any significant restraints on regional competition.[105] It seems that in such competition the future of the third world, particularly Southern Asia, would feature prominently.

CHINA AND NATIONAL LIBERATION

The breakaway of China from the Soviet ideological line of 1956 introduced a new variable in the power-configuration of Asia, which in the earlier days of the cold war was characterized by a simpler bipolarity with pockets of non-alignment thrown in between. The Sino-Soviet dispute, which started in the later half of the 1950's, culminated in violent border clashes on the Ussuri (1969) and the mobilization of the armed forces by both the communist giants along their long common frontiers.

The dispute started on a distinctly ideological note, although later a number of observers have attributed other factors to its perpetuation and intensification (e.g., China's resentment against the Russian expansion in the Far East in the nineteenth century, racial factors, the dynamics of Chinese nationalism, etc.). The fact remains, however, that the dispute is carried on by both sides in ideological terms. It is proposed here to examine China's challenge to the Soviet ideological authority and the assumptions and beliefs of the Soviet foreign policy, and its significance for the theoretical framework of this dissertation.

The Sino-Soviet ideological controversy, stripped to its bare essentials, reminds of the Lenin-Roy debate of 1920, mentioned earlier. It reveals that the crucial question hinges on timing. The whole intellectual history of operational communism — that is, from 1917 onwards — reveals the obsession with the analysis of "objective factors", of the relative progression, stagnation or retrogression of the "objective flows" of history. In accordance with their teleological view of history, the communists feel the need for constantly watching, analysing and assessing the incessant currents of reality. If there are signs of a "maturing" situation, the ideological line and tactics are adjusted accordingly in order to give the "objective forces" the residual "push" so that the desirable "objective situation" matures fully. If, on the other hand, an analysis reveals ebbs in the "objective progression", a different ideological and tactical line is formulated. The various types of ideological line available in the arsenal or Marxism-Leninism also reflect whether one is in a hurry regarding the transformation of the international system and processes or one can afford to wait for an indefinite period of time. The Chinese endorsed the former while the Russians adopted the latter attitude, and this, coupled with their correspondingly different ideological assessments, produced the now apparently irreparable split.

Stalin's policy in the postwar era towards the newly independent states, including India, was characterized by an ultra-leftist orientation similar to the subsequent Chinese stance. It was Malenkov who in his speech of August 8, 1953 ushered in a new era of the Soviet foreign policy. Khrushchev formalized the new paradigm in the twentieth CPSU congress of 1956. The net result of such a drastic reassessment of "objective" reality had a number of new implications for the third world. The revision of a fundamental Leninist thesis, that of the inevitability of war between the capitalist and socialist systems, came to draw the bulk of subsequent Chinese invectives. This, incidentally, also reveals how sacrosant "theory" in its narrower sense discussed earlier is perceived to be in the communist world. In the Chinese view, the Russian leaders had revised part of the immutable "theory" itself which on no account was to be confused with tactical ideological flexibility.

Since war in the thermonuclear age was unacceptable to the Soviet leaders,—even in theory—a new set of strategy and tactics had to be introduced into their bloc foreign policy —with the transformationist urge (the central dynamics) remaining a constant. Thus, "peaceful coexistence" of states with different domestic structures and philosophies, and the parliamentary road to socialism were considered possible— the latter explaining the subsequent loss of militancy of the CPI and its collaboration with India's central government. Since and ultra-leftist stance and active encouragement of violent uprisings against the existing governments of the third world would tend to attract Western military intervention— which in its turn could result in a deterioration of the situation to a point of no return and a thermonuclear apocalypse,—it had to be substituted for a more peaceful and congenial approach. A CPI working within the framework of parliamentary democracy in India, for instance, would be far more acceptable than if it operated outside it in open violation of the "rules of the game".

Consequently, non-aligned states, hitherto held by Stalin as disguised appendages to Western imperialism, were now accorded a genuine recognition of their status in the cold war. Also, the national bourgeois leadership pursuing non-alignment qualified for Soviet praise and support. All this was anathema to China. Although the latter professed to practice a "good neighbour" policy during the mid-1950's, her preference for a more radical leftist stance revealed itself in 1957. The Chinese disillusion with Khrushchev's ideological leadership of world communism and her consequent endeavour to modify the Soviet stance resulted in her ultimate challenge to the Soviet claim to ideological leadership itself. The seemingly irresponsible Chinese statements calling the U.S.A. a "paper-tiger" and defying thermonuclear war were, indeed, cleverly devised. They were meant to despise the enemy *strategically*, though not in a tactical military sense. The Soviet successes with the sputnik and ICBM experiments in 1957 were initially seen by the Chinese as a major triumph for communism. Since central pressure by the U.S.A. could henceforth be neutralized by the Soviet counterpressure, there would be nothing to prevent the encouragement of a more active radicalization of the communist movements in the third world. A corollary of the Chinese Weltanschauung was that the bourgeoisie of even the newly independent nations could not be trusted in furthering the cause of revolution. In this, the Chinese seemed to be guided by their own unpleasant experience of 1927 mentioned earlier, which ended the period of communist collaboration with the KMT under Moscow's guidance. In Chinese view, a communist party with a sufficiently radical programme which replaced nationalist leadership in the third world could bring about a genuine revolution. Further, the Chinese seemed to resent the subordination of third world-imperialism contradictions to those of capitalism-socialism by the U.S.S.R. In their view, as outlined by Lin Piao, the primary contradiction of the present stage of history is that between "world-cities" and "world-villages".[106] The Soviet cautiousness regarding war and the consequent gradualism were unpalatable to Peking, and this ultimately tore apart the Eurasian heartland.

The Sino-Soviet dispute has had an important bearing on the South Asian subcontinent, just as the initiation of U. S. military aid to Pakistan in 1954 had set off a series of processes there. From the 1960's, as the dispute gained in intensity and was increasingly becoming public, and as the U.S.A. started to become increasingly involved in Indochina and to lose interest in South Asia, China switched over to a policy of cultivating Pakistan's friendship, which was welcomed by the latter. India, frigid in her stance on the question of her borders with China, found it natural to strengthen further her ties with the Soviet Union, now a rival of China in Asia. The U.S. refusal to arm India following the latter's request in the wake of the 1962 border clash with China only helped in pushing India closer to the U.S.S.R., which cheerfully granted India's request. As the negative process of keeping China isolated from the world community of states ran out of its utility and as China emerged as a major rival to the Soviet Union in Asia, the U.S.A. switched over to a policy of normalizing relations with her beginning with secret talks in Warsaw. With the advent of the Nixon-administration in Washington, a detente atmosphere was introduced into Sino-American relations against the background of an impending "low profile" U.S. presence in Southern Asia. If the power configuration during the creation of Bangladesh in 1971 is any pointer to the future, it would seem plausible to imagine an as yet loose U.S.-Chinese-Pakistani political axis in Asia pitted against a similar Indo-Soviet axis, which was accorded official sanction in the 1971 Friendship Treaty. It seems probable that the U.S,A. would be willing to witness in future a Sino-Soviet rivalry within limits and to encourage a broader Japanese participation in the economic and political affairs of the region. Doak Barnett, for instance, recommends :

> We should avoid unduly alarming the Soviet Union—although creating a certain low level of uneasiness in Moscow is probably inevitable and not necessarily undesirable.[107]

The result of the Sino-Soviet rivalry coupled with the projected low profile of the U.S. presence in Southern Asia, hence, has been the closing of ranks by India with the U.S.-S.R.[108] For a time in the post-Khrushchev period, the U.S.S.R. seemed to be moving towards a more intermediate position between India and Pakistan against the background of the diminishing cold war importance of Kashmir. Unequivocal support for India, as used to be forthcoming during Khrushchev's tenure, was being replaced by a more conciliatory posture towards Pakistan. In 1965, President Ayub Khan visited the U.S.S.R. and returned with an agreement with the latter to expand trade relations between the two countries.

The May Day slogan for Pakistan that same year reflected the Soviet desire to cultivate Pakistani friendship. Moscow also urged both India and Pakistan to negotiate their dispute over the Rann of Kutch on a bilateral basis. Three years later, Kosygin paid an official visit to Pakistan, the first Soviet Premier to do so. He also offered Soviet assistance in establishing a metallurgical plant at Kalabagh (West Pakistan) and an atomic plant at Rooppur (the then East Pakistan). This visit took place a few days after Pakistani's note to the U.S. government that lease of the Badaber intelligence base at Peshawar was no longer automatically renewable and was henceforth to be negotiated annually.[109] A year later, Grechko, the Soviet defence chief, followed suit. A limited arms aid to Pakistan was initiated by the U.S.S.R.

This relative pro-Pakistani tilt by the U.S.S.R. was certainly due to a winding down of the U.S. presence and interest in that country in the 1960's as well as her own competitive relationship with China, which was concentrating on actively cultivating relationships with Pakistan, including military ones. Some amount of alarm and resentment was, consequently, inevitable in India, despite Soviet assurances that no basic change in relations with India was being contemplated.

The accentuation of the revolt in East Pakistan at the turn of the decade, however, performed a homeostatic function for Indo-Soviet relations in bringing them back, as least for a while, into the Khrushchevian track. The U.S.S.R., right till Mrs Gandhi's visit to Moscow in September, 1971, appeared to favour a compromise between the two wings of Pakistan. Among the chief reasons must have been her concern for stability in South Asia, for checking the spread of likely points of confrontation with the West and for avoiding antagonism with Pakistan.[110] The convergence of international political interests of West Pakistan, China and the U.S.A. during the crisis led finally to unequivocal Soviet support for both the revolt and India's role in it. Tashkent (1966), the Indo-Soviet Friendship Treaty and the emergence of Bangladesh (both in 1971) reflected the major influence that the U.S.S.R has come to exercise in the post-World War II years in a region which had for centuries been the traditional preserves of the British empire. The official Soviet estimate of India as a "peaceloving country" has been revised upward coinciding with Mrs Gandhi's consolidation of power at the turn of the decade.

The Domestic Economic Scene

Finally, a consideration of the Soviet economic scene is germane to understanding some of the forces that are operating to mould Soviet foreign policy within the broad theoretical framework of this dissertation. The lop-sided development of the Soviet economy has been widely noted, and even the Soviet leaders implicitly admit it. While the Soviet achievements in military and space technology have been spectacular, other sectors of the economy have suffered from relative chaos and inefficiency. One analyst suggests that the high performance level of the military and space sectors of industry is to be attributed to "pachrovye yaschiki" (post-boxes), which are highly privileged secret institutions not required to follow doctrinaire economic planning. In other fields like synthetics and computers, the U.S.S.R. stands well behind her capitalist rivals.[111] Inadequate innovations, despite many theoretical advances made by Soviet science, provide another cause for bottlenecks. Part of the blame must go to the massive bureaucracy. An article in *The Economist* points out that since drastic cuts in military expenditure and introduction of major decentralization measures in production are unlikely—despite SALT and an April, 1973 decree establishing new industrial associations supposedly free from ministerial control,—the Russians are going in for large-scale import of Western technology "to help the Soviet Union buy time".[112] The periodic crises appearing in the agricultural sector have also posed serious problems. Khrushchev's attempt to hold down privateplot production of the kolkhozniks led to an agricultural failure, which, incidentally, was one reason for his removal.[113] Unfavourable weather conditions affecting grain harvests forced the U.S.S.R. in 1972 to make "the largest grain deal in history" involving her purchase of 1,000 million dollars worth of American grains. Such unprecedented cornering of the international grain surplus set off fears of future shortages in the international market and consequent spiralling of prices.[114] Adverse weather alone, however, cannot account for the periodic crises; despite the fact that nearly half of the Soviet labour force is engaged in agriculture, compared to around 6% of the U.S. population, and that the U.S.S.R. has been the world's leading wheat producer, built-in deficiencies in the agricultural sector persist.[115]

An examination of high-level Soviet pronouncements on economic problems in the U.S.S.R. confirms the preceding arguments. During the twenty-third CPSU congress of 1966, Brezhnev complained about the retardation of the Soviet economic growth. He blamed "the bad harvests of 1963 and 1965" and the deterioration of the international situation (Vietnam), and listed other factors like defective management, planning, cost-accounting methods and the inefficient use of "moral and material stimuli" as the chief culprits. Unrealistic setting of production targets, he maintained, resulted in a wrong assessment of performance.[116] Brezhnev further complained about a loose sense of responsibility of "factory staffs" and stressed the need to shore up greater discipline and to introduce more material incentives.[117] He then took to task the government bureaucracy:

> We should like to warn those working in the ministries against attempts to revive the narrow departmental approach to business that was a frequent fault of the old ministries.[118]

He went on stressing the importance of "ability", "initiative", and "efficiency" of "executives, engineers and technicians", the ability to "mobilize factory staffs to fulfil plans" and achieve "the maximum efficiency" in production.[119] He seemed to be implying bureaucratic functioning when he expressed regret over "the slow introduction of the results of scientific research into production". According to him, "There is an unjustifiable gap between theoretical research and its technological and design development. Often, years pass before a a discovery is applied in production. ... Poor use of electronic computer techniques is one example of this."[120] Finally, the Soviet consumer could no longer be ignored. Brezhnev, hence, promised that the gap between the capital goods sector and the consumer goods sector "will be considerably narrowed down."[121]

An important reason behind halting the ABM race and allied arms competition under the SALT agreements has been economic. In 1971, it was hinted in the Soviet press that the percentage of defence expenditure might go down during the current ninth five-year plan (1971-1975).[122] Western analysts also seem to take the Soviet peace offensive more seriously than hitherto.[123] As has already been mentioned, the Soviet economy with its massive industrialization drive needs greater resources, relaxation of tension and closer contacts with the capitalist states for realizing its ends.[124] The official reports of the ninth five year plan reveal various unsolved problems of the rationalization of the economy in tackling which capitalist collaboration would be profitable.

> The main task of the five-year plan is to ensure a considerable rise of the people's material and cultural level on the basis of a high rate of development of socialist production, enhancement of its efficiency, scientific and technological progress and acceleration of the growth of labour productivity,

declared Kosygin on 6 April, 1971.[125]

For the first tsme in the history of the Soviet economy, the rate of growth of the consumers' sector of the economy is being allowed greater priority than the other traditionally high-priority sectors. The plan produces great emphasis on raising the standard of living of the Soviet citizens; salaries, wages, scholarships and social benefits are to go up considerably which, however, are not to be in exclusion of the continued development of heavy industry. The rate of growth of the purchasing power of the consumer, it is explained, is to be matched by a simultaneous expansion of the production of consumers' goods, the rate of which is to be even higher[126] so that the price structure is not adversely affected due to the classic problem of too much money chasing too few goods.

Hence, the need for the "enhancement" of "efficiency, scientific and technical progress" and the "acceleration" of the growth of labour productivity.

Productivity of labour is a much discussed topic today in the U.S.S.R. The growth of the Soviet GNP was particularly striking in the 1950-58 period (the rate of its average growth being variedly estimated at 6.4% on the conservative side and 10.9% on the liberal side ; the corresponding U.S. figure was 2.9%), but has tended to fall off since then. Since no corresponding retardation occured in the growth of the key inputs of capital and labour, the decline in the rate of the GNP growth must be ascribed to that in labour productivity. The latter is accounted for by a variety of factors, the analysis of which lies beyond the scope of the present narrative (they include Khrushchev's reduction of the working hours in 1956, the vicissitudes in Soviet agriculture, faulty planning, inefficient management, the limits to the post-war 'catch-up' phenomena, etc).[127]

In his March 30, 1971 report to the twenty-fourth CPSU congress, Brezhnev again pointed out the imperative need of streamlining and rationalizing production methods. The problem of raising productivity of labour was considered by him to be of "truly national importance."[128] At the fifteenth Trade Union Congress, held a year later, he was again complaining about the slow growth of labour productivity and new technology as well as about the substandard quality of certain products. He reminded the trade unions that wages should ever more be tied to the exact value of the individual worker's labour so as to discourage any complacency.[129] Nine months later, in the course of his report of December 21, 1972 on the occasion of the fiftieth anniversary of the formation of the U.S.S.R., the CPSU General-Secretary struck an all too familiar note in his lamentation over the persistent shortcomings affecting the Soviet economic growth. He repeated the familiar list of problems : slow rise in labour productivity, inefficiency of the ministries and the enterprises, flaws in planning and "the entire system of management", etc.[130] A few months later, Brezhnev, appearing on West German TV, frankly admitted that not all the problems of economic growth had been solved in the U.S.S.R.[131] No wonder, then, that the hard substratum of the economic factor explains much of the operational Soviet foreign policy vis-a-vis the West today.

NOTES AND REFERENCES

1. "A mechanism", as Parsons defines it, "is an empirical generalization about motivational processes stated in terms of its relevance to the functional problems of an action system." *The Social System*. Amerind Publishing Co., New Delhi, 1972 (Indian ed.) p. 6. fn.

2. The word "transformation" is used here instead of "revolution" since it is a more neutral and broader concept and able to cover a wide range of revolutionary urges, from the violent to the more peaceful ones. The word 'revolution', in Marxist context, tends to connote violence, which is largely inapplicable today in dealing with post-Stalin Soviet categories.

3. See Brzezinski. *op. cit.*

4. James N. Rosenau, *Linkage Politics*. The Free Press. New York. 1969. The Farrel volume. *op. cit.*, and Henry A. Kissinger, *American Foreign Policy*. A. H. Wheeler & Co., Allahabad, 1971 (Indian ed.).

5. Kissinger, *op. cit.*, p. 35.

6. Kissinger, *op. cit.*, p. 36.

7. See Morgenthau, *op. cit.*

8. Brzezinski, *op. cit.*, p. 112.

9. Brzezinski, *op. cit.*, p. 4.

* Author's note.

10. Brzezinski, *op. cit.*, p. 108.

11. V. I. Lenin, *Speeches At Congresses of the Communist International*, Progress Publishers, Moscow, 1972, p. 9.

12. J.V. Stalin, *Economic Problems of Socialism in U.S.S.R.*, Foreign Language Press, Peking, 1972, pp. 30-31.

13. *Mission of Friendship*, Soviet Land Booklets, New Delhi, 1973, p. 52.

14. See Robert Jervis, "The Costs of the Quantitative Study of International Relations", in Knorr and Rosenau, *op. cit.*, pp. 177-217, and Robert C. North, "The Analytical Prospects of Communications Theory", in James C. Charlesworth (ed.), *Contemporary Political Analysis*, The Free Press, New York, 1967, pp. 300-316.

15. Brzezinski, *op. cit.*, p. 113.

16. Shulman, *op. cit.*, p. 53.

17. Kissinger, *op. cit.*, p. 35.

18. See Gunther Nollau, *International Communism and World Revolution*, London, Hollis & Carter, 1961.

Gene D. Overstreet, Marshall Windmiller, *Communism in India*, Universsity of California Press, Berkeley & Los Angeles, 1959. David N. Druhe, *Soviet Russia and Indian Communism*, Bookman Associates, New York, 1959.

Zafar Imam, *Colonialism in East-West Relations. A Study of Soviet Policy Towards India and Anglo-Soviet Relations 1917-1947*, Eastman Publication, New Delhi, 1969.

Jayantanuja Bandyopadhyaya, *Indian National versus International Communism*, Firma K.L. Mukhopadhyay, Calcutta, 1966. Donaldson, *op. cit.*, Chapter I.

19. Nollau, *op. cit.*, pp. 44-45.
20. Nollau, *op. cit.*, p. 58.
21. Nollau, *op. cit.*, p. 56.
22. Issac Deutscher, *Stalin*, Penguin, Harmondsworth, 1968, and Nollau, *op. cit.*, p. 180.
23. Nollau, *op. cit.*, p. 179.
24. Nollau, *op. cit.*, pp. 202-203.
25. Marx and Engels, *Manifest der Kommunistischen Partei*, Dietz Verlag, Berlin, 1967, p. 43.
26. "Preface to the Russian Edition" of Marx, *Notes on Indian History*, Foreign Languages Publishing House, (no date), p. 8.
27. "Publisher's Note". Marx and Engels, *On Colonialism*, Foreign Languages Publishing House, Moscow, (no date), p. 7.
28. Karl Marx, "The British Rule in India", Marx and Engels, *On Colonialism*, op. cit., p. 36.
29. Marx, "The British Rule in India", *op. cit.*, n. 28, p. 39.
30. Druhe, *op. cit.*, p. 14.
31. Druhe, *op. cit.*, pp. 14-15.
32. Druhe, *op. cit.*, pp. 15-16.
33. Druhe, *op. cit.*, pp. 27-29.
34. Druhe, *op. cit.*, pp. 30-31.
35. Lenin, *op. cit.*, pp. 55-60.
36. Druhe, *op. cit.*, pp. 49-50, and Lenin, *op. cit.*, pp. 82-83.
37. Druhe, *op. cit.*, pp. 49-50.
38. Druhe, *op. cit.*, p. 52.
39. Druhe, *op. cit.*, pp. 50-51.
40. Overstreet, Windmiller, *op. cit.*, p. 45.
41. Imam, *op. cit.*, pp. 106-107.
42. Imam, *op. cit.*, pp. 162-163.
43. Overstreet, Windmiller, *op. cit.*, p. 50.
44. *Comintern and National and Colonial Questions. Documents of Congresses*, Communist Party Publication, New Delhi, No. 9, March 1973 (c. 86), p. 49.
45. Druhe, *op. cit.*, p. 66, and Overstreet et al., *op. cit.*, p. 70.
46. Imam, *op. cit.*, p. 203.
47. Druhe, *op. cit.*, p. 70.
48. Druhe, *op. cit.*, p. 70.

49. Overstreet, et al., *op. cit.*, p. 81.
50. Overstreet et al., *op. cit.*, p. 73.
51. Druhe, *op. cit.*, p. 71.
52. Druhe, *op. cit.*
53. Druhe, *op. cit.*, pp. 86-88.
54. See M N. Roy, *Revolution and Counter-Revolution in China*, Renaissance Publishers, Calcutta, 1946.
55. Overstreet et al., *op. cit.*, pp. 102-103.
56. Overstreet et al., *op. cit.*, pp. 107-108.
57. Overstreet et al., *op. cit.*, pp. 107-110.
58. Overstreet et al., *op. cit.*, p. 117.
59. Imam, *op. cit.*, p. 260.
60. Druhe, *op. cit.*, p. 104.
61. Druhe, *op. cit.*, p. 130.
62. Imam, *op. cit.*, pp. 279-281.
63. Druhe, *op. cit.*, p. 130, and Overstreet et al., *op. cit.*, p. 144.
64. Quoted in Druhe, *op. cit.*, p. 190.
65. Quoted in Druhe, *op. cit.*, p. 127.
66. Quoted in Druhe, *op. cit.*, p. 194.
67. Imam, *op. cit.*, pp. 337-338.
68. Quoted in Druhe, *op. cit.*, pp. 128-129, and Overstreet et al, *op. cit.*, pp. 151-152.
69. Druhe, *op. cit.*, p. 134.
70. Druhe *op. cit.*, p. 137.
71. Druhe, *op. cit.*, pp. 141-142 ; Imam, *op. cit.*, pp. 375-376, and Overstreet et al., *op. cit.*, p. 157.
72. Comintern..., *op. cit.*, p. 125.
73. Druhe, *op. cit.*, p. 151, and Iman, *op. cit.*, pp. 387-388.
74. Druhe, *op. cit.*, p. 145.
75. Druhe, *op. cit.*, pp. 146-147.
76. Overstreet et al., *op. cit.*, pp. 163-164.
77. Druhe, *op. cit.*, p. 197.
78. See Overstreet et al., *op. cit.*, pp. 184-185.
79. Quoted in Druhe, *op. cit.*, p. 210.
80. Druhe, *op. cit.*, p. 210.
81. Overstreet et al., *op. cit.*, pp. 194-195.
82. Druhe, *op. cit.*, p. 219, and Imam, *op. cit.*, pp. 439-441.
83. Both articles quoted in Imam, *op. cit.*, pp. 461-462.
84. Quoted in Druhe, *op. cit.*, pp. 269-271.
85. Druhe, *op. cit.*, p. 284.
86. Druhe, *op. cit.*, pp. 284-285.
87. Druhe, *op. cit.*, pp. 285-290.
88. Imam, *op. cit.*, pp. 309-313.
89. Michael Edwardes, *Nehru. A Political Biography*, **Praeger Publishers**, New York, and Washington, 1971, p. 267.

90. Brzezinski, *op. cit.*, p. 112.

91. Donald S. Zagoria, *The Sino-Soviet Conflict, 1956-1961*, Princeton University Press, Princeton, New Jersey, 1962, p. 5.

92. John H. Badgley, "The American Territorial Presence in Asia", in James C. Charlesworth (ed.), *A New American Posture Toward Asia, The Annals* (of the American Academy of Political & Social Science), Philadelphia, Vol. 390, July 1970, p. 44.

93. See Seymour Melman's views in his *Pentagon Capitalism. The Political Economy of War*, in Stephen J. Cimbala's review, "New Myths and Old Realities : Defence and its Critics" World Politics, Vol. XXIV, No. 1, October 1971, pp. 127-157, and Warren W. Unna, "The U.S. Military—A Steady Growth of Elitism", *The Statesman*, Calcutta, October 15, 1972.

94. Jules Davids, *America and the World of Our Time. United States Diplomacy in the Twentieth Century*, Random House, New York, 1970, p. 594.

95. Raphael Littauer and Norman Uphoff (eds.), *The Air War in Indo China*, Beacon Press, Boston, 1972, fig. 1-1, p. 11.

96. Kissinger, *op. cit.*, pp. 29-33.

* Author's note.

97. Shulman, *op. cit.*, p. 85.

98. Among the growing number of volumes dealing with the future of the U.S. policy and global changes are, *The Annals*, *op. cit.*, Robert E. Osgood, et al., *Retreat from Empire*, Johns Hopkins University Press, Baltimore and London, 1973, and Henry Owen (ed.), *The Next Phase in Foreign Policy*, The Brookings Institution, Washington D.C., 1973.

99. The disruptive potential of this growing gap was explicitly noted by U.S. Secretary of State Henry Kissinger in hearings before the Senate Foreign Relations Committee in September 1973. "Nomination of Henry A. Kissinger", *Hearings before the Committee on Foreign Relations, U.S. Senate, 93rd. Congress, 1st. Session*, Washington, D.C., U.S. Govt. Printing Office, 1973, Part 1, p. 84. See also the 1975 World Bank study as quoted in *Amrita Bazar Patrika*, Calcutta, August 11, 1975, p. 1.

100. See Ralph N. Clough, "East Asia", in Owen, *op. cit.*, pp. 49-69.

101. See Philips Talbot, "The American Posture Toward India and Pakistan", *Annals, op. cit.*, pp. 87-95.

102. George Liska, "The Third World : Regional Systems and Global Order", in Osgood et al., *op. cit.*, p. 340.

103. Z. Brzezinski, "The Politics of Underdevelopment", in Harold Karan Jacobson (ed.), *America's Foreign Policy*, Random House, New York, 1965, p. 596.

104. Brzezinski, in Jacobson, *op. cit.*, pp. 610-612.

105. Z. Brzezinski, "U.S.-Soviet Relations", in Owen, *op. cit.*, p. 126.

106. See Astatyev, G. V., and Fomichova, M. V., "The Maoist Distor-

tion of Lenin's Theory of the National Liberation Movement", in Sladkovsky, M. I., Kovalyov, Y. F., and Sidikhmenov, V. Y. (eds), *Leninism and Modern China's Problems*, Progress, Moscow, 1972, pp 206-232.

107. A. Doak Barnett, "The New Multipolar Balance in East Asia : Implications for United States Policy", *Annals, op. cit.,* p. 84.

108. The following empirical referents have been collated from, inter alia :

J. A. Naik, *Soviet Policy Towards India From Stalin to Brezhnev*, Vikas Publications, Delhi, 1970.

Pran Chopra, *Before and After the Indo-Soviet Treaty*, S. Chand & Co, New Delhi (no date), and Kaushik, *op. cit.*

109. Kaushik, *op. cit.*, p. 107.

110. See Bhabani Sen Gupta, "Moscow and Bangladesh", *Problems of Communism*, March-April 1975, Vol. XXIV, No. 2, pp. 56—68.

111. See David Bonavia. "The Soviet Economy", *The Times*, London, reproduced in *The Statesman*, May 29, 1972.

112. "The Soviet Economy", The Economist, reproduced in *The Statesman*, August 6, 1973.

113. This is discussed in Arthur W. Wright's review article, "Systemic Ills in Soviet Agriculture", *Problems of Communism*, January-February, 1975, Vol. XXIV, No. 1, pp. 51-55.

114. See Sam W. Morris, "The Soviet-U.S. Grain Deal—Its Global Impact", *The American Reporter*, New Delhi, November 1, 1972, Vol. XXII, No. 22, p. 1.

115. For more details, see Louis Heren, "Russia Reaps the Harvest of Marxist Mistakes", The Times, London, reproduced in *The Statesman*, Calcutta, December 17, 1972.

116. "Report of the Central Committee of the Communist Party of the Soviet Union to the 23rd. Congress of the CPSU delivered by L. Brezhnev on March 29, 1966", *23rd. Congress of the CPSU, 1966*, Novosti, Moscow (no date), p. 68, (henceforth *Brezhnev Report, 23rd. Congress*).

117. Brezhnev Report, 23rd, Congress *op. cit.*, p. 69.

118. Brezhnev Report, 23rd. Congress, *op. cit.*, p. 70.

119. Brezhnev Report, 23rd. Congress, *op. cit.*, p. 70.

120. Brezhnev Report, 23rd. Congress, *op. cit.*, p. 109.

121. Brezhnev Report, 23rd. Congress, *op. cit.*, p. 75.

122. See Valeri Savinov, "Der Neunte Fuenfjahrplan der UDSSR", *Neue Zeit*, Moscow, December 1971, No. 49, p. 7 (henceforth *NZ*).

123. See Abram Bergson, "Toward a New Growth Model", *Problems of Communism*, March-April 1973, Vol. XXII, No. 2, p. 9.

124. See "Report of the Central Committee of the Communist Party of the Soviet Union to the 24th. Congress of the CPSU, delivered by Leonid Brezhnev, General Secretary of the CC, CPSU, March 30, 1972" *Information Bulletin*, No. 7-8 (188-189), Vol. 9 (Special Issue).

Peace and Socialism. Publishers,' Prague, 1971, p. 74, (henceforth. *Brezhnev Report. 24th. Congress)*, and Bergson, *op. cit.*, p.8.

125. "Directives of the 24th. Congress of the CPSU for the five-Year Economic Development Plan of the USSR for 1971-1975. Report delivered by Alexei Kosygin, Chairman of the Council of Ministers of the USSR, April 6, 1971", *Information Bulletin, op. cit.* p. 145.

126. *Brezhnev Report, 24th. Congress, op. cit.*, p. 55.

127. See Bergson, *op. cit.*, pp. 1-4.

128. *Brezhnev Report, 24th. Congress, op. cit.*, p. 70.

129. Brezhnev's speech at the 15th. Trade Union Congress of the USSR, March 24, 1972, *Neue Zeit*, No. 14, April 1972, pp. 33-35.

130. *The Fiftieth Anniversary of the USSR, Report by L. I. Brezhnev* (December 21, 1972), Novosti, Moscow, 1972, pp. 72-76.

131. See "An einen amerikanischen Leser", *Neue Zeit*, No. 24, June 1973, p. 21, (reply to the letter of an American reader).

Chapter III

THE NODAL RESTRAINT AS REFLECTED IN THE SOVIET MILITARY AND DOCTRINAL POSTURE

THIS CHAPTER EXAMINES the question of whether the present nuclear age finds Soviet military policy in both theory and practice in a noticeable restrained state. If the finding is positive then the second major concept of the framework of this book is substantiated and the way is cleared to complete the global-strategic context, the synthetic scenario mentioned in Chapter 1. This context, it has already been submitted, is essential to fully grasp the significance of the post-Stalin orientation of the U.S.S.R. to India. Accordingly, this chapter sets itself the task of examining the nature and purpose of the Soviet military power, especially the characteristics of the post-Khrushchev arms build-up, the latter's link with the salient features of the Soviet politico-strategic doctrine, and the kind of bearing these have on the operative Soviet policy.

The "nodal restraint", as this chapter attempts to show, has weakened any Soviet impulse to be aggressive, despite the vast magnitude of destructive power assembled by the U.S.S.R. for the first time in the entire history of Russia. This factor in its turn has affected Soviet predispositions to the third world, including India. The fact that the U.S.S.R. in the post-Stalin era is encouraging state-level relations with developing states like India despite obvious ideological differences and that Soviet ideologues want the state in India to assume an ever increasing number of functions even while they note its severe limitations are all organically linked with the impact of the nodal restraint upon the central dynamics. The net effect of the latter "contradiction" is that Soviet foreign policy has set up longer-term moderate goals vis-a-vis the third world.

The Soviet arms build-up in the post-Khrushchev era has attracted considerable attention in the West and has been subjected to a spate of commentaries and analyses.[1] The overtaking of the U.S.A. by the U.S.S.R. in the number of strategic missiles on the one hand and the stepped-up Soviet naval activities on the other have led both academic and government circles in the West to devote a great deal of attention to such questions as : whether the U.S.S.R. has been aiming at acquiring a first-strike capability, whether the Soviet arms build-up after Khrushchev has caused perceptible shifts in the Soviet politico-strategic doctrine, and, if so, whether such doctrinal shifts are a prelude to a more vigorous, even aggressive, Soviet policy posture, etc.

Two major aspects of arms development in the U.S.S.R. have gained considerable publicity : the strategic forces (including the sea-based component) and the conventional naval forces. The following table reflects the result of the stragetic arms race between the superpowers during 1961-1972 :

STRATEGIC WEAPONS

Table 1[2]

(mid-years)

	1961	'62	'63	'64	'65	'66	'67	'68	'69	'70	'71	'72
US												
ICBM	63	294	424	834	854	904	1054	1054	1054	1054	1054	1054
SLBM	96	144	224	416	496	592	656	656	656	656	656	656
USSR												
ICBM	50	75	100	200	270	300	460	800	1050	1300	1510*	1530*
SLBM	Some	Some	100	120	120	125	130	130	160	280	440	560

* Including those in IRBM/MRBM fields

Table 1 reveals that after a period of distinct numerical inferiority in both land—and sea-based strategic missiles, the U.S.S.R. finally caught up with the U.S.A. and then overtook her at the turn of the 1970's in the production of land-based missiles while narrowing the gap rapidly in sea-based missiles. With the signing of the preliminary SALT agreements in the Vladimir Hall of the Kremlin on May 26, 1972, the strategic missile race between the two superpowers was halted and the U.S. ambition of attaining strategic superiority over the U.S.S.R. was given up. The remarkable fact to be noted in this connection, however, is not that the U.S.S.R. had been maintaining a steady lead over the U.S.A. in strategic missiles but that the U.S.A. had allowed the number of her missiles to remain frozen since 1967. Given the U.S. posture of "assured destruction", i.e., her declared policy to keep up her second-strike capability, this curious fact only indicates that the U.S.A. had been shifting her strategic emphasis to some other realm. This is the qualitative development of her strategic missile forces.

The U.S. MIRVing programme envisages the replacement of 550 land-based ICBMs with Minuteman-III, each capable of carrying three independently targetable nuclear warheads. Further, 496 Poseidon-type SSBMs, each with a payload of ten strategic warheads, are coming into operation in the place of the Polaris. Even these new developments are dwarfed by the envisaged ULMS programme, which, incidentally, former Secretary of Defence Melvin Laird promised to carry out despite SALT-I, apparently to use it as a strong bargaining counter in the following SALT negotiations.[3] The Under-sea Long-range Missile System envisages the development by 1978 of the 16,000 ton super-submarine called the "Trident", each to be equipped with twenty-four improved SLBMs of 8,000 km. range. The U.S.S.R., judging by available reports, has little as ambitions as the ULMS.

It is true that the U.S.S.R. has been expanding her nuclear submarine fleet at the rate of eight per year[4] and has already surpassed the U.S.A. in this field[5], but the submarines she has built have been of the "Yankee" class corresponding to the U.S. Polaris/Poseidon types. Hence, although the Moscow summit succeeded in freezing the number of modern submarines of the two superpowers at 44 and 62 respectively, the advent of the U.S. Trident must be borne in mind while comparing their respective strategic advantages. The Russians are only belatedly catching up with the U.S.A. in their MIRVing programme. Their otherwise versatile SS-9, capable of lifting a 25-megaton bomb, can at best be fitted out with the less sophisticated MRV (multipled re-entry vehicle). The picture of the U.S. strategic offensive power projected for 1973 is contained in Table 2 (excluding aircraft-carried strategic warhead).

Table 2[7]

	No. of Nuclear Warheads
10 Polaris submarines, each with 16 MRBMs (each MRBM carrying 1 warhead)	160
31 Poseidon submarines, each with 16 MRBMs (each MRBM with 10 warheads)	4960
504 Minuteman II and Titan ICBMs with 1 warhead each	504
550 Minuteman III ICBMs with 3 warheads each	1650
Total :	7274

The mid-1972 figures for the strategic nuclear weapons at the disposal of the U.S.A. have been estimated at 5,700 and those of the U.S.S.R. at 2,500[8]. These figures, hence, completely change the picture obtained from Table 1. In the actual strike power in terms of launchable warheads, the U.S.A. enjoys overwhelming superiority over the U.S.S.R. In fact, the U.S. policy has been so designed as to make sure that each of the three Strategic strike components (land-based ICBMs, sea-based SLBMs and the bomber fleet) would be able to inflict unacceptable damage upon the adversary. It is not the number of delivery vehicles which counts in the esoteric strategic calculations but the payload, the effectiveness of the nuclear punch. This also explains the relative US indifference to the quantitative aspect of the missile race since 1967.

The number of strategic weapons does not count after a certain level of stockpiling has been reached ; a stockpile increasing beyond that level only represents overkill capacity. But the figures presented above certainly reveal that the allegation regarding the increase of the Soviet nuclear threat is a matter of presentation.[9] The Western sources upholding the threat theory commit, in Morgenthau's term, the fallacy of absolutizing Soviet strategic power.[10] While it is undeniable that the Soviet strategic power has increased following the Cuba crisis of 1962, its magnitude appears in exaggeration due to the slackening of the U. S. effort to keep up the numbers race—as distinct from the race for qualitative improvements (e. g., MIRV, reduction of the "circular error probability", etc.). Further, the SALT talks indicate that neither of the two superpowers takes the concept of the "first strike" capability seriously—if they ever did. Even if hard ICBM bases consisting of underground silos could conceivably be wiped out in a carefully synchronized nuclear attack, the problem of tackling sea-based mobile deterrents would still remain, not to speak of the strategic air force units at a continuous ready status.

The record of the conduct of the U.S.S.R. at the SALT talks and the preliminary agreement, as pointed out by Benjamin S. Lambeth and John Newhouse, showed her seriousness of purpose,[11] hardly befitting a power allegedly bent upon threatening the nuclear balance. If anything, the Soviet strategic effort has been to create a more equitable balance. The overall defensive nature of the Soviet military policy is further reflected in the reluctance to supply Egypt with advance offensive weapons, which seriously strained the relations between the two countries. Consequently, in July 1972, President Sadat ordered the 20,000 Russian advisers and technicians out of Egypt.[12] He also implied that the U.S.S.R. was trying to restrain the Arabs from reopening military conflict with Israel in the course of an address to the Central Committee of the Arab Socialist Union.[13] Further, despite Western anticipation of a Soviet "surgical strike" against China, the Soviet posture vis-a-vis the latter country is characterized by the same overall defensiveness.[14]

Conventional Navy

A number of Western analysts have taken an alarmist view of the Soviet activities in the sphere of the conventional navy following the Cuba crisis of 1962.[15] It is true that the Soviet navy has achieved impressive results in the recent past in this sphere. The increasing tonnage of the Soviet merchant fleet, which places the U.S.S.R. among the leading maritime nations of the world, the rise in the naval transport tonnage, the development of amphibious landing capabilities (including the resuscitation of the naval infantry in 1964), the appearance of the Moskva-class helicopter-carriers for ASW operations and that of heavy missile-cruiser have shown the Soviet desire to play a greater role in the seas and the oceans of the world, hitherto monopolized by Western naval units. The U.S.S.R. has reportedly been building a 20,000-30,000-ton ship at the Nikolayev yards in the Black Sea, presumably her first aircraft-carrier.[16] In addition, she has at her command the largest submarine fleet in the world—both conventional and nuclear—and has acquired the giant AN-22 turbo-prop aircraft for long-range logistics operations.[17]

The statistics certainly seem impressive. At the same time, however, the inherent weaknesses of the Soviet navy should not be overlooked. In terms of air cover and strike power, the latter remains at a disadvantage vis-a-vis the Western navies with their aircraft-carriers. The Soviet navy is handicapped in its strike power in terms of adequate aircraft-carriers. It possesses Shaddock missiles of around 400 nautical miles range, and smaller styx missiles which, incidentally, proved their worth in the Arab-Israeli war of 1967 and the Indo-Pak war of 1971. But they cannot entirely make up for the absence of air cover; the U.S. nuclear-powered aircraft-carriers have a complement of 100 aircraft apiece. Also, the U.S.A. has developed the most sophisticated ASW gadgets which can neutralize much of the effectiveness of the Soviet numerical superiority in submarines. Above all, the Soviet navy is also handicapped in the absence of large foreign bases as opposed to the U.S. navy's worldwide bases. The U.S.A. is also spending about 1,700 million dollars on new fighter-bombers (the B-1) and attack submarines.[18]

The Mediterranean Theatre

It is the Mediterranean and the Indian Ocean regions which recently caught world attention in connection with the allegedly increasing Soviet naval threat. It is true that the

SOVIET MILITARY AND DOCTRINAL POSTURE

Soviet policy in the Middle East has been characterized by considerable political, economic and military penetration. Since 1967 elements of the Soviet Black Sea fleet have been stationed in the Mediterranean and this naval presence has been considerable, particularly in view of the fact that it was insignificant in the earlier decades. The Russians also have berthing facilities available at Latakia in Syria and Port Said and Alexandria in Egypt.[19] Nevertheless, the Soviet Mediterranean fleet remains at a disadvantage in relation to its Western counterparts. Some of the major reasons affecting the operational capability of the Soviet navy have already been offered. The MiG-21 with a range of around 500 nautical miles and operating from Arab airfields would provide cover only in the eastern Mediterranean. In addition, among the three gateways to the Mediterranean, the Dardanelles and Gibraltar are controlled by NATO members. As to the third gateway, Egypt has demonstrated to the U.S.S.R. that the latter must not take her friendship for granted. Further, much of the naval build-up of the U.S.S.R. has been a process of modernization with actually a reduced number of ships.[20] In numbers, the Italian navy alone exceeds the Soviet Mediterranean fleet.[21] While the West has been facing difficulties over the British base in Malta, the U.S.A. has secured her naval presence in the eastern Mediterranean in the form of the Pireaus base in Greece.

The Russians must also be aware of their weaknesses as seen, for example, in their cautious use of power in the Middle East.[22] The significance of the Soviet naval presence in the Mediterranean, hence, does not lie in its preponderance of power over Western naval power but rather in its role as a counterpoise, in its denial of the monopoly of Western naval presence in the region. In the view of one analyst :

> ...the effect of the increase of the Soviet naval force on the military balance has not been decisive, for the Soviet squadron is inferior to the US Sixth Fleet in striking power......[23]

Another commentator, reflecting a similar sober view, points out :

> ...the thought is compelling that in situations of limited conventional conflict in the Middle East, Soviet ships could strongly inhibit—if not interdict—US naval actions in the Mediterranean.[24]

Inhibition, not interdiction, then, is the likely role of the Soviet navy in the Mediterranean. This implies that risks of intervention like the landing of U.S. Marines in Lebanon in 1958, mentioned earlier, have enhanced in view of the Soviet naval presence in the region. It reflects the deterrent role of the Soviet navy—perhaps at least partly in response to the positive feedback phenomenon provided by China, as will be discussed at the end of this chapter—but hardly a "threat" as such. The interdiction role was reflected, for instance, in the increase of the number of the Soviet vessels stationed in the Mediterranean from around 50 to about 70 during the Arab-Israeli conflict in late 1973.[25]

The Indian Ocean Theatre

Regarding the Soviet naval activity in the Indian Ocean, an even more exaggerated assessment has been made by certain sections of the Western governments. During the Indo-Pak war of December, 1971, the U.S. Commander-in-Chief in the Pacific, John S. McCain, Jr., stated in connection with the cruise of the Enterprise into the Bay of Bengal that the U.S. Seventh Fleet would henceforth play a greater role in the Indian Ocean "to counteract Russian strategy".[26] The following month reports of the U.S. acquistion of a naval base in Bahrein became public. This was in addition to another new naval base that the U.S.A. has been developing in Diego Garcia, initially described as a communication centre.[27] The U.S. Defence Department sources also reported the presence of 21 Soviet ships including 2 guided-missile cruisers.[28] However, it must have been the "right-wing radicals" of the Pentagon who played up the Soviet "threat". U.S. intelligence sources reported in 1973 that the average Soviet naval presence in the Indian Ocean was about 8 ships, with an average composition of one submarine, one destroyer, one landing vessel, one mine-sweeper and about four escort ships. This

was considered by more sober U.S. leaders to be in keeping
with the Soviet defence needs, given the long closure of the
Suez canal.[29] Several experts in the U.S.A. specializing in
South Asian affairs came out against the Soviet naval menace
theory. Philip Talbot, a former U.S. Assistant Secretary of
State for Near East and South Asian Affairs, and Columbia
University's expert on South Asia, Howard Wriggins, asserted
that the reports of a Soviet naval build-up in the Indian
Ocean were exaggerated.[30] Their views tallied with the assessment of British intelligence, which, in addition, estimated that the
Soviet naval vessels present in the region as of early 1972
have been actually less in number than those present in 1970.
Enquiries conducted by Australian MPs have also confirmed
that the Soviet naval presence was over-estimated by Western
government officials.[31] While it is likely that the Russians
are interested in the Indian Ocean for more reasons than
merely ensuring safe descent of their spacecraft, as cryptically explained by the Soviet naval chief, Admiral Gorshkov,
during his visit to India in April, 1972,[32] they do not as
yet have a military treaty with any of the Indian Ocean
littorals. In one view, the hue and cry over the Soviet naval
presence in the Indian Ocean has been motivated.[33]

The admission of the U.S.A's top military man, Chairman
of the Joint Chiefs of Staff, Admiral Moorer, that the reports
regarding the U.S.S.R.'s acquisition of base facilities in Vishakapatnam had no basis, is another pointer to the over-estimation of the Soviet presence in the Indian Ocean.[34] The
Russians do have deep-water berthing facilities in two areas
in the western Indian Ocean at Hodeida in Yemen and at
Berbera in Somalia. For the past few years they have also
maintained a permanent mooring buoy at Fortune Banks
south of the Seychelles.[35] They have also concluded a fishing
agreement with Mauritius and have shown interest in Singapore's port facilities. The power significance of these activities,
however, have generally been overestimated in certain circles
of the Western governments. Britain at a stage went so far
as to justify her sale of arms to South Africa as a response
to the alleged Soviet threat.[36]

The character of the Soviet fleets would be largely strategically defensive, meeting the threat posed by the Western carrier strike forces and missile submarines. An authoritative source confirms the above description and adds that the Soviet "challenge" in the sea is the result of "more forward deployment rather than more rapid naval building in the East than the West."[37] Yet another reputed source maintains:

> Soviet surface ships and submarines were originally sent into the Mediterranean to counter the strategic strike capability of the US Sixth Fleet. Their primary task is the defence of the homeland and the Soviet Fleet's composition is consistent with this ... the fleet has no strategic strike role.[38]

The generally defence-orientedness of the U.S.S.R. was further reflected in the territorial air defence arrangements as represented by the ABM code-named Galosh and the high-performance Tallinn system based on the SA-5 missile.[39] Ten thousand SAMs and three thousand interceptor aircraft are available for defensive operations.[40] Morton H. Halperin points out in this connection that "The Soviets have continued to the present time to spend a much greater percentage of their defence budget on active defence than the United States does"[41] It was also the U.S.S.R. which initiated the ABM as a real defence effort against strategic missile strikes. Long-range bomber forces have dwindled on both sides. However, the U.S.A. still commands over 500 of them, about 72 being the modern F-111. The U.S.A. is re-equipping the large number of ageing B-52s with short-range attack missiles (SRAMs) and concentrating on making the supersonic B-1 bomber fleet (250 in number) operational by the end of the 1970's, each of them costing 31 million dollars not counting its elaborate avionics and missile armaments.[42] The U.S.S.R., on the other hand, has about 150 strategic bombers and there is no sign of her developing a new version or increasing the already existing types. The variable-geometry bomber, NATO code-named Backfire/Flogger, which it is reportedly developing, is a short-range one.[43] Thus both in strategic arms as well as in conventional naval build-up, the Soviet policy seems to have been based on denial to the U.S.A. of the latter's supremacy. This assessment finds further confirmation in Senator J.W. Fulbright's assertion that the U.S.S.R may not be nearly as militarily expansive as the U.S. cold war doctrine made her out to be.[44] The defence-consciousness of the U.S.S.R. was also seen in her insistence during the SALT negotiations on inhibiting offensive weapons systems.[45] Finally, U.S. analyses also reveal that the U.S.S.R. has traditionally spent much more money on defence than offence, the ratio being about 3 : 1, compared to the U.S. ratio of 1 : 1.[46]

Politico-Strategic Doctrine

The purpose of a consideration of the Soviet politico-strategic doctrine is to determine its essential characteristics and to examine them against the background of the foregoing analysis. The outcome would then explain a large part of operative Soviet foreign policy today. Millitary theory, created by policy, builds in its turn a broad framework of military-strategic goals with reference to which policy formulation takes place. It defines situations in the abstract in which threat of force may be made or actual resort to force may be undertaken. Policy, therefore, has to take cognizance of military theory whenever confronted by latent or actual crisis situations. In this sense, Clausewitz's celebrated dictum that war is the continuation of policy by other, i.e., violent means has not lost its validity. Robert E. Osgood, for example, defines the relationship between force and policy as follows :

> (The) principle of political primacy is basic to all forms and all uses of military power, whether employed overtly, covertly, or only tacitly......In order that military power may serve as a controllable and predictable instrument of national policy, it must be subjected to an exacting political discipline.[47]

For Morton H. Halperin :

> ......force does continue to play a role despite the development of the thermonuclear weapons...War very much remains a thinkable and possible instrument of policy.[48]

What the two experts are stressing is essentially the time-honoured Clausewitizian formula. In this connection, the controversy between one section of Western thinkers and Soviet ideologists as to whether war can still be designated as a valid instrument of policy seems misplaced. The theoretical Leninist position, according to which war is the continuation of policy, is based on certain socio-economic tenets of Marxism. It generally provides valuable insights into the socio-economic factors that, inter alia, shape governmental policy. By no means does it imply, however, that war is a *rational* policy choice. Western scholars, however, tend to impute precisely that implication to the Soviet theoretical position.[49] If it be granted that war does not appear from the blue but breaks out in accordance with policy (barring accidents), then the Soviet ideological views of war might give an insight into the current Soviet policy. In fact, some prominent Western scholars have adopted this approach to the study of the Soviet foreign policy and military thinking.[50]

Strategic doctrine, cautions Henry Kissinger, "must not be thought of as something theoretical or dogmatic. Its role is to define the likely dangers and how to deal with them, to project feasible goals and how to attain them."[51] It is proposed to ascertain in the following section the degree and nature of violence sanctioned by the Soviet politico-strategic doctrine so as to throw further light upon the true purposes of the post-Khrushchev arms build-up.[52]

While the Soviet public stance minimised the significance of nuclear weapons under Stalin, it adopted a maximalist position on the issue under Khrushchev. During the latter's tenure, the Soviet strategic line harped on the theme that any armed clash involving the superpowers would inevitably grow into a central war, i.e., full nuclear exchange. Thomas W. Wolfe claimed in 1964 to have discerned preliminary signs of flexibility in the hitherto rigid Soviet strategic doctrine.[53] Analysing *Military Strategy* edited by Marshall Sokolovskii (first published in 1952 and revised in 1963) and other Soviet military publications, Wolfe came to the conclusion that the Soviet military doctrine was undergoing a transformation in several aspects, an important sign of which was the de-emphasizing of the "inevitability" of the central war in the event of a superpower confrontation of any degree.

In 1969, Wolfe in another article took up the discussion of Soviet military activity and showed that the Soviet armed forces were growing more versatile, but he failed to pursue the theme of Soviet doctrinal flexibility.[54] This was presumably because even his perspicacity could not detect any further significant changes in the Soviet military doctrine, e.g., the concern that central war must be avoided and the belief that deterrence is the best guarantee against nuclear war.

The cautious and security-first approach in defining strategic objectives has been a steady trend in Soviet history from the time the "permanent revolution" doctrine was discarded in favour of "socialism in one country". Even Khrushchev's adventurism and verbal fireworks were never based on any bridge-burning tactics; the line of retreat was kept wide open as noted earlier. Hermann Kahn's assessment that the U.S.S.R. under Khrushchev was fully appreciative of "committal strategy", which keeps no lines of retreat open and advertises this to the adversary so as to compel him to give way, was wrong.[55] As Raymond L. Garthoff has pointed out, "The Soviet policy was never based on reliance on war as the chief means of achieving the triumph of Communism."[56] A similar line of thinking is noted in Halperin who suggests that the NATO has been based on the false assumption of Soviet aggressive policy. And, according to Edward L. Warner III, the conservative concern with the security of the Soviet state will most certainly be weighed against great power and ideological aspirations for expanded political influence in the world.[57]

The U.S. doctrine of "flexible response" has no Soviet counterpart. As Western commentators like Wolfe, Garthoff, Warner, et al. have pointed out, the Russians have been reducing their stress on the inevitability and automaticity of escalation of local wars involving the superpowers; a recent Soviet ideological study states, "Not that every local conflict will inevitably develop into a world conflict; but ... there is always the danger that it will ... ."⁵⁸ But for this rather ambiguous revision of a major tenet, the Soviet strategic doctrine at present is hardly characterized by any great novelty. There is nothing, for example, which even faintly resembles those U.S. theories which are based on the concept of "credible irrationality". Thomas Schelling's "compellence" theory and Hermann Kahn's "chicken strategy" and "escalation ladder" with its 44 rungs⁵⁹ have no doctrinal counterparts in published Soviet military thought.

The Chinese appreciated the rigidity of the Soviet strategic doctrine and urged the U.S.S.R. in effect to shake off her obsessive concern with the central war and introduce greater flexibility into her outlook.⁶⁰ This has been noted in more details in the preceding chapter. In their public defiance of nuclear weapons, the Chinese seem to have adopted the same "credible irrationality" which is the key to the theories of Kahn and others. "This is partly a recognition on their part", observes Halperin, "that to play the role of lunatic can be in some situations a source of strength, if their opponents are convinced that the Chinese are not afraid of their opponents' weapons."⁶¹ Kahn's contention that the Chinese clearly underestimate the effects of nuclear war and that time will bring them greater wisdom is untenable. It is all the more surprising that the propounder of "chicken strategy" should fail to grasp its Chinese version.

The Soviet doctrine thus sanctions no such bold moves as the large-scale U.S. bombing of Vietnam, the blockading and mining of Haiphong and other North Vietnamese ports and harbour installations, the open demonstration of power in ordering the prestigious nuclear-powered aircraft-carrier, the Enterprise, to the Bay of Bengal, and the like.

WAR TYPOLOGY

The tenets that war is a deliberate policy choice to achieve policy goals by violent means and that it has a class-dimension inextricably linked with it set the major premises of the Soviet war typology. Since exploitation is the fundamental reality of imperialism and since the latter never ceases to attempt to erect new structures of exploitation or to defend existing ones, wars perpetrated by it are ipso facto "unjust". They are, however, "just" on the side of those historically progressive forces which are engaged in destroying, or preventing the reintroduction of, exploitative systems. The Soviet war typology thus spells out the following kinds of war which, with one exception, are both "just" and "unjust", depending on the historical role of the respective adversaries. The classification which follows also corresponds to the major "contradictions" of the current phase of history.[62]

(a) wars between opposing social systems ;

(b) civil war between the proletariat and the bourgeoisie ;

(c) wars between colonialists and the peoples fighting for national liberation, and

(d) wars between capitalist states.

The major contradiction of the present epoch, in Soviet view, is that between the two opposing social systems. This is an improvement upon the previous capitalist-encirclement psychosis and reflects the growing confidence of the U.S.S.R. in her assessment of the global distribution of power. While the First World War had given birth to the first socialist state of the world, the Second World War paved the way for the creation and consolidation of the socialist community of states. The inevitable result of this was the serious weakening of global imperialism and colonialism. Added to the discomfiture of imperialism was the socio-political awakening of its vast hinterland. the continents of Asia, Africa and Latin America. Hence, so goes the Soviet argument, the U.S.A., which is the leading imperialist power, has taken upon herself a kind of Hitlerite task of unleashing war upon the U.S.S.R. and her socialist partners "with the aim of stopping the forward march of history".[63] However, it is the growing might of the socialist community led by the U.S.S.R. which deters U.S. imperialism from carrying out such a drastic policy. With an argument reminiscent of the Hegelian dictum that the rational is the real, Yuri Krasin, a Soviet scholar, justifies the consequent peaceful coexistence in the following words :

Lenin's comments on inevitable conflicts with imperialist states do not run counter to the peaceful coexistence principles : they are a sober judgement of the actual situation that then prevented the realisation of principles advocated by socialism.[64]

It is noteworthy in this connection that the Soviet doctrine categorically rejects the concept of "limited war" propounded by U.S. theoreticians. Unlike the U.S. theories of target discrimination in central war, e.g., the distinction between "counterforce" and "countervalue", the Soviet target philosophy refuses to recognize the possibility of selective nuclear strikes. As a recent Soviet textbook puts it :

> The use of nuclear missile weapons makes it possible to attain decisive military results in a very short time... In the event of war not only groupings of the enemy's armed forces will be subjected to destructive nuclear strikes, but also his industrial and political centres, communication centres, everything that feeds the arteries of war.[65]

Further :

> The propaganda of limited wars is intended to pacify public opinion, to accustom people to the thought that nuclear war is possible. At the same time all talk about confining nuclear strikes only to military objectives is intended to camouflage the plans for a preemptive war (first strike) against the socialist countries.[66]

What is the Soviet image of the central war ? The Soviet doctrinal position ascribes first strike intentions to imperialism. While admitting that a full nuclear exchange would inflict tremendous damage not only on imperialism but also on the socialist community, it stresses the need for keeping up a high degree of morale among troops so as to enable them to survive the holocaust psychologically. It further emphasizes the need to train and condition troops with the help of simulation techniques. The emphasis on the survival of troops seems to indicate the Soviet belief that while nuclear strikes would be the chief feature, they would not necessarily be the alpha and omega of central war. Followup operations by surviving military formations could also be decisive. To what extent Chinese militancy has evoked this viewpoint it is difficult to determine. Also, whether this line of a post-central war operation would replace to a considerable degree the hitherto frozen Soviet attitude of unacceptability of central war remains to be seen. The predominant viewpoint, however, is still centred on the avoidance of central war.

Civil war between the proletariat and the bourgeoisie, in Soviet view, is the most acute of all forms of struggle between the two classes and breaks out only when the proletariat has exhausted all other non-violent means of struggle for state power. Armed struggle, assures the Soviet doctrine, is not an inevitability in all countries as a prelude to socialist revolution. Naturally, the bourgeoisie would not be inclined to hand over state power on a silver platter. Nevertheless, "the considerably greater strength of the working class, the wider social basis of the revolution and the existence of the powerful socialist community open up the possibility for a peaceful transition of some countries to socialism."[67]

The Soviet doctrine has revived a relatively obscure chapter in history to substantiate the thesis of peaceful transition to socialism. The Bela Kun-government, which came to power in Hungary in March, 1919, without resort to violence and lasted four months, has been described as a model for "the revolutionary movement of the European proletariat".[68] Krasin, quoted earlier, reproaches Western scholars for amplifying Lenin's idea of an armed seizure of power and playing down his admission of the possibility of a peaceful transition to socialism.[69]

Wars of national liberation have achieved historic importance, so asserts the Soviet doctrine, following the October Revolution of 1917 in Russia. They received an added stimulus from the creation of the socialist states following the Second World War. While recognizing wars of national liberation as one of the major contradictions of the present epoch, the Soviet doctrine refuses to accord them prime importance unlike the Chinese doctrine. "The might of the world socialist system is a decisive factor in the struggle of the people in the colonies and dependent countries for their liberation from imperialist oppression", asserts the Soviet doctrine.[70] The Sino-Soviet dispute regarding the doctrinal position on wars of national liberation has been covered in the foregoing chapter and need not be repeated here. Suffice to mention at this juncture that the Soviet ideologues have been joining issue with the Chinese and have stated, for instance, that "a revolutionary situation does not arise merely because some people desire it, or on the order of 'brilliant personalities'." Attacking the Maoist thesis that political power grows out of the barrel of a gun, they polemically put the question as to where the guns would come from in aid of national liberation forces unless the latter are "firmly linked" with world socialism.[71] From the Soviet standpoint, the Lin Piao strategy of rural encirclement of the urban centres is erroneous since only the liberation army reared in the city, not peasant guerrillas based in villages, can be the vanguard of national liberation.[72] This view, apart from the different historical experiences of the Russian and the Chinese communists in fighting for liberation of their countries, also reflects the contempt which a highly advanced industrial power feels for the potentialities of rural areas as the focus of future revolutionary movements. The city-optimist, village-pessimist outlook of the Soviets, and its opposite with the Chinese, reflect the varying levels of the economic development of the two states.

The cautious policy of the U.S.S.R. is also seen in her adoption of, in Zagoria's terminology, the "classical right" strategy regarding the liberation of the colonial areas.[73] It envisages, under the pressure of the nodal restraint, struggle in the colonial areas for bourgeois-national and democratic goals rather than radical social demands from the outset. Unlike the "independent right" strategy adopted by the Chinese, which, although recognizing the two-stage revolutionary process, stresses the need for prominence and leadership of the communist party throughout, the Soviet model does not require communist leadership in national coalition. It is, hence, based on the ideas of a united front-from-above in which the communist party is willing to accept bourgeois leadership. An application of this strategy, for example, was made in Iraq in 1971 when under Soviet encouragement and in view of the signing of the 15-year Iraqi-Soviet Treaty, Aziz Mohammed, the communist leader, announced that his party was ready to forego any reservations regarding the formation of a national front in Iraq, on which the ruling Ba'ath party was keen. The Kurdish rebels also adopted a conciliatory attitude towards government.[74] The classical right strategy is particularly important in relation to India, but that problem will be examined in greater details in the following chapters.

The final type of war, according to the Soviet doctrine, results from inter-imperialist contradictions. It breaks out chiefly over the division of markets and is, therefore, "unjust" in an all-round sense. A classic example was the First World War. Following the Second World War, Stalin professed that the inter-imperialist contradiction was an inevitability. Speaking of the vanquished imperialist powers, Germany and Japan, he declared:

> Yet only yesterday these countries were great imperialist powers and were shaking the foundations of the domination of Britain, the USA and France in Europe and Asia. To think that these countries will not try again to get on their feet again, will not try to smash the US "regime", and force their way to independent development, is to believe in miracles.[75]

At present, although the Soviet doctrine keeps up the theme of inter-imperialist contradictions (those between the U.S.A. on the one hand and Japan and the EEC on the other), it excludes the possibility of an inter-imperialist war as "extremely unlikely".[76]

The overall impression conveyed by the Soviet arms build-up, politico-military doctrine and operative policy is, hence, that of an obsessive concern with the security of the U.S.S.R. The massive Soviet peace offensive in Europe, discussed earlier, is in line with the security-first stand of her foreign policy. The desire to avoid involvement in a conflict situation containing the potentialities of contradiction number one is unmistakably present in Soviet operative policy. In none of the treaties concluded in the early 1970's with Egypt (May 27, 1971), India (August 9, 1971) and Iraq (April 9, 1972) is there a military assistance clause or any categorical undertaking to provide military aid. Aspaturian's assertion that these are proto-military alliances[77] overlooks the other possibility that they may also serve for Moscow as mechanisms of restraint.[78] Indeed, the U.S.S.R. risked a severe diplomatic setback with her refusal to supply Egypt with MIG-23 and other advanced offensive war materiel.[79] Further, the absence of matching Soviet response (except increased arms aid to North Vietnam) to spectacular U.S. demonstration of power in the Vietnam war and during the Bangladesh crisis is still another indicator of the Soviet concern for security. Direct and determined Soviet armed intervention has occurred only when the cohesion of the socialist bloc has been threatened (Hungary, Czechoslovakia). Two factors seem to have been primarily responsible for the Soviet security-consciousness. One is technology, a collateral of the nodal restraint. Kissinger has described it as the "basic paradox" of the contemporary age. To quote him :

> Power has never been greater ; it has also never been less useful. In the past, the major problem of strategists was to assemble superior strength ; in the contemporary period, the problem more frequently is how to discipline the available power into some relationship to objectives likely to be in dispute. Yet, no matter what spectrum of power the major contenders may have at their disposal, the fear of escalation is inescapable.[80]

The historical factor inhibiting the adoption of a more flexible strategic doctrine and action based on greater risk-taking is the doctrinal belief of "imperialist conspiracy" to destroy world socialism. The appeasement of Hitler by the

West in the 1930's and, as mentioned earlier, the Nazi determination to raze the young Soviet state to the ground only reinforced this conviction. While the U.S.S.R. is now confident of her own power, she appears to be keen on giving no latitude to the imperialists to start off a central war. As Gromyko put it showing clearly the Soviet concern with the nodal restraint :

> The report of the Central Committee (at the 23rd. CPSU Congress) emphasizes the enormous role of the socialist community in world affairs. No statesman who looks at the situation with open eyes can deny the growing importance of the foreign policy conducted by the socialist countries, whose aim is to prevent a new war and repulse the designs of aggressors.[81]

Khrushchev had appreciated the need of the U.S.S.R. to outgrow the traditional continental limits of Russian power and to transform Soviet power into a truly global one. However, he proceeded to achieve that goal from an inadequate power base. The post-Khrushchevian triumvirate has been trying to accomplish the same by different means. Hence, there appears to be no "threat" as such to the global balance of power from the Soviet side in an immediate millitary sense ; the recent Soviet endeavours have been geared to equalization with the Western powers.

Central Dynamics, Nodal Restraint and Positive Feedback

An examination of the parameters discussed above in terms of the theoretical framework of the Soviet foreign policy is now in order. A number of important consequences start flowing from their interplay. The most significant contribution of the U.S. policy of containment and the concomitant nuclear arms race was to force a major paradigm-shift of the Soviet foreign policy. The step-function, introduced by Malenkov in his famous speech mentioned earlier, was developed and enshrined by his more successful rival, Khrushchev, in 1956. That foreign policy paradigm has continued to the present day without essential modification. The prospect of the thermonuclear war, hence, has led to major changes in the Soviet foreign policy-orientation which has been spelt out with particular care to avoid risks of confrontation with the West that could run out of control. This is the component of the "nodal restraint" that has significantly conditioned and modified the other component of "central dynamics". It has been widely noted even by Western experts that the Soviet foreign policy has generally been cautious and security-conscious.[82] With the single exception of perhaps Khrushchev, the Soviet leaders have avoided taking unduly risky foreign policy moves in the face of Western opposition. In this, there is a remarkable similarity between the Chinese and the Soviet foreign policies. Despite verbal fireworks, the Chinese have a foreign policy record unblemished by risk-taking vis-a-vis the West. Their Korean involvement does not contradict this since the U.S. crossing of the 38th. parallel was interpreted by them as the probable crumbling of a vital buffer. The shelling of the offshore islands—as distinct from their invasion—has to be seen also in the light of China's conviction that two Chinese states could not exist. Even Khrushchev, while he precipitated a number of crises in Berlin and one in Cuba taking full political advantage of the then widely perceived "missile gap" between the U.S.A. and the U.S.S.R., never pushed the former too far. Time and again, ultimatums were postponed and allowed to lapse. Rhetorics, not rockets, were the most frequently used means against the West.

The Soviet ideological line and foreign policy towards India, which remained in consonance with each other during the post-Stalin period, can be properly grasped against the background of the interaction between the central dynamics and the nodal restraint. The apparent precipitate drop in the revolutionary elan of the Soviet ideology and foreign policy, against which the Chinese have been so vociferous, cannot be explained otherwise statisfactorily.

To be sure, "peaceful coexistence" was played up for a number of times before 1956 by the U.S.S.R. But the chief and more fundamental difference between the earlier versions and the current one is generated by a completely new kind of reality: the lurking presence of the power of destruction on an unprecedented scale with equally unprecedented swiftness. Emerging from a war in which the U.S.S.R. had to bear the brunt of the offensive thrust of a mighty foe for four years at the cost of twenty million lives and great material loss, it was small wonder that she would not be keen for long to hold on to the Leninist thesis of the inevitability of war.[83] The U.S.S.R.'s sensitivity, for instance, to the possibility of rearming West Germany with nuclear arms reflects her wartime experience with Nazi Germany. As the U.S.A. started toying in 1965 with the idea of a multilateral sharing of nuclear arms by her NATO partners, including West Germany, the U.S.S.R. registered her strenuous opposition to such schemes. Remarkable was the "unflagging attention" devoted not so much to the NATO as to "the West German revenge-seekers".[84] The new technological reality shaped by the spiralling nuclear arms race between the two superpowers acted as a nodal restraint and called for a basic revision of the Soviet ideology. In Shulman's words, this "process of adaptation" of the Soviet foreign policy to the external environment, which is "partly conscious and partly unintended—by which the Soviet leadership seeks to make its efforts effective under changing conditions, has had a transforming effect upon Soviet policies and the Soviet system, and has been an important factor in opening up the dispute with the Chinese."[85]

In terms of the theoretical framework at hand, it is the pressure generated by the nodal restraint upon the Soviet central dynamics that led to the Sino-Soviet dispute on the ideological plane. It has already been mentioned that the difference between the Soviet and the Chinese ideological positions turned out to be that of *timing*, a problem which has far-reaching implications in terms of tactics, assessments and contexts. While the nodal restraint successfully forced the central dynamics out of its Zhdanov-mould and metamorphosed it into a gradualist process, China refused to be daunted by it on the politico-strategic plane. With the initiation of the space age by the U.S.S.R. in 1957, including her first successful testing of an ICBM, the U.S.A. for the first time became vulnerable to a thermonuclear attack from Eurasia. China felt greatly encouraged. She began emphasizing in effect that the U.S.S.R. encourage national liberation revolutions and other communist uprisings around the globe more actively and in defiance of the West. While the Soviet Union hardly hid her sense of triumph in her latest technological achievements, the Chinese went further and declared that the new developments made the east wind prevail over the west wind. Unlike the Russians, the Chinese proclaimed the overwhelming superiority of the socialist forces over the Western forces.[86] The operational significance of these varying assessments became apparent a number of times in the following year. The Iraqi coup of July 13, 1958 attracted Anglo-American landings in Lebanon and Jordan, and evoked the fear of intervention against the new Iraqi government in the U.S.S.R. and China. The former hastily proposed a summit conference with Indian participation and later accepted a Western counterproposal for a summit within the framework of the Security Council. The Chinese reaction to these events was initially hostile; although subsequently Peking came to accept Khrushchev's appeal for an emergency summit, this happened not before she had harped on the familiar theme of teaching the West a violent lesson.[87]

A month after the Middle East crisis, China launched a limited venture in the Taiwan Strait. Although a variety of motives may have impelled her in this, she must have felt encouraged by her own perception of the recently acquired superiority of the socialist bloc. On August 24, one day after the Chinese began shelling the offshore islands of Quemoy and the Matsus, Khrushchev in a speech surveying the possibility of war completely ignored the very topical Far Eastern crisis. The Soviet media rather belatedly began reiterating support for China. Khrushchev's subsequent communication to Eisenhower that an attack on China would be treated as an attack on the U.S.S.R. came only *after* the relaxation of the crisis on September 6.[88] As Donald Zagoria concludes :

> In Mao's view, because Bloc military superiority constituted an absolute deterrent to general war, the deterrent threat could be publicly invoked by Khrushchev without risk to Moscow. Khrushchev evidently did not agree. ... Throughout the crisis, Soviet statements betrayed a genuine concern over the prospects of a nuclear war.[89]

The subsequent development of China's "paper tiger" concept and Lin Piao's scenario of "world-villages" pitted against "world cities" was but a logical linear outcome.

The nodal restraint, hence, not only modified the Soviet global policy but also precipitated the schism with China. The China parameter, however, has important implications for the theoretical framework of the Soviet foreign policy. By posing a challenge to the credibility of the Soviet revolutionary purity it may very well act as a *positive feedback* to the central dynamics component. It is possible to visualize that China's claim to the monopoly patronage of the third world might embarass the Russians into more energetic and competitive involvement. Already, Southeast Asians perceive themselves as the object of Sino-Soviet competition with neither side likely to gain decisive influence in exclusion of the other. While her geographical proximity, and ethnic and ideological ties give China an edge over the U.S.S.R., the latter has a cleaner record in matters relating to ideological support for insurgents (except in the extraordinary Indochina scene).[90] As Shulman suggests :

> In local conflict situations, the present greater Soviet militancy is an effort to maintain its leadership in the Communist movement by refuting the Chinese charge of lack of enthusiasm for local revolutionary developments. Even more broadly, it is a response to the competition of the Chinese for leadership of the nationalist movements in the underdeveloped areas......

He goes on to conclude that :

> ...the combination of continued turbulence in the underdeveloped areas and the emergence of a

Maoist radical revolutionary drive works against the prospects for a conservative Soviet policy in these areas, and has a secondary disturbing effect upon the prospects for stabilization elsewhere, since it leads the Soviet Union to give a militant inflection to its policies with regard to the campaign for "anti-imperialism" and support for "wars of national liberation".[91]

Reorienting itself under the nodal restraint, the central dynamics of the Soviet foreign policy in its post-Stalin phase struck out in a number of new directions. Major emphasis was placed on socialist bloc unity to arrest fissiparous trends, in which, incidentally, Chinese support was forthcoming in the 1950's. The Soviet ideological line began emphasizing that the primary contradiction of the epoch was that between capitalism and socialism and that the latter bloc would spare no efforts to achieve massive economic power to break the economic and political monopoly of the West. A successful challenge to the economic power of capitalism would also set an example before the uncertain third world which was groping for its future identity. Khrushchev, invoking the example of Soviet scientific and technological achievements, declared that the aim of the CPSU was to achieve for the U.S.S.R. a standard of living higher than that of the United States. Two days after his arrival in the U.S.A., on September 17, 1959, Krushchev in the course of a speech in the grand ballroom of the Waldorf-Astoria in New York, took up that theme :

> For a long time nobody ventured to dispute your supremacy. But the time has now come when a country has appeared which accepts your challenge, which takes into account the level of development in the United States and in its turn challenges you. You may rest assured that the Soviet Union will hold its own in this economic competition and it will overtake you and leave you behind.[92]

Apart from responding to domestic economic needs as

discussed earlier, the new course of the Soviet foreign policy charted in 1956 signalled quick recognition of the significance of nationalism in the third world. While the U.S. took up a foreign policy position vis-a-vis the third world reminiscent of Stalinist outlook, the post-Stalin Soviet leadership shifted their policy from a minimalist to a maximalist position. Any newly independent state which was not an ally of the West was now considered friendly. Although the Anlass, the immediate occasion for the more congenial Soviet attitude was the U.S. involvement in the Korean war and the subsequent extension of the line of containment to Asia, the deeper and long term Ursachen should not be overlooked. The dramatic revision of the official Soviet historiography and commentary containing unfavourable assessments of the nationalist leaders like Gandhi and Nehru symbolized the new Soviet desire to encourage nonalignment and anti-Western sentiments in the third world as a step towards containing—and eventually rolling up—Western influence in the region. The Soviet ideological recognition of third world nationalism as a potent factor preceded similar recognition by the U.S.A. Consequently, state-level relations with the young nations were rapidly built up and indigenous communist parties like the CPI were accorded a subsidiary role. It will not be perhaps too far-fetched to establish a correlation between the advent of the thermonuclear bomb and the ICBM on the one hand and the rather meek role of the CPI operating within the legitimate framework of parliamentary democracy in India on the other. The U.S.S.R. is certainly inclined today to orchestrate movements of the faithful in the third world in accordance with the accepted "rules of the game", especially if the governments concerned enjoy some measure of popular legitimacy and are non-aligned. Motivated by the twin objectives of consolidating domestic economy and extending economic and political support to young nations in competition with the West, the U.S.S.R. today sends abroad, not the professional revolutionary types of the 1920's and 1930's, but engineers, technicians, scientists and military experts. Gone are the days of Karl Radek, Michael Borodin and M. N. Roy, travelling abroad incognito and conspiring to spark off social cataclysm in Germany and China; instead, the central dynamics of the Soviet foreign policy has decisively shifted in favour of building new monuments to the Soviet economy and technological power abroad as symbolized by such names as Aswan, Bhilai, Ghorasan, Aliaga and Bokaro.

The Soviet endeavour to encourage and cultivate relationships with the nationalist governments of the third world also fits into the overall paradigm of the Soviet foreign policy. Instead of taking a hard line against the various shades of indigenous socialism, the U.S.S.R. encourages them. Even though they are far from being "scientific", as Soviet scholars do not hesitate to point out, the U.S.S.R. approaches them with abundant sympathy since they all have one substratum in common : their anti-capitalist and hence anti-Western bias. A characteristic assessment of, for instance, "Islamic socialism", is as follows :

> It cannot be easy for the non-proletarian strata to go over to the positions of the working class, for, objectively, they cannot at once embrace the ideas of Marxism-Leninism in all their dimensions, although they do reject the capitalist road of development because it has no future. This inevitably leads to interpret socialism in nationalistic, religious and other—most frequently petty bourgeois—senses and forms.[93]

As David Morison aptly concludes, the "socialist" orientation of the developing states "is valued (by the USSR) only quite secondarily for its effects on domestic policies ; its prime virtue lies in producing a pro-Soviet orientation of foreign policy."[94] Such Soviet tolerance of "utopian socialism" becomes readily comprehensible in the light of the Soviet perception of contradiction alpha of the present age. The Soviet policy of befriending the third world nations flows from the concern to "push" history in the desired direction within the limits of generally recognized legitimacy so as not to attract risks and dangers latent in the primary contradiction. The policy of encouraging a broad "anti-imperialist" and "peace-loving" front regardless of the varied sociological background of the strata involved, although it has greater potential of success in the generally fluid situation of the third world than in the advanced capitalist nations, is nevertheless not confined to the former area. The Soviet leaders do not shrink from making distinctions even within the bourgeoisie and other ruling strata of the advanced capitalist states. As early as 1959, during his U.S. sojourn, Khrushchev sought to make this distinction :

> Like the bourgeoisie of other countries, the American bourgeoisie is far from being homogeneous. The comparatively small but still influential top monopoly group continues to regard the mad arms race almost as its only source of profit and enrichment. But those American companies and corporations that have no access to the "military pie" are less interested in fanning war hysteria and preserving international tensions. ... This circumstance alone could not but give rise to bitter debates and disagreements in the American business world concerning the further trend of US foreign policy and the means of stimulating the American economy.[95]

In his Central Committee report to the twenty-fourth CPSU congress of March, 1971, Brezhnev indicated the desirability of cooperation between the CPSU and the left socialist parties throughout the world. Special mention was made of the intention to cooperate with the Social-Democrats on questions of "peace", "democracy", and "socialism", and it was noted that "this line of the Communists has been meeting with stubborn resistance from the Right-wing leaders of the Social-Democrats."[96] Willy Brandt is, accordingly, hailed as "progressive", since during his tenure as the Foreign Minister of West Germany he introduced the Ostpolitik which, subsequently under his government culminated in Bonn's recognition of the Order-Neisse line, the burial of the Hallstein doctrine, the recognition of the Munich Pact of 1938 as presently invalid, and the conclusion of a number of treaties with the Soviet bloc, the most prominent of them being the Soviet-FRG Treaty of August 12, 1970. The Austrian Social-Democratic leader, Bruno Kreisky, on the other hand, is classified as a "right-winger" for his more tough anti-communist stand.[97]

In a similar vein, the struggle between the two factions of the ruling Congress Party in India at the turn of the present decade was assessed by an *Izvestia* article as one between pro and anti-imperialist forces. Having stated that "events in India have the attention of the entire world," because this vast country "has for years been an influence in the balance of progressive and reactionary forces in the international arena", it goes on to conclude :

> The intensification of the domestic political struggle in India, therefore, is by no means prompted by individual persons, as Indian reaction and its overseas protectors claim. It is the result of objective causes rooted in the present phase of the development of the new India.[98]

A serious imbalance characterized the development of the armed forces in the U.S.S.R. during Khrushchev's tenure. While strategic rocket forces had been established to meet the challenge of the U.S. strategic strike power, the U.S.S.R. still largely remained a continental power on the level of conventional forces, particularly navy. The built-in tension between such a composition of the armed forces and the Soviet policy of supporting its overseas clients became evident during the 1958 Middle East crisis and again during 1961 and 1962 in Cuba. While the central Soviet pressure remained paralyzed in the face of equivalent U.S. strategic pressure, the U.S.A. had a clear advantage in conventional naval forces which gave her police-role adequate material content and flexibility. Further, official U.S. policy was also based on the philosophy that strategic superiority over the U.S.S.R. must be attained. The post-Khrushchev leadership, drawing appropriate conclusions, concentrated on expanding Soviet naval role on a global scale while at the same time denying the U.S.A. her aspired strategic superiority. As Brezhnev explained in the twenty-third CPSU congress in March, 1966 :

> Nor must the deterioration of the international situation be ignored. The aggressive acts of the US imperialists forced us in recent years to make additional and substantial allocations to strengthen our country's defences.[99]

It can be maintained that the Soviet foreign policy scored a number of successes in this decade in matters concerning her relations with the West, while suffering diplomatic setbacks in the Middle East in July, 1972 (Egypt) and in the U.S. befriending of China. As mentioned earlier, the West German drive for normalization of relations with the Soviet bloc countries ran parallel to the Soviet diplomatic position. No less important were the SALT agreements of May, 1972, which were based on the assumption of strategic "parity" of the two superpowers. They implied a downward revision of the hitherto held U.S. concept of "strategic superiority". As Lawrence W. Martin comments:

> SALT had its origins in the Soviet erosion of American superiority and in a consequent deeper American sense that the option of strategic nuclear war had become a negative instrument, capable only of deterring nuclear aggression.[100]

The peace offensive launched by the twenty-fourth CPSU congress was followed by the dramatic 35-nation European conference in Helsinki in 1975, while the prospects of a mutual balanced forces reduction (MBFR) in Europe are being seriously considered. Thus, while her European flank north of the Mediterranean has been stabilized, the unstable Asian flank tends to attract rivalry and competition with the U.S.A. and China.

Despite growing functional and regional cooperation between the U.S.S.R. and the capitalist states, especially the U.S.A., the third world generally remains the major battlefield. It is the latter which turned the existing reality in the international scene into that of competitive coexistence. As early as 1969, Brezhnev vaguely floated the idea of a collective security for Asia[101] which, perhaps because of the lack of enthusiasm for it among Asians, has not been imparted a definite shape. If the idea was floated with a view to containing

China, as has been widely suggested,[102] it was still-born right at its inception.

It is interesting to note that even though time and again a revolution in the advanced West appeared to have null prospects, at no point of time in her half-century history has the U.S.S.R. considered a Marxist-type transformation of the third world (previously colonies) to be the most important factor. Indeed, M. N. Roy's theses in the second Comintern congress were substantially watered down by Lenin precisely because they sought to emphasize the point that metropolitan revolution was predicated upon the revolution in the colonies. The national liberation movements of the backward areas are ideologically considered to be important but subsidiary to the contradiction alpha between capitalism and socialism. It is also the problem of how much ideological weight to allot to the third world in the overall transformational process that keeps China ideologically alienated from the U.S.S.R.

Detente and technical cooperation with the West are not to be confused with an eclipse of the central dynamics of the Soviet foreign policy. Given the post-Stalinist Soviet proclivity to rely more on "spontaneous" socio-economic forces to bring about transformation, rather than on more "conscious" (and more radically left) agents of history, there cannot be room for doubt that the central dynamics will continue to operate. So long as the Soviet leadership remain convinced of the inexorable laws of history, they may switch between positions defined respectively by the "spontaneity" and "consciousness" factors which have a long history of succeeding each other in Marxist-Leninist thought, but it is their conviction that would feed the central dynamics of their foreign policy. To conclude this chapter with Brzezinski :

> ...the Soviet approach to international affairs is characterized by an intense preoccupation with change. This awareness of continuing change, and the conviction that the inner nature of that change is understood only by them, creates the basis for the faith of the Soviet leaders that they have unravelled the internal logic of history...[103]

NOTES AND REFERENCES

1. See J. I. Coffey, "Soviet ABM Policy : The Implications for the West", *International Affairs*, Chatham House, London, Vol. 45, No. 2, April 1969. Malcolm Mackintosh, "Soviet Strategic Policy", *The World Today*, London, Vol. 26, No. 7, July 1970. Joseph J. Baritz, "The Soviet Strategy of Flexible Response", *Bulletin*, (Institut zur Erforschung der UdSSR), Munich, Vol. 16, No. 4, April 1969.

For Nixon's argument for increasing US defence expenditure in third "State of the Union" message, see *The Statesman*, Calcutta, 21 January 1972. For Melvin Laird's report to the Senate on Soviet military activities, see *The Statesman*, 16 February 1972.

The British government's alarm at the Soviet arms built-up has been reported in *The Statesman*, 17 February 1972.

2. Compiled from *The Military Balance 1971-72*, p. 56 and *1972-73*, p. 67, International Institute for Strategic Studies (JISS), London.
3. *The Statesman*, 27 May 1972.
4. *The Military Balance 1972-73*, op. cit., p. 3.
5. *The Statesman*, 14 January 1972. The USSR reportedly started construction of her 42nd. nuclear submarine, while the USA possessed 41.
6. Joachim Schwelien, "ABM Accord in Moscow and ULMS Program in the USA", *Aussenpolitik*, Vol. 23, 3/72, Hamburg, p. 274.
7. Adapted from Schwelien, op. cit., p. 277, and *The Military Balance 1972-73*, op. cit., p. 3.
8. Schwelien, *op.cit.*, p. 278.
9. For Western fear of alleged Soviet threat, see Coffey, *op. cit.*, pp. 205-206. See also the views of Nixon, Laird, and the British Government, *op. cit.*
10. Morgenthau, *op. cit.*, pp. 153-155.
11. For a sober assessment of the Soviet arms build-up policy, see Benjamin S. Lambeth, "Moscow and the Missile Race", *Current History*, Vol. 61, No. 362, October 1971. See also John Newhouse, *Cold Down. The Story of SALT*, Holt, Rinehart & Winston, New York, 1973.
12. *The Statesman*, July 19, 1972.
13. *The Statesman*, July 20, 1972.
14. See Thomas W. Robinson, "Soviet Policy in East Asia" *Problems of Communism*, November-December 1973, Vol. 23, No. 6, pp. 35-36.
15. For a typically alarmist attitude, see Patrick Wall, "A Threat to Europe's Supply Routes", *The Statesman*, 19 February 1973.
16. *The Statesman*, 3 May, 1972.
17. For an informative discussion of the Soviet naval build-up, see Edward L. Warner III, "The Development of Soviet Military Doctrine and Capabilities in the 1960's" in Mark E. Smith III and Claude Johns, Jr. (eds.), *American Defense Policy*, Johns Hopkins, Baltimore, 1968, and Ciro Zoppo, "Soviet Ships in the Mediterranean and the US-Soviet

Confrontation in the Middle East", *Orbis*, Spring 1970, Vol. 14. No. 1.

18. See *The Statesman*, 23 February, 1972, and Newhouse, *op. cit.*, pp. 39-40.

19. The Egyptians seem to have had initially difficulties with the Russians over the terms and conditions governing the base facilities to be made available to the latter ; however, by April 1972, these difficulties had been solved. See *The Statesman*, 27 March, 1972 and 26 April 1972.

20. *The Mititary Balance 1971-72, op. cit.*, p. 2, and *1972-73*, p. 3.

21. See Curt Gasteyger, "Moscow and the Mediterranean", *Foreign Affairs*, New York, Vol. 46, No. 4, July 1968, pp. 679-680.

22. See Gasteyger, *op.cit.*

23. John C. Campbell, "The Communist Powers and the Middle East. Moscow's Purposes", *Problems of Communism*, No. 5, Vol. 21, September-October, 1972, p. 41.

24. Zoppo, *op.cit.*, p. 126.

25. *The Satesman*, October 19, 1973.

26. *The Statesman*, 18 December, 1971.

27. *The Times of India*, Bombay, 7 January, 1972.

28. *The Statesman*, 12 January, 1972.

29. See Russell Warren Howe, "Moves on Rhodesia," *The Statesman*, July 16, 1973.

30. *The Times of India, op.cit.*

31. *The Statesman*, 25 February, 1972.

32. *The Statesman*, 9 April, 1972.

33. Devendra Kaushik, *The indian Ocean* : *Towards a Peace Zone*, Vikas, in "Book Review", *The Statesman*, 16 April, 1972.

34. *The Statesman*, 9 April, 1972.

35. *The Statesman*, 25 February, 1972.

36. *The Statesman*, 25 February, 1972.

37. *The Military Balance 1971-72 op.cit.*, p. 81.

38. "The Middle East. The Soviet Union in the Mediterranean", *Strategic Survey, 1971.* IISS, pp. 31-32.

39. Newhouse, *op.cit.*, pp. 11-12.

40. *The Military Balance 1971-72*, op.cit., p. 2.

41. Morton H. Halperin. *Defense Strategies for the Seventies*, Little, Brown & Co., Boston, 1971, p. 56.

For details of active defence, see Lt. Col. J. B. Meyers "Soviet Airmobility", *US Army Aviation Digest*, September, 1971, p. 1.

42. Newhouse, *op.cit.*, pp. 39-40.

43. Schwelien, op.cit., p. 276, and *The Military Balance 1972-73*, op.cit., p. 3.

44. *The Statesman*, 25 February, 1972.

45. Newhouse, *op.cit.*, p. 90.

46. Newhouse, *op.cit.*, p. 107.

47. Robert E. Osgood, "The Theory of Limited War", *American Defense Policy*, op. cit., p. 157.

48. Morton H. Halperin, "The Role of Force in the Nuclear Age", *American Defense Policy*, op.cit., p. 15.

49. For Western attitude, see Thomas W. Wolfe, *Soviet Strategy at the Grossroads*, RAND Corporation, Cambridge, Massachusetts, 1964, p. 4. For Soviet arguments, *Problems of War and Peace* (authors unknown), Progress Publishers, Moscow, 1972, Chapter 4.

50. See, for example, Wolfe, *op.cit.*, and William Zimmerman, *Soviet Perspectives*, op.cit.

51. Henry A. Kissinger (ed.), *Problems of National Strategy : A Book of Readings*, Praeger, New York, 1965, p. 9.

52. In studying this aspect, the following publications from the USSR and the USA have been mostly consulted : *Problems of War and Peace*, op. cit., *Marxism-Leninism : On War and Army* (authors unknown), Progress Publishers, Moscow, 1972, Wolfe, op.cit., and Raymond L. Garthoff, *Soviet Military Policy : A Historical Analysis*, Praeger, New York, 1966.

53. Wolfe, *op.cit.*, and Wolfe, "Shifts in Soviet Strategic Thought", *Foreign Affairs*. New York, Vol. 42, No. 3, April 1964.

54. Wolfe, "The Soviet Military since Khrushchev", *Current History*, Philadelphia, Vol. 57, No. 338, October, 1969.

55. Hermann Kahn, "Alternative National Strategies", *American Defense Policy*, op.cit., pp. 85-86.

56. Garthoff. *op.cit.*, p. 24.

57. Halperin, *Defense Strategies...*, op cit., p. 60, and Warner III, *op.cit.*, p. 319.

58. *Problems of War...*, op.cit., pp. 90-91.

59. For these theories, see Thomas C. Schelling, "Compellence", and Kahn, "Some Possible Sizes and Shapes of Thermonuclear War" and "Escalation as a Strategy", *American Defense Policy*, *op.cit*.

For the influence of "think tanks" on U. S. Government, see Paul Dickson, *Think Tanks*, New York, Atheneum, 1972.

60. Cf. Garthoff, *op.cit.*, pp. 191-192, and p. 106.

61. Halperin, *Defense Strateiges...*, *op.cit.*, p. 63.

For a similar assessment of China's policy, see Davis B. Bobrow, "Chinese Views on Escalation". *American Defense Policy...*, *op. cit*.

62. See *Marxism-Leninism*, *op. cit.*, Chapter 2.

63. *Marxism-Leninism*, *op.cit.*, p. 99.

64. Yuri Krasin, *Sociology of Revolution. A Marxist View*, Progress Publishers, Moscow, 1972, p. 232.

65. *Marxism-Leninism*, *op.cit.*, p. 393.

66. *Marxism-Leninism*, *op.cit.*, p. 100.

67. *Marxism-Leninism*, *op.cit.*, p. 109.

68. *Marxism-Leninis n*, *op.cit.*, p. 108.

69. Krasin, *op.cit.*, p. 24.

70. *Marxiem-Leninism,op. cit.*, p. 117.

71. N. Simoniya, *Peking v. National Liberation*, Novosti, Moscow, 1970, p. 13.

72. Simoniya, *op. cit.* pp. 12-13.

73. Donald S. Zagoria, "Russia, China, and the New States", in Donald W. Treadgold (ed.), *Soviet and Chinese Communism*, University of Washington, 1967.

74. *The Statesmam*, 11 April, 1972.

75. Stalin, J. V., *Economic Problems of Socialism in the USSR, op. cit.*, p. 34.

76. *Marxism-Leninism, op. cit.*, p. 128.

77. Vernon V. Aspaturian, "Moscow's Options in a Changing World", *Problems of Communism*, Vol. 21, July-August 1972, p. 3.

78. See William J. Barnds, "Moscow and South Asia", *Problems of Communism*, Vol. 21, May-June 1972, p. 25.

79. For Moscow's caution regarding arms supply to the Middle East, see Gasteyger, *op. cit.*

80. Kissinger, *Problems of National Strategy*, op. cit., p. 5.

81. A. Gromyko, *Policy of Realism*, speech at the 23rd. CPSU Congress, April 2, 1966, Novosti (no date), p. 6.

82. For a detailed analysis, see the earlier sections of this chapter.

83. Edward Crankshaw puts it eloquently, "Nobody who did not live through that first terrible starvation winter with the Russians can have the least conception of the suffering of the people and the total ruin of the Soviet economy.... These things are too easily forgotten over here (the West), if only because they were never properly understood. They were not forgotten in the Soviet Union, and they are not yet forgotten. *Khrushchev's Russia*, Pelican, London, 1962, p. 14.

84. *Brezhnev Report, 23rd. Congress, op. cit.*, pp. 46-48. A. Gromyko, the Soviet Foreign Minister, speaking at the same Congress on 2 April, devoted nearly half his speech to the problem of "revanchism" in West Germany. See A. Gromyko, *Policy of Realism, op. cit.*

85. Shulman, *op. cit.* p. 31.

86. Zagoria, *op. cit.*, p. 160.

87. Zagoria, *op. cit.*, pp. 195-199.

88. Zagoria, *op. cit.* pp. 206-217.

89. Zagoria, *op. cit.*, pp. 216-217.

90. Dick Wilson, "Sino-Soviet Rivalry in Southeast Asia", *Problems of Communism*, September-October, 1974, Vol. XXIII, No. 5, pp. 39-51.

91. Shulman, *op. cit.*, pp. 69-70.

92. A. Ajubei et al., *Face to Face With America*, Foreign Languages Publishing House, Moscow, 1960, p. 175.

93. I. I. Garshin, "The Evolution of Socialist Ideas in the UAR", quoted in "UAR and USSR : The Dialogue on Socialism", *Mizan*, Vol. X, No. 1, January-February, 1968, p. 39.

94. David Morison. "USSR and Third World" (first instalment), *Mizan*, Vol. XII, No. 1, pp. 7-25.
95. *Face to Face with America*, op. cit., p. 170.
96. *Brezhnev Report*, 24th. Congress, op. cit., p. 28.
97. V. Shumsky and V. Kachanov, "Social Democracy at the International Crossroads", *International Affairs*, Moscow, No. 12, December, 1971, pp. 40-41.
98. V. Kudryavtsev, "Observer's Opinion : A Blow to the Plans of Reaction in India", *Izvestia*, November 15, reprinted in *Current Digest of the Soviet Press*, Vol. XXI, No. 46, p. 16, Ohio, 1969.
99. *Brezhnev Report*, 23rd. Congress, op. cit., p. 68.
100. Lawrence W. Martin, "Military Issues : Strategic Parity and Its Implications", *Retreat from Empire*, op. cit., p. 139.
101. Chopra, *op. cit.*, p. 71.
102. Chopra. *op. cit.*, pp. 71-78.
103. Brzezinski, *Ideology and Politics in Soviet Foreign Policy*, op. cit., p. 103.

Chapter IV

THE NON-CAPITALIST PATH AND INDIA

The Foregoing Chapters have dealt with the characterization of certain basic dynamics of the Soviet foreign policy with a number of references to the Indian context. They have endeavoured to substantiate the basic framework of this book out of the melange of an incessantly evolving reality. The conceptual framework thus established, the focus now shifts in the succeeding sections to certain fundamental ideological tenets which have a direct bearing on the developing nations with India cast in the role of a model. The crucial tenet here is that of the "non-capitalist path" with "national democracy", "the formative sector" and the like as important correlates. The non-capitalist path thesis will be traced back to its origin and development in some details so as to cast it in a perspective proper to its understanding. Its relevance today along with the correlates mentioned will be brought out for identifying India's place in the Soviet conceptualization of the third world. It is timely to bear in mind that the playing up of these tenets in current Soviet publications and official documents ought to be scrutinized "dialectically", i.e., a) in their mutual relationships, and b) in their relationship with the current direction of the Soviet foreign policy as sketched in the earlier chapters. Only such a perspective can guarantee a comprehensive and an indepth appreciation of the Soviet foreign policy towards India. The aetiology of the expanding and multidimensional Soviet ties with India, the perception of certain objective forces of change at work and their ideological encoding, and a whole array of related factors discussed before or to be discussed in the following chapters can never be adequately grasped merely from a chronicle of the surface flurry of events. It is to be noted that the following sections, which describe and analyze in the Indian context the non-capitalist path and Soviet activities and perceptions hinging on it, reflect passim, as it were, the outcome of the "contradiction" between the "central dynamics" and the "nodal restraint" components. In the following sections, the non-capitalist path will be studied diachronically as well as in the Indian context. The next chapter will follow with a brief correlative discussion of the role of the state in Marxist thought and its modified Soviet version in the Indian context, the latter forming the heart of the otherwise largely unadumbrated non-capitalist path idea. These largely ideological-theoretical analyses will be followed by detailed quantitative depiction of the multidimensional economic and military exchanges taking place between India and the USSR.

THE NON-CAPITALIST PATH : A DIACHRONIC PERSPECTIVE

The non-capitalist path to socialism is a much used phrase of the current Soviet litany. Soviet ideological writings and statements play up the theme before the newly independent nations as an alternative to capitalism. The question which arises anew in this connection is at least a century old, namely whether the classical Marxist scriptures necessarily take the infralapsarian view of the inevitable capitalistic destiny of nations in the present industrial age as a sine que non of the eventual evolution to socialism. If it is asserted that nations at a certain historical stage of development can skip the capitalist stage in the current era of supposed general transition to socialism – which, in fact, the Soviet ideologues have been doing—then the orthodox Marxist scheme with its neatly juxtaposed stages of history is considerably loosened. The present investigation is designed to throw light on this problem. Further, it will serve as an indispensable background to the application of the thesis to India.

The doctrine of the non-capitalist path to future development was first formulated by a non-Marxist German scholar with regard to the peculiarities of the Russian village commune. Baron von Haxthausen, commissioned by the Prussian government in the 1830's to draw up a report on the peasantry so as to facilitate legislation, found in western Germany remnants of institutions bearing the stamp of Slavonic character. This stimulated his interest in the Slavonic village communes, especially those of Russia, and he made a direct study of the latter for about a year in the early 1840's. An ardent admirer of the earliest known human idiosyncracies, he concluded that

> Russia has...nothing to fear from the revolutionary tendencies which threaten the rest of Europe. Its own internal healthy organization protects it against pauperism, and the doctrines of communism and socialism.[1]

The Moloch of industrialization, from which no forms of backwardness could ultimately escape, contraposed the social forces in Russia in the second half of the nineteenth century which either championed the future large-scale industrial concerns or preferred continuation of the age-old rural commune system. The Russian intelligentsia now abandoned its ethereal preoccupation with German metaphysics and allowed itself to be irresistibly drawn into the vortex of more mundane matters. The burning question of the day concerned Russia's socio-economic destiny : could Russia afford, on the basis of her peculiar rural institutions, to circumvent the capitalist phase of history and establish socialism ? The almost sadistic diatribes incessantly exchanged between the Narodniks and the Russian Marxists were reflective of the apparent antipodal theories of Haxthausen and Marx. Or so thought Marx's Russian disciples who brushed aside all contentions which did not tally with their thesis springing from the orthodox Marxist schema of historical stages. The Narodniks, resenting the thesis of the inevitability of capitalism in Russia, accused Marx of devising a theory which served to steamroll over all peculiarities and local conditions of the nations of the world and condemned all to the evils of capitalism. This Narodnik allegation placed Marx, who had been studying Russian condition in 1870's with keen interest, in a position where he felt compelled to clarify his theoretical stand.

In his letter of 1877 to the *Otechestvennye Zapiski* (henceforth "Mikhailovsky letter"), published posthumously, Marx categorically rejected the view that his major work on capitalism contained a historico-philosophical theory of universal applicability. He went on to state that contrary to the charges of the Narodnik writer, Mikhailovsky, he had hitherto uttered nothing either in favour of or against the Narodnik thesis of Russia's unique, non-capitalist future. The conclusion which Marx reached in the letter was conditional : if Russia continued along the path taken by her since 1861, she would "lose the best chance which history has ever offered a nation and would have to undergo all the attendant vicissitudes of capitalism."[2]

Since the letter was not published in Marx's lifetime, his opinion on the controversy could not be immediately known either to his admirers or to his adversaries. In early 1881, Vera Zasulich, who had shot a Tsarist official and had escaped to Switzerland, took it upon herself to seek the master's opinion as to whether "all countries of the world have to pass through all the phases of capitalist production."[3] The query was more easily made than answered. The unenviable intellectual torments which the master had to undergo are recorded in the three lengthy draft replies which he cancelled one after another before deciding upon a fourth, brief version. In the cancelled drafts, Marx prepared a case in favour of Russia's non-capitalist destiny taking the controversial commune as his starting point. In an implied attack on his own followers, who rejected the commune lock, stock and barrel as the possible foundation of a future society, Marx put together all its "progressive" features and recommended a revolution for its preservation and development.[4] In his actual reply to Vera Zasulich the same year, Marx pleaded his inability to give a convincing reply and went on to reiterate his earlier stand first outlined in the Mikhailovsky letter, viz. his theory of the origin of capitalism was confined to western Europe and was not meant to be automatically applied elsewhere. He then expressed his conviction that "the village community is the basis of social regeneration of Russia", although it was already exposed to baneful influences.[5]

The ideas that crystallize from above are, firstly, that Marx's scheme of historical stages (especially the juxtaposing of feudalism-capitalism-socialism) was not intended to be as rigid as was generally believed,[6] and secondly, that the village commune of Russia was far more "progressive" than the

Russian Marxists presumed. Since it was subject to adverse forces, a revolution to counter the latter was necessary. Engels, however, by no means shared these views. Only two years before the composition of the Mikhailovsky letter, he ruthlessly debunked the Russian village commune in his reply to a critic and made no bones about how he looked down upon its effete nature. However, as if on second thought, he admitted that some possibility of Russia's non-capitalist development still remained, the sine qua non of which, he maintained, was a proletarian revolution in the more advanced western Europe.[7] Writing to N.F. Danielson about two decades later, Engels reflected that Russia could have perhaps avoided the capitalist route to social progress only if western Europe had experienced a prior revolution and had served as an example. Since that condition remained unfulfilled, he hastened to console, not without a touch of condescension, a despairing Danielson—almost like the doctor who coaxes his patient into swallowing bitter medicine—by drawing his attention to the brighter aspects of capitalism which had struck roots in Russia.[8]

Engels, hence, held the potentialities of the Russian village commune in low esteem and saw little possibility of Russia's non-capitalist development. He would reluctantly recognize its "progressive" aspects only upon the fulfilment of his unflinching precondition of a proletarian revolution in the industrially advanced western Europe. This prerequisite was, interestingly enough, conspicuous by its absence from any of Marx's writings on the subject, with the single exception of the Preface to the second Russian edition of the *Communist Manifesto* (1882), where Marx and Engels jointly mention it,[9] the text reflecting a compromise between the "Marxist" Engles and the "Narodnik" Marx, with a tilt in favour of the former. Marx appears to have believed in the prospects of an independent socialistic revolution in Russia till the very last moment of his life; only a year before his death he came around to the theoretical position maintained by his alter ego. Whatever the differences in their predispositions and theoretical nuances, the co-founders of Marxism were agreed on one basic point, viz., that the non-capitalist path to socialism was theoretically tenable.

Marx's personal involvement in loosening his own theoretical framework, supplemented by his views on the question of the commune, reinforced the Narodnik line of argument. This considerably embarrassed his Russian disciples. Both Plekhanov and Lenin, while paying lip-service to the shocking contents of the master's contentions hastened to prove by means of a heavy dose of theoretical sophistry that the possibility of the non-capitalist road no longer existed in Russia.[10] Lenin was quite correct in maintaining that Marx avoided a definite answer to the problem—although Lenin himself avoided examining the reason—but was distorting facts accessible to him when he went on to assert that Marx similarly "avoided examining Russian data".[11]

With the question of Russia's future having been settled in favour of capitalism, the tenet of the non-capitalist path suffered a temporary eclipse. With the establishment of the Bolshevik rule, the doctrine reappeared and was applied with renewed vigour for charting the future course of the colonial and semi-colonial areas of Asia, Africa and Latin America. The doctrine thus underwent a readjustment in its context and a reinvigoration in its content. Marx had written profusely on colonial problems of contemporary significance but avoided precise and specific prognostications regarding the future of the backward areas. As Engels explained in 1882, "I think we today can advance only rather idle hypotheses."[12] It was otherwise after the Bolsheviks came to power. The colonial peoples were already becoming conscious of their bondage and signs of unrest were in the air. Bolshevik Russia in her effort to survive in a suspicious and hostile environment launched a political counter-offensive of veriable intensity against the colonial appendages of the metropolitan European powers, as described earlier.[13] In this, the non-capitalist path concept came in handy. While Lenin was dead opposed to the concept in the Russian context,[14] by the time of the Second Comintern Congress in 1920 he came round to its enthusiastic acceptance in the context of the colonial and other backward countries. Reopening the question of the inevitability of the capitalist road for the backward nations, Lenin confidently asserted,

> If the victorious revolutionary proletariat conducts systematic propaganda among them [backward nations]* and the Soviet governments came to their aid with all the means at their disposal—in that event it will be mistaken to assume that the backward people must inevitably go through the capitalist stage of development.

Further,

> ...the Communist International should advance the proposition, with the appropriate theoretical grounding, that with the aid of the proletariat of the advanced countries, backward countries can go over to the Soviet system and, through certain stages of development, to communism, without having to pass through the capitalist stage.[15]

Lenin here seemed to be sticking to Engel's precondition to non-capitalist development, viz., that of a west European revolution. The Leninist reaffirmation of the thesis in a different and wider context meant the "creative development" of Marxism—or further loosening of its scheme initiated by its own creator.

Meanwhile, Bolshevik hopes of a revolution in western Europe—also the sine qua non of the non-capitalist path thesis —were dashed on the banks of the Vistula by the Polish counter-offensive. The Fourth Comintern Congress, however, reiterated the tenet in late 1922, repeated the familiar precondition and recommended the Soviet system as the least painful form of transition to the backward nations.[16]

The theopneustic vision of a capitalist apocalypse in western Europe during 1922-23 was not translated into practice; the ever vigilant Reichswehr scotched the attempt of the German communists to make political capital out of the Ruhr crisis. With the failure of the repeated Bolshevik attempts at fomenting revolution in western Europe, Engels' sine qua non was changed in form but not in essence. Soviet Russia, although still backward vis-a-vis the west European states, was more advanced socio-economically than the colonies of the Western powers. It was, hence, the new socialistic Russia which was now expected to attract by the sheer force of its example the backward areas to the non-capitalist path. Six years later, the Sixth Comintern Congress dropped the tenet of the west European proletarian revolution and took up the more credible theme of the USSR as the future centre of revolutionary aspirations of the peoples in bondage.[17]

The tenet again disappeared during the decades marked by Stalin's rule. Like a number of other correlated tenets and concepts, it reappeared after Khrushchev took over in the post-World War II period. Khrushchev's controversial reconstruction of the world political scenario made enough room for manoeuvres vis-a-vis the third world; the non-capitalist path thesis turned out to be a major edifice of the Soviet theory of the third world and has remained so ever since.

In his report to the Twenty-Second CPSU Congress, delivered on October 18, 1961, Khrushchev pointed to the problem of ensuring a genuine, socio-economic liberation of the newly independent states where "the heritage of colonialism is making itself felt very strongly". As he explained,

> ...the upper crust of the bourgeoisie and the feudal landlords, who have linked their destinies with foreign capital, are doing all they can to keep the underdeveloped countries in the system of world capitalism.

Having thus posed the problem, he went on to provide the solution :

> What is the way out ? History provides a clear answer to this question : the way out should be sought along the non-capitalist path of development.

He was also in a position to cite results :

> Those who want to know what fruits are to be gathered on this path should take a glance at the flourishing republics of Soviet Central Asia and at the other parts of our country that, after the October Revolution, bypassed the thorny path of capitalist development.

Further elaborating on his theme, Khrushchev went on to

assert that Soviet theory had created a form of state which reflected the interests of broad strata of the people and which was capable of accomplishing the task of anti-imperialist revolution for the purpose of real national liberation. That form was "national democracy". He congratulated the emergent nations on their good fortune which was possible in the contemporary era of retreating imperialism and the growing power of socialism.[18]

National democracy forms a nodal point of the Soviet doctrine of non-capitalist development. It made its maiden appearance in the Moscow Conference of Eighty-one Communist Parties held in November, 1960. The national democratic state was defined as one which "consistently upholds its political and economic independence, fights against imperialism and its military blocs, against military bases on its territory; ...a state in which the people are ensured broad democratic rights and freedoms, the opportunity to work for the enactment of an agrarian reform and other democratic and social changes...".[19] It is apparent from the above definition that the USSR strove to arrange the means and purposes of the national liberation struggles of the emergent nations in accordance with what she considered to be contradiction number one of the current phase of history, viz., between imperialism and socialism. The term *national* democracy was preferred to *people's* democracy precisely because the Kremlin was more concerned with the horizontal politico-economic relations among nations than with the vertical socio-economic structure of the developing states. Containment and rolling up of imperialism — albeit in a gradualistic fashion and without risking dangers contained in the contradiction—with the help of the third world nations, hence, became by far the primary goal than carrying out an immediate and drastic shake-up of the socio-economic structures of the latter.

An earlier discussion pointed to the Soviet latitudinarianism towards the third world as a major irritant in the Sino-Soviet ideological relations. It has beed argued that the Soviet gradualistic policy towards the colonial flanks of the West grew out of a perennial security psychosis characterized by an ardent desire to keep out of all direct armed confrontations with the West.[20] The official Soviet view presents the matter in a different light by asserting that since socialism has been successfully balancing imperialism, the latter is deterred from dictating policies to the newly independent states or from actively intervening in their internal affairs.

A major reason why the non-capitalist path thesis is at the forefront of the Soviet doctrinal arsenal at present is that proletarian revolutions did not take place where they should have, i.e., in the developed capitalist states of western Europe and America. This greatest of all paradoxes contained in Marxist theory had already confounded Lenin. Although he did not agree with Roy's thesis that the proletariat in the advanced states of the West could not bring about a revolution since Western imperialism handed over to them their entire surplus value while ruthlessly expropriating in compensation huge superprofits from the colonies, he did hint at a parallel explanation in the Second Comintern Congress for the stabilization of the citadels of world capitalism. Lenin's criticism of the "labour aristocracy" in Europe and the imperialist expropriation of "superprofits" as "the economic basis of opportunism in the working-class movement" had a Royist flavour.[21]

In the Soviet view, the non-capitalist path provides the correct alternative for the thorny problem of modernization faced by the third world nations. Orthodox Marxism recognized capitalism as the only method which could develop the latter at unprecedented rate before exhausting its own potentialities and turning into fetters on them. Today, so goes the Soviet ideological explanation, the emergent nations in endeavouring to modernize, to develop their productive forces, are able, thanks to the "victorious advance" of the world socialist system, to bypass the capitalist way. The non-capitalist path, hence, is characterized by an external factor :

> ...consolidation and development of the socialist countries and extension of all round links with them and with the other states taking the non-capitalist path,

and an internal one :

> ...a steady growth of the revolutionary movement of the people, in the course of which constant activity and initiative from below are combined with a firm state policy of progressive socio-economic change, leading to socialism.[22]

Genuine sovereignty, as distinct from its formal Austinian connotation, can be achieved by the emergent nations "only by abolishing the domination of monopoly capital, breaking up the colonial structure of the economy, setting up a firm and viable economy....".[23]

The Indian Context

India represents today the objective trend towards the non-capitalist path in the eyes of the Soviet ideologues. It is true, as G. K. Shirokov in his work on India's industrialization observes, that "Of all the developing countries, India has probably the most powerful national bourgeoisie."[24] That does not prevent V. Trubnikov, another Soviet publicist, from pointing out that "though imperialism promotes a limited development of capitalist relations in the economically backward countries this tendency should not be exaggerated.... The basic policy of imperialism continues to be the policy of subjugating these countries, retarding their development and perpetuating their position as adjuncts supplying agricultural and other raw materials to the industrially developed imperialist states."[25] He adds that this is even more true at present when capitalism has lost its free competitive nature and has turned into a monopoly-imperialistic phenomenon.[26]

India's "mixed economy" with its constituent element of the private sector can hardly provide a hindrance to its identification with the tendency towards the non-capitalist path of development. Indeed, it is the existing *trends* in the economy and foreign policy, rather than the absence of the private sector, that seem to be among the decisive criteria of the tenet. Particularly since Indira Gandhi took over power, the Soviet assessments of India's objective tendencies have been, on the balance, very favourable. R. Ulyanovsky and V. Pavlov in their book on South Asia, in which they cross swords with

Gunnar Myrdal, write of the non-capitalist path in the obviously Indian context :

> The non-capitalist path presupposes a mixed economy, with the public sector playing an increasing and ultimately decisive role. This provides an economic basis on which wide circles of the petty and middle national bourgeoisie are prepared to co-operate with national democrats.[27]

Another scholar points out that many a third world state represents, what he calls, the "transitional society".[28] He perceives an intricate and contradictory process in the multi-structural socio-economic pattern of these societies, "a process of converting the public sector into the leading or, as it is usually called, the formative sector of the economy."[29] He further observes that "transitional forms of non-capitalist production relations are arising, in which different elements of state, state-private, cooperative group and other types of property are being integrated."[30] Such theoretical formulations have doubtlessly affected the nature of the Soviet exchanges and transactions with India. The Soviet ideologues draw satisfaction, for instance, in that despite Keynesian influence on India's economic architects, the latter accepted the principle of the priority development of the heavy and manufacturing industries beginning with the Second 5-Year plan. Even the First 5-Year plan, in Soviet view, was "a fundamentally new phenomenon" in the economic policy of the state in that the scale of the planned expenditure of state resources far exceeded the volume of enterprise of any monopoly.[31] The state sector industrial expenditure jumped from Rs. 60 crores during the First Plan to Rs. 690 crores during the Second.[32] This is perceived, not entirely without justification, as "a tremendous victory for the practical example and influence of socialist planning..."[33]. Carrying their argument further, they observe that "all progressive social forces" can be rallied together under the non-capitalist path slogan so as to set up a national democratic front and stem the further growth of big and monopoly capital prior to its nationalization, as in India.[34] As noted earlier, Indira Gandhi's phenomenal rise to power in the teeth of unsuccessful Congress (O) opposition was hailed by the Soviet press symbolic of the victory of progressive forces in India over those of reaction.[35] It served, as it were, as an indicator of India's increasing gravitation towards the desired direction. The nationalization of 14 indigenous banks and 106 private Indian and Foreign general insurance companies was hailed by the Soviet ideologues as "timely and natural".[36] Without nationalization of the credit institutions, it is maintained, it would be wellnigh impossible for developing states to control and guide economic development. While before nationalization, the share of the Indian banks in providing credit to the economy did not exceed 10%, by 1971 the Indian government had access to about Rs. 20,000 million for financing developmental projects.[37] Further, the abolition of the privy purses to former princes was acclaimed as a fine coup d' grace to a long effete stage of history. That Indira Gandhi's leftist stances and slogans conjure up in Soviet eyes visions of India taking to the non-capitalist path with all the consequences for the rest of the world is reflected in the general sympathy shown to her policies—despite large realms of the Indian scene that show little sign of falling into a predictable pattern :

> By having long-term planning as the basis of its economic programme, Indira Gandhi's Government has been trying to combat the haphazard nature of private capital in the economy. India's plan is a well-based effort to ensure the planned growth of production, to carry out social changes on a vast scale and develop science and technology, the transport system and foreign trade.[39]

A crucial question of theoretical import now shows up : what social forces and classes are expected to make the non-capitalist path successful ? This is interwined with the nature of the present epoch in which developing countries like India find themselves. In Soviet view, the present epoch of the history of the young nations reveals the telescoped nature of two stages of revolution, the general democratic, anti-imperialist movement and the struggle for social progress. The classical anti-colonial bourgeois-democratic revolution has transcended its own boundary and taken on additional features of the trend towards social progress. The resulting symbiosis is vested with some attributes of both the bourgeois-democratic and the socialist revolution. As it is explained,

> This type of revolution, previously unknown in newly-free countries, leads to the establishment of a revolutionary-democratic dictatorship of semi-proletarian and middle strata, which opens up the possibility of non-capitalist development.[39]

The semiproletarian and petty bourgeois strata thus provide leadership in the place of the as yet inchoate proletariat. While such leadership can hardly be expected to be genuinely revolutionary, it is capable, nevertheless, of laying the foundation of socialism under certain conditions.[40]

> One must consider the fact that in many, if not most of the developing Asian and African countries, there are no forces today more influential than national democracy whose prestige, organization and support among the masses would enable them to head the struggle for realizing the aims of the present stage of the revolution on a national scale.[41]

To be sure, the ideology of national democracy itself presents baffling contradictions. It is a congeries of indigenous and imported ideas and concepts reflecting the interplay and clash between past and future. The entire spectrum of the ideology of the Indian National Congress party, for instance, fits this description. According to the Soviet ideologues, the existing material basis and mode of production in young states of the third world cannot necessarily explain the success of the national democratic ideology—a line of thinking that is essentially Marxist. Particularly in countries with a "socialist orientation", it is maintained, the political superstructure "runs ahead" of the economic basis, "towing" the latter through a process of revolutionary changes.[42] It takes time for advanced ideas from the vanguard superstructure to percolate through ever-widening circles of the masses down to the economic substructure itself. The idea of this "ideological conveyer" system is also reflected in the work of an East German ideologue :

> The influence of the subjective factors must not begin only when all objective conditions for a socialist revolution have matured. The latter will not happen on its own accord without the influence of the subjective factors. That is why the revolutionary forces in the liberated countries which have entered the road to a non-capitalist development must create consciously and in an organized manner the necessary objective and subjective factors in order to pass over to the socialist stage of revolution.[43]

The point here is the age-old Spinozian controversy over the primacy of consciousness v. spontaneity. The Soviet ideological line clearly favours here the conscious, voluntarist factor in view of the high level of economic and organizational entropy in the newly independent states.

Admittedly, religious and cultural roots in countries like India are so deep and strong that it would be folly to attempt a hasty superimposition upon them of ultra-progressive ideas and interaction patterns. Instead, progressive ideas have to be selected from the religious-cultural milieu and played up carefully for the purpose of creating a stable ideological conveyer system. Information thus encoded can be assumed to reach its destination and correctly decoded. Otherwise, the probability of channel distortion and entropy would remain high. As the Soviet ideologues observe,

> (The revolutionary-democratic parties and organizations)* seek to base themselves on some of the humanist customs of collectivism, mutual assistance and solidarity which originated in the traditional institutions, to link them with the concrete tasks of the socio-political, economic and cultural development of their countries.[44]

It is by such "nurturing" of "the shoots of genuine socialism" in the developing states that the way to socialist millenium would finally be paved.[45]

Albeit with a certain amount of misgivings, the Soviet ideologues have not fallen short of describing the state in the third world as containing "progressive" potentialities. It is stressed, for example, by Semyon Skachkov, Chairman of the State Committee for Foreign Economic Relations, USSR Council of Ministers, as follows :

> Public ownership of big property holdings is particularly essential in order to resist the pressure of foreign monopolies and the local bourgeois groups which seek to collaborate with them. When the public sector is absent or proportionately insignificant, the economic advancement of the young states is bound to be unstable and dependent on uncontrolled capitalist private enterprise.[46]

This optimism is, of course, intricately linked with similar outlook on third world nationalism, and they grew out of the contradiction between the central dynamics and the nodal restraint components of the theoretical framework of this study. As two of the leading Soviet ideological exponents explained :

> Soviet Indologists held long discussions on the question of the role of the national bourgeoisie in the national liberation movement. As a result many Soviet historians were obliged to revise to some extent their interpretations.[47]

This is understandable in the light of the contradiction mentioned above as well as because the Soviet government could not possibly hope to befriend the existing governments of the third world, particularly India, without being prepared to cooperate with the classes which formed them. This, of course, needed a theoretical adjustment and redefinition. Thus the Soviet perception of contradiction number one of the present age, viz., between capitalism and socialism, led to a variety of theoretical reformulations. As the former Soviet ambassador to India, N. M. Pegov, put it :

> Thus we can assert with complete confidence that the Soviet-Indian political, economic and cultural

cooperation, having begun from zero at the time of establishment of these relations, has acquired during the last 25 years such volume and scale, that it would be difficult to find a parallel to it in the history of development of relations between states with different social systems.[48]

In the Soviet conceptualization, India is perceived to be a state with uneven development, with vestiges of feudalism intermingling with capitalism. The redeeming features consist of the phenomena like central planning and the public sector, which exhibit the spirit of socialism and do inhibit, if not eliminate, unbridled growth of capitalism. The chief enemies of India's progress are stated to be the feudal landowning classes and monopoly capital in league with Western imperialism. The Jan Sangh, Swatantra and Congress (O) are held to be their representatives.[49] The Indian government has pseudo-socialistic aspirations and, although these are by no means "scientific", they need to be encouraged.[50] Out of the womb of utopian and voluntaristic socialism will emerge, it is hoped, "scientific" socialism. Thus, a *Pravda* assessment of Nehru stated that he was an outstanding fighter for peace who had grasped that the future of India lay in socialism, without, however, understanding "scientific" Marxism.[51]

The Soviet theorization of India's class structure varies, especially when it comes to an analysis of the classes that form the government. In fact, official Soviet government pronouncements are almost always more concerned with the course of foreign policy of the third world states—the two-fold classification of pro- and anti-imperialism is, again, in terms of contradiction number one—rather than a rigorous analysis of their class structure. This has also been noted, for instance, by David Morison, who does not, however, advance any reason for the Soviet behaviour.[52] Considerable vacillation seems to exist among Soviet ideologues on the "progressiveness" of the ruling circles of India. Since the official ideological framework is quite loose in terms of class analysis of India, the Soviet ideologues gain considerable leeway in their analytical endeavour. The official ideological framework, concerned as it is primarily with contradiction number one, is largely based on certain imprecise concepts like the non-capitalist path, forces of anti-imperialism, etc. Hence, evaluations of India by the Soviet scholars vary. Charles B. McLane confuses somewhat this dual aspect of the Soviet conceptualization of India.[53] His argument that while ideologically the Soviet theoreticians are critical of India, the Soviet government nevertheless keeps up massive aid programmes for her, revealing the primacy of Soviet national interest over ideology, misses the mark. The latter problem has been dealt with in earlier sections of this dissertation and need not be repeated here. Suffice to mention here that while the vagueness of official guidelines regarding India's class structure remains—and is deliberately tolerated for the sake of Indo-Soviet friendship—Soviet analysts do gain for themselves wide latitude. But contrary to what McLane thinks, India as part of the international system of states is considered quite favourably by the Soviet leadership in their public pronouncements. Brezhnev in his report to the Twenty-Fourth CPSU Congress on 30 March 1971 made the doctrinal observation that "the main thing is that the struggle for national liberation in many countries has in practice developed into a struggle against exploitative relations, both feudal and capitalist". He provided illustrations from India's bank nationalization and the victory over the right-wing forces in the Lok Sabha.[54] In another important speech, the General Secretary of the CPSU stated :

> The friendship between the Soviet Union and India —one of the largest peace-loving states on our planet—is having an important positive influence on the international situation as a whole. The Soviet Union and India have already accumulated considerable experience in fruitful cooperation. We think that now, when our relations are developing on the basis of the Treaty of Peace, Friendship and Cooperation, they will become still deeper. This is indicated by the strengthening of the position of the progressive, anti-imperialist forces in India. It is also indicated by the policy

of the Indian government, headed by Indira Gandhi.[55]

In line with the above statement indicating the importance attached to contradiction number one, the faithful Communist Party of India maintains that its major task is to unite the left and democratic forces in the struggle against rightist reactionary forces supported by foreign imperialism and for strengthening the national independence of India and for the country's development on the path of economic and social progress.[56] In other words, the CPI's role today is that of a homeostat trying to counter deviation of India's political system from an equilibrium inclined to the left. Such a role becomes clear in the light of the course of the Soviet foreign policy which has largely been arranged in accordance with the nodal restraint (contradiction one).

NOTES AND REFERENCES

1. Baron Von Haxthausen, *The Russian Empire* : *Its People, Institutions and Resources*, (transl.), Chapman & Hall, London. 1856, Vol. I. p. 135.

2. Karl Marx, Brief an die Redaktion der 'Otetschestwennyje Sapiski' (Mikhailovsky letter), in Marx & Engels, *Werke*, Dietz Verlag, Berlin, Vol. XIX, pp. 107-112 (author's translation).

3. Marx & Engels, *op. cit.*, (note No. 1), Note No. 155, p. 572

4. Ibid. Marx's draft replies (cancelled) to Vera Zasulich, pp. 385-403.

5. Marx, Brief an V. I. Sassulitsch, Marx & Engels, *op. cit.*, (note No. 1), pp. 242-243.

6. Marx appeared to be somewhat less orthogenetic in his views than many of his followers in this regard ; he frankly admitted that contingent events could also influence history, retard or facilitate its course. See Marx's letter to Ludwig Kugelmann in Hannover (1871), Marx & Engels, *Ausgewaehlte Werke*. Verlag Progress, Moscow, 1972, p. 700.

7. Friedrich Engels, "Soziales aus Russland", in Marx & Engels, *Ausgewaehite Schriften in zwei Baenden*, Dietz Verlag, Berlin, 1972, vol. II, pp. 39-50.

8. Engels to Nikolai Franzewitsch Danielson in Petersburg (Auszug), 1893, in Marx & Engels, *Ausgewaehlte Schriften*, op. cit., pp. 469-471.

9. Marx & Engels, Vorrde zur zweiten russischen Ausgabe des "Manifests der Kommunistischen Partei", *Werke, op. cit.*, p. 296.

10. V. I. Lenin, "What the 'Friends of the People' Are and How They Fight the Social-Democrats", *Collected Works, 1893-1894*. Foreign Languages Publishing House, Moscow, 1960, vol. I, pp. 265-266, and G. Plekhanov (N. Beltov), *The Development of the Monist View of History*, Progress, Moscow, 1972, pp. 238-241.

11. Lenin, *op. cit.*, (note no. 10), p. 266. Lenin refers here to the Mikhailovsky letter which contained Marx's own statements on his familiarity with the Russian language and source materials. For the text of the letter, *op. cit.*

12. Engels' letter to K.Kautsky (1882), Marx & Engels, *On Colonialism* (collection of articles and letters), Foreign Languages Publishing House, Moscow, Second Impression (no date), p. 341.

13. See Chapter 2.

14. In 1894, Lenin had written :

How can one accept Marx's economic theory and its corollary—the revolutionary role of the proletariat as the organizer of communism by way of capitalism—if people in our country try to find ways to communism other than through the medium of capitalism and the proletariat it creates ? (Lenin, *op.cit.*, note no. 10, p. 293). A decade later he had declared again : ...the idea of seeking salvation for the working in anything save the further development of capitalism is reactionary. In countries like Russia the working class suffers not so much from capitalism as from the insufficient development of capitalism. The working class is, therefore, most certainly interested in the broadest, freest, and most rapid development of capitalism. (Lenin, "Two Tactics of Social-Democracy in the Democratic Revolution", *Selected Works*, Progress, Moscow, 1970, vol. I, p. 488).

15. "Report of the Commission on the National and the Colonial Questions" July 26, 1920, in Lenin, *Speeches at Congresses of the Communist International*, Progress, Moscow, 1972, p. 59.

16. "Fourth Congress. Theses on the Eastern Question", *Comintern and National and Colonial Questions*. *Documents of Congresses*, a Communist Party of India publication, No. 9, March 1973 (C86), New Delhi, p. 51.

17. "Sixth Congress 1928. Theses on the Revolutionary Movement in the Colonies and Semicolonies", *Comintern...*, *op. cit.* p. 66.

18. N. S. Khrushchev, "On the Programme of the Communist Party of the Soviet Union. Report delivered to the 22nd. Congress of the CPSU, October 18, 1961", Supplement to *Soviet Land*, New Delhi, No. 24, Dec. 1961, pp. 98-99.

19. *Pravda*, Dec. 6, 1960. Quoted in Donald S. Zagoria, *The Sino-Soviet Conflict. 1956-1961*, *op. cit.*

20. See Chapter 3.

21. Lenin, "Report on the International Situation and the Fundamental Tasks of the Communist International", (1920), *Speeches ...*, *op. cit.*, pp. 45-46.

22. *The Newly Independent States* : *Problems of Development*, Novosti, Moscow, 1972, p. 91 (author ?).

23. V. Tyagunenko, "World Socialism and National Liberation Revolutions", *Soviet Military Review*, Krasnaya Zvezda, Moscow, No. 10, Oct. 1973, p. 9.

24. G. K. Shirokov, *Industrialisation of India*, Progress, Moscow, 1973, p. 9.

25. V. Trubnikov, "Non-Capitalist Path : From Theory to Practice", *Soviet Review*, No. 43, Vol. XI, Sept. 19, 1974, pp. 20-21.

26. Trubnikov, *op. cit.*, p. 21.

27. R. Ulyanovsky & V. Pavlov. *Asian Dilemma* : *A Soviet View and Myrdal's Concept*, Progress, Moscow, 1973, p. 161 (henceforth *AD*)

28. Vi. Li, "Social Movements in Developing Countries", *International Affairs*, No. 6, 1974, p. 14, Moscow.

29. Li, *op. cit.*, p. 14.

30. Li, *op. cit.*, p. 14.

31. *AD*. p. 94

32. Dhiresh Bhattacharya, *India's Five-Year Plans, 1951-61*, Udayan Granthagar, Calcutta, 1968, pp. 55-56.

33. *AD*, p. 95.

34. *AD*, p. 154.

35. See chapter 2.

36. E. Gryaznov, "India : Main Tendencies of Socio-Economic Development", *International Affairs*, No. 12, 1971, pp. 53-54, Moscow.

37. Gryaznov, *op. cit.*, p. 53.

38. Gryaznov, *op. cit.*, p. 54.

39. *AD*, p. 158.

40. *AD*, p. 159.

41. *AD*, p. 159.

42. Li, *op. cit.*, p. 15.

43. Gerhard Powik, "Objective and Subjective Factors in the Current World Revolutionary Process (II), *German Foreign Poilicy*, Vol. X. No. 4, 1971, Institute for International Relations, Berlin, p. 320.

44. Li, *op. cit.*, p. 18.

45. *AD*. p. 166.

*Author's note.

46. Semyon Skachkov, "Economic Cooperation of the USSR with the Developing Countries", *Socialism. Theory and Practice*. No. 2, February 1974, Novosti, Moscow, p. 94.

47. V. Balabushevich and A. Dyakov, "Some Problems of the Contemporary History of India in Soviet Ideological Studies", in Litto Ghosh and Kartar Singh (eds.), *Unity in Diversity : 50 Glorious Years of Union of Soviet Socialist Republics*. Indo-Soviet Cultural Society, New Delhi date ?), p. 119.

48. N. M. Pegov. "In the Interests of Peace and Progress", in Jagadish Bibhakar (ed.), *A Model Relationship—25 Years of Indo-Soviet Diplomatic Ties*. Punjabi Publishers, New Delhi, 1972, p. 90.

49. Victor Mayevsky, "Son of India", *Pravda*, 14 Nov. 1969, reprinted in *Current Digest of the Soviet Press*, vol. XXI, No. 46, p. 15. Ohio (henceforth *CDSP*).

50. See, for instance, G. F. Kim, A. S. Kaufman, "Certain Problems of National Liberation Revolutions in the Light of Lenin's Ideas", (summary), *Narody Azii i Afriki*, No. 2, 1972, Moscow.

51. Mayevsky, *op. cit*.

52. "The 'socialist orientation' of the developing states is valued [by the USSR] only quite secondarily for its effects on domestic policies ; its prime virtue lies in producing a pro-Soviet orientation of foreign policy". David Morison, "USSR and Third World" (first instalment) *Mizan*, vol. XII, No. 1, p. 23.

53. "The record of Russia's relations with India is from one perspective a classic illustration of the pre-eminence of national interest over ideology in Soviet foreign policy. India at no time during the 17 years reviewed here aroused the enthusiasm of Russian ideologues...its social structure and economic policies were often criticised, sometimes sharply." Charles B. McLane, *Soviet-Asian Relations*, Vol. II of *Soviet-Third World Relations*, London, Central Asian Research Centre, 1973, p. 60.

54. Brezhnev's report of the 24th. CPSU Congress, March 30, 1971, *Pravda*, 31 March, 1971, *CDSP*, vol. XXIII, No. 12, pp. 3-9.

55. Brezhnev's speech on the occasion of the 50th. Anniversary of the USSR, 21 Dec. 1972, *Pravda*, 22 Dec. 1972, *CDSP*, vol. XXIV, No. 51, p. 5.

56. *Pravda*, 18 Nov. 1970, *CDSP*, vol. XXII, No. 46, p. 26.

CHAPTER V

INDIA'S FORMATIVE SECTOR IN SOVIET IDEOLOGY

MARXIST DOCTRINE In its classical and Soviet manifestations has regarded the state at best as a necessary evil.[1] The only kind of help it can be to revolution is negative, that of protection against counter-revolutionary trends. The Soviet Marxist thought at present makes striking shifts from this general pattern in the case of newly independent nations like India. Indeed, Soviet ideologues point out that the state in India constitutes an outstanding example—a "model"—for Soviet theoretical tenets concerning the third world. As Shirokov puts it,

> Soviet and foreign economists believe that only a few of the major developing countries could possibly introduce industrialization approximating the Soviet pattern. They refer to the large territories and populations of these countries and to their fairly developed economic base capable of guaranteeing a sufficient demand for the modern means of production. The primary task in those countries is the establishment of heavy industry. India, which holds a prominent place in terms of population, size of territory, etc., stands out in the indicated group of countries.[2]

It is, therefore, worthwhile to make a study of the current Soviet views and analyses of India as a proving ground for ideology, most of the latter being concentrated on theoretical and practical aspects of the role and performance of the state sector in the economy, and to determine how they appear in the light of the overall framework of this study.

The state sector in India was created, not primarily consequent upon nationalization, but as a result of the entrepreneurship of the state itself. Further, both public and private enterprises in India today work in a sheltered atmosphere, protected from international competition by a system of exchange controls and tariff bans, and from undue domestic competition by the system of industrial licensing. Selective protectionism of India's industries was first introduced by the colonial government of British India following the First World War in order to blunt the edge of competition offered by continental Europe and Japan. Indigenous capital played a crucial role in the inter-war industrial build-up in India, despite obstructionist tendencies of the colonial government at times (as in the case of dismantling India's first locomotive plant in 1924 and refusal to a group of Bombay-entrepreneurs to set up an automobile plant with US collaboration in the 1930's).[3]

The line of thinking that the state should protect and aid indigenous industrial development and provide correctives to the manifold weaknesses of such a multistructural economy as in India was hardly novel at the time of India's independence. M. G. Ranade and G. K. Gokhale, among others, were prominent exponents of the formative sector.

The Industrial Policy Resolution of April 30, 1956, divided India's industries into three groups and assigned the state sector an exclusive and predominant role, respectively, in the first two of them. It certainly gave the state sector a far wider latitude of role and responsibility than did its 1948 predecessor. The result was the strategy of state control of the "commanding heights of the economy", viz., infrastructure and strategic sectors. The "commanding heights" concept, first propounded by Britain's Chancellor of Exchequer Hugh Gaitskell, implies not only that the state endeavours to channelize resources and investments into the desired productive directions by means of a complex system of controls and licensing but also that the state itself steps into the key areas and undertakes the direct productive effort. According to Soviet estimates, the state sector at the end of the 1960's accounted for 12.5% of GNP in India.[4] And as the following table[5] shows, the growth of India's state sector industrial and commercial enterprises has been impressive.

Growth of Investment in Central Government Industrial and Commercial Enterprises.

End of First 5-Year Plan	Rs.	81 crores
End of Second 5-Year Plan	Rs.	953 crores
End of Third 5-Year Plan	Rs.	2415 crores
As on March 1973	Rs.	5571 crores

But problems abound. Investments in a multistructural economy as India are essentially required in long gestation industries which require enormous capital investments and which in the initial stages constitute areas of low profitability. The following charts[6] illustrate this.

TABLE I

Top 10 Public Sector Firms (in terms of investment)

Crores of Rupees
Total for Top 10 Firms : Rs.3665 crores.
Total for All Enterprises : Rs.5571 crores.

Hindustan Steel Ltd.	Bokaro Steel Ltd.	Fertiliser Corpn.	Heavy Engineering Corpn
1030	795	344	283
Food Corpn.	National Coal Dev. Corpn.	Oil&Natural Gas Commission	Neyveli Lignite Corpn.
240	223	221	187
Shipping Corpn.	Bharat Heavy Electricals Ltd.		
186	156		

Data : Bureau of Public Enterprises, 1962-73

TABLE II

Top 10 Public Sector Firms (in terms of Profits)

(Crores of Rupees)

Indian Oil Corpn.	Bharat Heavy Electricals Ltd.		Heavy Electricals India Ltd.
19	8		7
Shipping Corpn.	Oil&Natural Gas Commission		Minerals & Metals Trading Corpn.
7	6		6
Hindustan Aeronautics Ltd.	State Trading Corporation	Fertiliser Corpn.	Bharat Electronics
5	5	5	3

Data : Bureau of Public Enterprises, 1972-73.

As P. J. Fernandes, Director General, Bureau of Public Enterprises, points out, the private sector is not in a position to face up to such tasks and cities J. R. D. Tata's statement to US Senators to the same effect.[7] For instance, according to British estimates, the Bharat Heavy Electricals Ltd. would take at least 10 years to break even, and during this period it would incur inevitable losses.[8] According to Fernandes, the minimum acceptable return on industrial investments in the Indian context should be 10%. In contrast, the following figures reveal the actual returns in the public sector[9]:

Year	Return on Capital Employed in Running Enterprises
1968-69	2.7%
1969-70	3.9%
1970-71	4.0%
1971-72	4.2%
1972-73	5.1%

The figures above reflect at once the dilemma that faces the Soviet ideology of the third world today : while state entrepreneurship in industrialization is welcome, its performance is severely limited by a variety of complex factors, over most of which control is inadequate or nonexistent. In the following sections, the Soviet line of analysis of those inhibiting factors in the context of India is to be discussed.

R. Ulyanovsky and V. Pavlov in their work on South Asian problems commend the organizational efforts made by the Indian state in building up the national economy. Their theoretical position on the role of the state in India is unlike the latter's place in classical Marxism, as has already been noted. They point out that

> The state in independent, but economically less developed countries, in view of the objective necessity for strengthening national economic independence and resisting neo-colonialism, will play a still bigger part in economic growth. This function of the state is a deeply progressive factor in the given historically concrete conditions.[10]

The authors then draw attention to their viewpoint that

the "national bourgeois state" is incapable of eliminating the crises and the basic contradictions of capitalist production and class conflict. This bleaker aspect does not prevent them from cheering, however, the capability of the state of reconstructing the economy on the basis of industrialization and countering neocolonial intrusions.[11] They reflect the official Soviet line shaped by the nodal restraint (contradiction number one) component when they assert in the Indian context that

> (A Marxist)* must remember not only the true class nature of a state—which is not everything—but also the tangible, progressive efforts of this state directed against colonialism, imperialism and the monopolies in conditions of the confrontation, between the two world systems.[12]

The degree of the development of state capitalism in the third world states like India and its nature depend, it is maintained by Soviet ideologues, not so much on the level of capitalist development as on "who stands at the helm of the state", i.e., on the nature of state power. The more radical the class forces in power, the faster state capitalism develops with the increasing possibility of its "democratisation" and transition to the path of non-capitalist development.[13]

In multistructural economies as in India, the state sector, while serving the interests of definite structures, acts as a regulator conditioning interactions among the existing structures. In the latter capacity, it not only assumes an important role in the economic direction but also in the sphere of effecting political cohesion as well.

Soviet scholars draw satisfaction from the fact that since it is the state which takes up the task of building the economic and political foundations of most third world nations, it has to fall back on aspects of socialist economic organization (planning, nationalization, etc.), which, in their turn, bring the state closer to the socialist bloc-orbit. As A. Levkovsky observes,

> The growth of the state sector in a number of basic branches of the economy also inevitably determines the reconstruction of the economic ties of a country with the outside world.[14]

It is little wonder that state capitalism in third world countries like India is seen as kind of an "incubator" of material production and class prerequisites for preparing the building of socialism.[15]

Turning to the specific problems of India's state sector and its philosophy, Soviet scholars perceive Keynesian influence in Indian economic thinking which, for them, serves little purpose other than camouflaging existing class and property relations.[16] Economically, technically and socially, two radically different structures are perceived in India, one comprising the small peasant and artisan, and the other comprising industrial capitalism. The latter by its concentrated economic and labour power is able to exploit the former. The state in effect helps industrial capital. According to Soviet estimates, during 1956-66 the private capitalist sector received from state organizations Rs. 8,700 million in the form of credits, deferment in payments and through the sale of shares, and Rs. 3,700 million working capital in the form of credits from state banks.[17]

73 groups of big capital united in monopoly associations received during 1956-66 more than 50% of all the resources redistributed from the state treasury to the private capitalist sector.[18] It is stated that

> Whatever democratic trappings embellish the intensive financial support given by the state to the private capitalist sector, this support inevitably strengthens big capital which ultimately turns into a gigantic force striving to subjugate everything to its interests and, first of all, state power. In this respect India is no exception...'[19]

Another Soviet estimate puts 95 representatives of big capital in the position of 114 out of 445 directorships in India's state enterprises, the most prominent of them being Tata, Birla, Goenka, Sahu Jain, J. Henderson, Scindia, Modi, B. N. Ellias, ICI, etc.[20] These powerful groups, according to the Soviet assessment, are trying to influence the economic policy of the Indian state.

An article in the authoritative journal *Mirovaya Economika i Mezhdunarodnye Otnoshenia*, makes a thorough analysis of the role of private capital in the developing countries.[21] Firstly, in such countries, capital has flown mainly in the directions of usury and trade to the neglect of industry—the pet sector in Marxist ideology. The technetronic revolution has had its impact on specific sectors of the developing societies which has aggravated class contradictions and forced socio-economic changes. The "green revolution" in India, for instance, has rapidly turned a part of the landowners, the recipients of precapitalist rent, into capitalist type farmers. "It is here that the connection between the development of capitalism in the Third World and the world scientific and technological revolution reveals itself clearly and directly," observes the article.[22] The consequent contradiction between pre-capitalist modes of production and pockets of advanced capitalism becomes acute. The state, which tries to act as a regulator and to balance the different structures of the economy, tends to favour the private capitalist sector by its massive investments in building the infrastructure. Without such state investments in agronomical services, provision of electricity, fertilizers, pesticides and farm equipments at reduced prices, the "green revolution" could hardly take place. However, private capital fully utilizes state credits and subsidies to finance the secret hoarding of grain, thus making high profits on artificial grain shortage on the market.[25]

Such being the case, the article draws the conclusion that "the introduction of contemporary productive forces in the agriculture of the developing countries stimulates the growth of capitalism which (and herein lies its specificity) assumes, since the very beginning, features of parasitism even to a greater extent than in the West and which causes even sharper social conflicts than in the Western countries".[24] The article perhaps hits the nail on the head when it goes on to observe that private capital in the developing countries, be it in industry or in agriculture, is incapable of effecting technological progress independently. In the sphere of material production, private capital in these countries uses not the most efficient technology but the one that would fetch quick and high profits, and this is made possible by "protectionism" which keeps the tense atmosphere of international competition out. It would be wishful thinking, states the article, if the state is expected to solve the peculiar problems posed by private capital when the national economy is solidly based on private capitalism.[25] The article here hints at the official Soviet Weltanschauung of a growing state sector in countries like India in alliance with the Soviet bloc as the only way out.

While pointing up other evils created by the private sector in India, Soviet ideologues nevertheless do not wish the latter out of existence. They stress that in view of the severely limited economic power and scale of accumulation of capital in India, all available instruments have to be utilized for the swift expansion of industrial and agricultural output, including private enterprise, controlled, of course, by the state.

Provided the state is consolidated, and it gains key economic positions and ensures efficient control, accumulation and initiative of the private sector can play an important positive part in solving questions of the supply of goods and expanding the service sphere, and also raising the overall economic growth rates.[26]

As a successful illustration of "controlled" growth of the private sector, Lenin's New Economic Policy of the 1920's in the USSR is cited.

The qualified tolerance of the private sector gives rise to the question of the role of foreign capital in an economy like India's and what, in Soviet view, should be the proper attitude towards it. Proceeding from their ideological position of "neocolonialism", the Soviet ideologues do not mince their words in calling foreign capital evil. Its exploitative nature in third world economies can only be countered by outright nationalization, which would bring added benefits like the solution of the problem of capital accumulation, strengthening the national state, and weakening imperialism and its indigenous collaborative classes.[27]

However, the Soviet ideologues hasten to add, almost "dialectically", that nationalization of foreign assets is not *always* and under all circumstances a wise move. Hasty nationalization without adequate political, economic and administrative preparation would lead to a disaster. Foreign capital may also have a major role to play in the developing economies in such spheres as organizational experience, markets, technical know-how, financial and material resources, and the like.[28]

> The main thing is that assistance be given without fettering terms, without political discrimination, without political strings that gradually lead to neo-colonial dependence. ...The issue is not whether to attract foreign capital for purposes of economic growth or not, but how to reduce to a minimum the attendant outflow of resources and to make this capital serve national economic development.[29]

Productive re-investment of profits obtained in a given country, rather than their withdrawal by foreign capital, is what the Soviet ideologues recommend to the third world to best exploit the necessary evil. After all, Lenin himself had been eager to attract foreign capital and technology into Soviet Russia under the NEP, not to mention Brezhnev's initiative in this direction at present.[30] Where nationalization of foreign capital is desirable but not feasible, "mixed" enterprises comprising foreign capital and public sector in a given country are recommended.[31]

A concomitant feature of state capitalism in India is planning. Over time, planning has come of age from being based merely on a list of construction projects to becoming a more sophisticated and comprehensive socio-economic blueprint. In adopting the balanced method of planning, which enables planners to establish rational material and financial proportions in economy, India along with Algeria, Guinea, Congo, etc. has been emulating the method pioneered by the USSR.[32]

The idea of planning in the public sector, it is explained, has gained much ground in the third world. This, in theory, reflects the growing consciousness of the developing nations of the need to shake off their age-old inertia, to seize the reins of their hitherto passive destiny and to establish themselves as the subjects of history and initiators of economic progress. This line of thinking finds support also in the West, e.g, in Myrdal's work.[33]

However, borrowing only selected devices of socialist economy like planning cannot be expected to produce panaceas since "to make this element 'work', even in its own sphere, it must be accompanied by a whole set of complementary and reinforcing measures in all spheres of social life".[34] Also, it is conceded, in conditions of a multistructural economy with a preponderance of pre-capitalist forms in the economic and social spheres, purely economic regulation as the only method of transformation would be sheer utopia.[35] As one Soviet analyst puts it bluntly,

> Mixed economies and a great variety of production relations are characteristic of all developing countries. And so is the constant breaking down of the socio-economic structure and the striving to transform the productive forces and production relations of society.[36]

Asserting that "planned targets are rarely met", he goes on to examine the complicated causes, many of which, like weather, condition of the export market, etc. are beyond the control of the state. The fact remains, however, that

> Failure in reaching plan-targets for mobilizing resources, developing industries and economic areas, and for the building of industrial projects lead, in actual fact, to systematic violations of economic proportions... Increasingly frequent are cases when enterprises work at a fraction of their capacity and construction falls behind schedule.

The sober conclusion that follows :

> Plans and schemes in most of the developing contries have failed to improve the employment situation or to check the process of unequal distribution of incomes, concentration of industries in a few centres, etc.[37]

The most cheerful effect of planning which this analyst could find in the third world was a negative, political one, viz., its role in stimulating mass consciousness of the direction of policies adopted by the ruling circles.[38]

In the wide range of Soviet scholarly literature on India and the third world, even un-Marxist lines of thinking can be detected. The changed conception of the third world state has already been noted. Kudryavtsev in an *Izvestia* article strikes an explicitly critical note on India's massive population problem :

> The enormous annual increase in population "consumes" the economic successes, as it were.[39]

Other Soviet scholars stress that this problem limits the utilization of the modern means of production in the semi-natural, small-commodity and even small-scale capitalist structures. The lower structures rely on their primitive means of production and factory-made intermediate goods. "For this reason the formation of a single cycle of reproduction is a slow process, and is not accompanied by any substantial increase in labour productivity", observes Shirokov.[40]

The angle of vision presented above makes a break with the official Soviet tendency of blaming all the ills of the third world states on their colonizers and with the official Marxist tenet that since population represents labour it can never be a problem but an asset, and that any population problem must be ascribed to the social system prevalent.

Concentrating on economics, Tiulpanov and Weiz maintain that while it has been markedly growing, India's state sector is not yet the leading one in the economy. Upon the assumption of the leading role, it has to reach a high state of effectiveness, by which is meant not profitability but influence on the formation of the present-day structure of the economy and the capacity to transform a static economy into a growing and dynamic one. Then the authors go on to conclude that far-reaching social reforms would be necessary to enable the state sector to function effectively[41]—a statement that sounds like Gunnar Myrdal's "institutional approach" and that accords relatively greater weight to non-economic elements.

Admittedly, despite all its theoretical potentialities and progressiveness, the state sector in countries like India is beset with numerous problems affecting profitability, optimization, underutilized capacity, efficient management, access to steady markets, and the like. As an Indian government official, quoted earlier, frankly admits,

> In a poor country like ours, we cannot afford waste, and yet we must admit that there is a great deal of waste in our total system—governmental, public sector etc..... . Are we getting the maximum out of every rupee which we invest in public enterprise ? We cannot, with due honesty, say that this is the present situation. ...We are faced with large unutilised capacities, unduly inflated inventories, inadequate prudence in the use of working capital, problem of over-staffing and unproductive management and labour, and a lack of adoption of sufficient modern teechniques of management.[42]

All this is reflected in current Soviet thinking on the performance of the state sector in India and the third world. One scholar mentions that the state sector is "noted" for its "bureaucracy and low efficiency". In the concluding chapter of his study on India's industrialization, he mentions the likelihood that with the growth of the share of the state sector in the total capital investments, an already low efficiency social production might diminish accompanied by greater capital-intensity and a more slackened rate of development.[43] There seems to be little ground for questioning this scenario in retrospect since the USSR herself has had abundant experience with similar problems relating to bureaucracy and labour productivity.[44]

The non-capitalist path thesis envisages a growing state sector in a developing economy like India's. The facts tend to corroborate this vision. During 1972-73, India's growing public sector had an investment in the neighbourhood of Rs. 6,000 crores, excluding the Railways and the Post and Telegraph. It employed approximately 1.5 million workers directly, and many hundred thousands indirectly through ancillaries.[45] According to 1971 census, about 18 million were employed in terms of total employment in the organized sector of the economy (including the civil service), out of which nearly 12 million were in the public sector. Roughly one-half of that number worked in government enterprises (the rest being in the administrative services).[46] According to Bazle Karim, production adviser of the Bureau of Public Enterprises in India, the latter country ranks at present among the top 10 industrial nations of the world. The public sector with its 120 enterprises has made a substantial contribution to achieving that position.[47]

While these facts are carefully studied by the Soviet ideologists, they temper their jubilation by the observation that expansion of the state sector as such does not provide an automatic guarantee of fulfilling national interests. Invoking Myrdal's authority, they point out that public enterprises may actually help swell the coffers of the private sector, as discussed earlier. India's case is specifically cited as an example.[48] They also show little illusion in their observation that despite substantial growth in the state sector private capitalism in India may actually consolidate its real position in the economy behind the facade of concepts like "restricted capitalism", etc.[49] Shirokov, indeed, appears to be more cautious than others in this regard. The concluding sentences of his work on India's industrialization run as follows :

> It is not yet possible to state with any certainty what the result of the new state-capitalist measures will be... It can only be noted that the planned measures introduce no radical changes in the general trend of the industrial revolution and the industrialization. There has been a slight change in the orientation of the industrial development, but the results of that change can be assessed as yet only in the most general form.[50]

All the problems and difficulties of the state sector in developing societies like India admitted, the Soviet ideological line remains overwhelmingly committed to backing it, particularly if it shows signs of, what is perceived to be, "anti-imperialism" and fits the Soviet conception of social and economic progress. This is amply illustrated by the recent endeavours to dovetail the Soviet and the Indian economies and aim at production collaboration. An overview of this phenomenon follows while a more detailed survey of the specifics of Indo-Soviet economic relations, which flow from the Soviet conceptualization of India, follows in the next chapter.

PRODUCTION COLLABORATION

Production collaboration, itself a reflection of Soviet influence on the Indian economy, started as early as 1966, when a trade agreement provided that India would develop certain branches of consumer industries, the products of which were marketable in the USSR, while the latter would also take into account India's need for capital goods in her own industrial development programmes.[51] In February 1970, an Indo-Soviet protocol was signed in New Delhi establishing production collaboration between the state machine-building enterprises. Next year, following Indira Gandhi's visit to the USSR, the Joint Indo-Soviet Statement referred to the establishment of an inter-governmental commission on economic, scientific and technical cooperation. Two years later, when the Brezhnev team visiting India counted among its members N. K. Baibakov, who holds, among other prominent positions, the chair of the USSR State Planning Committee, and S. A. Skachkov, Chairman of the USSR Council of Ministers' State Committee for Foreign Relations, a further augmentation of Indo-Soviet economic relations was to be expected. More agreements on widening economic cooperation were signed. The most interesting was the one envisaging cooperation between the State Planning Committee of the USSR and the Planning Commission of India. It was also agreed that joint recommendations were to be issued in 1974 by the appropriate organs of the two sides on "new forms of mutually advantageous cooperation", including "production specialisation" and cooperation in certain types of industrial items.[52] Article 2 of the Agreement on the Further Development of Economic and Trade Cooperation between the USSR and the Republic of India states :

> The cooperation...shall have as its goal the study of possibilities for the development of the two countries' economies and for production cooperation....[53]

The envisaged dovetailing of the economies of the two countries reflects the influence the USSR wields over India's state sector. The "reciprocal supplementing of our economic potentials", as Brezhnev put it,[54] certainly also involves a conscious ideological manoeuvre on the part of the USSR, viz., to bolster the state sector in India's economy so as to enable her to counter the expansive tendencies of the private sector and especially to neutralize Western capitalistic participation in the latter. This is but the micro aspect of a macro strategy : fighting private, and especially Western, capitalism at the micro level would contribute ultimately, to the global collapse of capitalism and imperialism. As a Western scholar put it so incisively :

> All Soviet efforts in foreign aid, from the Aswan dam to the humblest grain elevator, were intended to end the monopoly of Western investment in developing nations.[55]
> He admits that the USSR has often succeeded through her policies in denying the West any monopoly power position in the third world and goes on even to assert that "India, for instance, is today beyond the reach of significant economic pressure from any Western state, thanks to Soviet aid".[56]

The decade 1951-70 saw the Soviet bloc-third world trade turnover rise from 1·7 milliard roubles to 5 millard roubles. Out of the total allocated credits of 8 milliard roubles, the USSR alone accounted for 5 milliard roubles. The Council for Mutual Economic Assistance is cooperating with the third world states in the spheres of industrial and other forms of development. The Complex Programme for Development of Socialist Economic Integration attaches special importance to further extension of trade, economic, scientific and technical cooperation with the third world.[57] India finds a prominent place in the Soviet bloc's third world programmes and represents, both in terms of ideology and economic investment, a model situation evolving slowly but surely towards the non-capitalist path.

NOTES AND REFERENCES

1. See Daniel Tarschys, *Beyond the State*, The Swedish Institute of International Affairs, Stockholm, 1971.
2. Shirokov, *op. cit.*, pp. 8-9. To be sure, Soviet scholars admit that all Afro-Asian countries cannot be treated as one entity. For a four-fold classification of these countries, see *Oriental Countries Today*, Vol. I, Statistical Publishing Society. Calcutta 1975, pp. 7-8. India represents the group with some of the industrially most advanced states.
3. Shirokov, *op. cit.*, p. 25.
4. Gryaznov. *op. cit.*, p. 53.
5. Table on p 88LVI, supplement on public sector, *Readers' Digest*, Sept. 1974, Bombay.
6. Adapted from tables on pp 88LV-88LVI, supplement on public sector, *op. cit.*
7. P. J. Fernandes, "Public Sector in Perspective", *Readers' Digest, op. cit.*, p. 88 XX.
8. Fernandes, *op. cit.*, p. 88 XX.
9. Fernandes, *op. cit.*, p. 88 XX.
10. *AD, op. cit.*, p. 96.
*Author's note
11. *AD. op. cit.*, pp. 96-97.
12. *AD. op. cit.*, p. 97.
13. A. Levkovsky, "Social Aspects of the Development of the State Sector in Newly-Independent Countries", *Soviet Review*, New Delhi. No. 27, Vol. XI, June 13, 1974, p. 23 (henceforth *SR*).
14. Levkovsky, *op. cit.*, p. 24.
15. Levkovsky, *op. cit.*, p. 28.
16. *AD*, p. 99.
17. *AD*. p. 106.
18. *AD.*, p. 106.
19. *AD*, p. 106.
20. Gryaznov, *op. cit.*, pp. 55-56.
21 M. Volkov, "Contemporary Productive Forces and Peculiarities of Development of Capitalism in the Third World," *Mirovaya Ekonomikai Mezhdunarodnya Otnoshenia*, Nov. 10, 1974, reprinted in *Soviet Review*, No. 57, vol. XI, Dec. 12, 1974, pp. 17-23, 26-28.
22 Volkov, *op. cit.*, p.19.
23. Volkov, *op. cit.*, p. 26.
24. Volkov, *op. cit.*, p. 26.
25. Volkov, *op. cit.*, p. 27.
26. Volkov, *op. cit.*, p. 28.
27. *AD*, p. 133.
28. *AD.*, p. 134.
29. *AD*. p. 134.

30. See also A. Kiva's views, *USSR and Third World*. London, Vol.I, No. 3, 15 Feb-21 March, 1971, pp. 131-132. Kiva speaks out against indiscriminate nationalization.

31. *AD*. 135, 137.

32. V. Popov, "Soviet Planning Experience and Third World Countries", *Soviet Review*. No. 4. Vol. XII. Jan. 23. 1975. p. 58. and *AD*. p. 100.

33. Gunnar Myrdal. *Asian Drama* : *An Inquiry into the Poverty of Nations*. Pelican. 1968. vol. II. p. 726.

34. V. I. Pavlov. "Theory and Practice of Planning in Third-World Countries". *Soviet Review*. No. 14. vol. XII, March 27, 1975, p. 37.

35. Pavlov, *op. cit.*, p. 40.

36. V. Kollontai, "Problems of Planning in the Third World". *National Liberation Movement* : *Current Problems*, Novosti, Moscow (no date), p. 57.

37. Kollontai., *op. cit.*, pp. 69-70.

38. Kollontai, *op. cit.*, p. 74.

39. Kudryavtsev, *op. cit.*

40. Shirokov, *op. cit.*, p. 312.

41. S. I. Tiulpanov and G. M. Weiz, "Problems of India's State Enterprises" (summary), *Narody Azii i Afriki*, No. 3, 1970, p. 251.

42. Fernandes, *op. cit.*, p. 88 XXIV.

43. Shirokov, *op. cit.*, p. 313.

44. See chapter 2.

45. Fernandes. *op. cit.*, p. 88 VIII.

46. S. R. Mohan Das, "Industrial Relations in India's Public Sector", supplement of the public sector in India, *Readers' Digest*, Oct. 1975 p. 108 XVI.

47. *Amrita Bazar Patrika* Friday, Nov. 14, 1975.

48. *AD*. p. 131.

49. *AD*. p. 99.

50. Shirokov, *op. cit.*, p. 314.

51. Dietmar Rothermund, Indien und die Sowjetunion, Arbeitsgemeinschaft fuer Osteuropaforschung, Boehlau Verlag, Tuebingen, 1968. pp. 79-81.

52. *Pravda*, 1 Dec. 1973, *CDSP*, Vol. XXV. No. 49, pp. 11-12.

53. For text of the agreement, *SR* No. 58, Vol. X, December 6, 1973, pp. 28-31.

54. Brezhnev's speech in New Delhi, *Pravda*, 28 Nov. 1973, *CDSP*, Vol. XXV, No. 48, p. 1.

55. Mclane, *op. cit.* p. 248.

56. Mclane, op. cit., p. 249.

57. I. Z. Zevin, "Socialist Economic Integration and Cooperation with Third World Countries" (Summary) *Narody Azii i Afriki*, No. 2, 1972, pp. 21-42.

CHAPTER VI

TRADE, ECONOMIC AID AND COLLABORATION WITH INDIA

THE INDO-SOVIET TRADE, began with the 5-year trade agreement of December, 1953, rapidly became tenfold by 1958.[1] It levelled off, according to a knowledgeable Western source, during the mid-1960's[2], but picked up momentum following the Brezhnev tour of India in November, 1973, when a 15-year economic agreement was signed. Of the many protocols signed on the Soviet assistance in India's development of oil, coal, and other industries, the trade protocol of January 21, 1974—one of the largest trade agreements signed by India—figured prominently. The USSR undertook to supply under it goods worth Rs. 270 crores. The agreement envisages an increase in trade turnover by 35% in 1974, from Rs. 430 crores in 1973 to Rs. 630 crores in 1974. It was agreed that trade turnover between the two states was to be doubled by 1980. The supply of Soviet raw materials for India's industrial enterprises was to increase fourfold. The USSR would supply 325,000 tonnes of fertilizers, 35,000 tonnes of asbestos, copper, pallodium, machinery, etc. for the Fifth 5-year Plan of India. In addition, she would supply 1 million tonnes of kerosene and 100,000 tonnes of diesel as well as vegetable oil.

India was expected to diversify her exports to the USSR which would leave India with a favourable trade balance. Among traditional items of Indian exports were : tea, spices, coffee, tobacco, castor oil, oil cakes, cashewnuts, and jute products ; among non-traditional items : manufactured items like engineering goods, cotton textiles, readymade garments, garage equipments, storage batteries, detergents, power cables, surgical instruments, woollen knitwear, footwear, etc. . Also included in this list were Rs. 1.7 crores worth of pharmaceutical products and 50,000 tonnes of alumina of the Korba plant. The long-term trade agreement for 1976-80 will take into account the long-term needs of the two states on the basis of projections prepared by the sub-committee appointed under the joint Indo-Soviet Commission for Economic, Scientific and Technical Cooperation.³

The Russians point with satisfaction to the growing diversification in Indo-Soviet trade. As Ivan Grishin, Deputy Foreign Trade Minister of the USSR, points out, earlier Soviet exports to India consisted largely of plants and machinery while at present they include a notable amount of raw materials reflecting the increasing pace of India's industrialization. The reverse is true for India's exports, as sketched earlier.⁴ A December 26, 1970 agreement laid down that non-traditional products in India's exports to the USSR were to go up to 60%, with engineering goods accounting for 16%.⁵ It is noteworthy in this connection that India's finished and semifinished products comprised 25% of her exports to the USSR in 1960, but climbed to 50% in 1970's.⁶ India has found in the USSR one of the biggest markets for tea, a traditional export item which now faces competition from a variety of substitutes ranging from soft drinks to coffee, and other tea-exporting states. From 7% in 1961-62, the USSR's share in India's total tea export grew to 21% in 1971-72. This is stated to have at least partly offset the decline of India's tea exports to the UK, her traditional market for tea. Indian tea accounts for 91% of the Soviet tea imports, while Sri Lanka accounts for only 4%. Indian coffee is also bought in significant quantities by the USSR and her socialist allies which, it is maintained, enables India to hold on her own against stiff competition from Brazil, Colombia and Angola. India's cashew nuts exports to the USSR jumped from 4,000 tonnes in 1960-61 to 25,000 tonnes by the end of the 1960's.⁷

In fertilizers, the USSR supplied India with 5,000 tonnes of urea in 1973—a scarce commodity in the world market. The following year, on January 28, an agreement was concluded under which the USSR undertook to supply India with, as already mentioned, 325,000 tonnes of fertilizers containing 200,000 tonnes of urea, 50,000 tonnes of muriate of Potash, and 75,000 tonnes of ammonium sulphate during 1974.⁸

Under another agreement of February 10, 1975, signed in New Delhi between the Minerals and Metals Trading Corporation of India (MMTC) and the "Soyuzpromexport" of the USSR, the latter is to provide 267,000 tonnes of fertilizers during 1975, including 2000,000 tonnes of urea and 67,000 tonnes of ammonium sulphate.[9]

Ever since the 1958 trade agreement which followed the first long-term agreement of 1953, all accounts between India and the USSR are settled in rupees, which eases India's foreign exchange burden. During recent years, according to V. I. Smirnov, Counsellor and Trade Representative of the USSR in India, the USSR has met India's entire requirement of kerosene, 50% of her need for asbestos, 25% of fertilizers, and 20% of newsprint. She has also been the first country to provide markets for India's engineering products. During 1972-73, the USSR accounted for 20% of India's export of jute and woollen products, 25% of leather shoes and sheep wool, 28% of castor oil, 35% of tobacco and cashew nuts, and 40% of pepper.[10] Other products of India have also found access to the Soviet and East European markets. According to Balraj Kumar, Managing Director of the York Hosiery Mills, Ludhiana, the hosiery industry of northern India has been helped by the Soviet foreign trade organization, "Raznoexport", in finding such markets. The following figures of hosiery export have been supplied by Mr Kumar :

Year	Value of hosiery exports to the USSR
1964-65	Rs. 18 lakhs
1967-68	Rs. 231 "
1968-69	Rs. 391 "
1968-69	Hosiery exports to Czechoslovakia : Rs. 76 lakhs.

During 1968-69, the combined Soviet-Czechoslovak markets accounted for 70% of the woollen hosiery exports from India. Currently the annual woollen knitwear export to the USSR is valued at Rs. 16 crores.[11]

Among other prominent features of the Indo-Soviet trade scene is the negotiation of an Indian delegation headed by Dr P. C. Alexander, Foreign Trade Secretary, in Moscow in

October, 1975 over 38 additional items of import from the USSR and 73 items of export from India to that country. Agreement had already been reached on 17 items of import from the USSR and 28 items of export from India in earlier talks. The Indian delegation is also exploring the possibility of exporting pig iron to the USSR.[12]

According to press reports, K. I. Gelaushin, the USSR Minister for Paper and Pulp Industry, assured India of the readiness of his Ministry to supply newsprint greater in amount than the previously agreed amount of 45,000 tonnes for 1975-76. The USSR would reportedly also "thoroughly consider" any Indian request for Soviet help in setting up newsprint mills in India. In view of India's newsprint crisis this was a timely promise.[13] Other recent press reports suggest that India was keen on entering the Soviet market with synthetic fabrics at the second round of trade talks in Moscow during October, 1975. The synthetic fabrics market in the USSR has been hitherto supplied by the UK, France, Japan and other leading industrial states. Since India was already selling synthetic fabrics to Canada, the USA, Poland and Japan, she stood a fair chance of entering the Soviet market as well.[14]

By 1973, India became the biggest trade partner of the USSR among the third world nations. Simultaneously, the USSR moved into the leading position in India's export trade.[15] This does not necessarily reflect *only* the Soviet keenness to bolster India's trade—as Soviet publicity materials are prone to suggest—but rather the prominent position of barter between the two trading states. Bearing this in mind one should turn to the following statistics relating to the Indo-Soviet trade :

Year	Value of turnover in roubles[16]
1953	1.7 million
1960	104.0 ,,
1973	589.0 ,,
1974	616.0 ,,

A more detailed breakdown in terms of India's exports and imports in crores of rupees is as follows :

Indo-Soviet Trade

Year	Imports	Exports
1951-52	1.39	6.92
1969-70	171.33	176.37
1970-71	104.68	209.85
1971-72	81.66	208.70
1972-73	105.72	304.76

The production collaboration between the USSR and India is expected to give a new fillip to trade between the two countries. As D. P. Chattopadhyaya, India's Minister of Commerce, put it :

> One of the important features of our future economic relations is the production in India of new goods to meet the increasing requirements of the USSR and vice of versa.[18]

ECONOMIC AID

While the U. S. economic aid to India, first enacted in May 1950 as the Technical Assistance Programme under Point Four, has been comprehensive in scope ranging across rural electrification, public health, education, multipurpose projects, and massive food aid programmes, the Soviet assistance has almost exclusively concentrated on India's industrial development in the public sector. The U.S.A. had to channelize most of her aid into India's public sector, a fact which placed her on the horns of a dilemma. The USSR, on the other hand, had no such compunctions and in fact welcomed collaboration with the sector in accordance with her ideological proclivity. Most Soviet economic aid has been in the shape of long-term interest-bearing credits, not grants. Of the total aid of 1,022 million dollars' equivalent extended to India from 1954 through 1965, only 156 million dollars represented grants.[19]

Generally, Soviet credits are provided for the purchase of machinery, equipment and other materials for specific projects requiring Soviet assistance. Many agreements cover the cost of training local personnel in the USSR. The latter finances the foreign exchange component of construction projects but rarely the local costs of the Soviet-financed projects. The local currency component of such projects are expected to be provided by the beneficiary state.[20] Leo Tansky, a US government economist, declines to join critics of the Soviet aid programmes in terming them "impact type" projects, which is intended to mean that they fetch quick returns in terms of finance and publicity. He raises a dissenting voice and opines that "The bulk of Soviet assistance actually is being channeled into basic industrial facilities and overhead investment."[21] Tansky also lends credence to the Soviet claim that the USSR accepts repayment of credits in commodities from the developing nations which, besides saving their scarce foreign exchange reserves, helps boost their exports. It may be noted here in passing that according to a reliable British estimate, although India's rate of utilization of Soviet credits has been rapid during 1955-69, it has stood at 75%.[22] The low rate of interest (around 2.5%) on Soviet credits, admits Tansky, also enables savings for the developing nations.[23]

Although within a certain time-frame (1954-65) the US economic assistance to India has been several times the size of its Soviet counterpart (5,901 million dollars : 1,022 million dollars),[24] the impact of the Soviet programmes has been more lasting. Soviet aid programmes for India together with those for the UAR accounted for 51% of the total Soviet aid by the mid-1960's.[25] About two-thirds of the Soviet assistance for industrial facilities have been concentrated on India and the UAR. The latter also take the lion's share of the Soviet heavy industry aid.[26]

McLane, however, points out that by 1970 India was paying more to the USSR in the form of debt service than she was receiving in new aid. Further, difficulties arose on fixing the price of manufactured goods which India wished to export to the USSR in payment of debt, since the Soviet market was already "glutted with goods that could not be sold abroad". The reinvigoration of Indo-Soviet trade in the present decade removed some of these irritants.[27] A breakdown of Soviet aid to India and economic cooperation with her follows below.

Industry

True to their ideological inclination for the priority creation of an industrial infrastructure—particularly that of heavy industry—the Russians have concentrated on assisting India in building her heavy industry. The Soviet-assisted steel plants in Bhilai and Bokaro, the heavy machine-building plant in Ranchi, and the heavy electrical plant in Hardwar (the latter producing 100,000 to 200,000 kw turbogenerators) are among the biggest in the third world.[28] A summary of the history of Soviet assistance in the sphere under consideration is given in the chart below.[29]

Year of Agreement	Amount of aid	Projects
1955	135.9 mil. dollars	Bhilai steel plant.
1957	125.0 ,, ,,	Machine-building plant, Ranchi. Coal-mining machinery plant & optical glass factory, Durgapur. Thermal power plant, Neyveli.
1959	20.0 ,, ,,	Pharmaceutical plants.
1959	375.0 ,, ,,	Expansion of Ranchi plant. Expansion of Bhilai plant. Expansion of coal-mining machinery plant, Durgapur. Expansion of thermal power plant, Neyveli. Heavy electrical equipment plant, Ranipur. Thermal power stations, Korba & Obra. Precision instruments plant, Kota.
1961	125.0 mil. dollars	Hydel station, Bhakra; Oil refinery, Koyali; Coal Washery, Kathara; Protocol on Neyveli power station.
1962		Protocol on technical aid. Protocol on expansion of

			Bhilai works. Protocol on additional oil refineries. Contract for pharmaceutical plant.
1963			Expansion of Neyveli's capacity. Expansion of refineries in Barauni and Koyali. Bhakra dam completed. Pharmaceutical plant completed. Ranchi & Durgapur works completed.
1964	211.0	,, ,,	Bokaro steel plant.
1966			Protocol on additional oil refineries.
1968			Protocol on aid.
1969			Antibiotics plants completed. Cooperation in ferrous, non-ferrous industries.
1970			Power plant at Aligarh completed. Bhilai expansion. Protocol on precision instruments plant, Kota.

Against the background of the above chart the more recent prominent features of the Soviet assistance in the heavy industries sector is to be considered. The discussion now concentrates on salient Soviet-assisted plants in India, starting off with the earliest one, Bhilai.

Bhilai: The Bhilai steel plant was established under a February 2, 1955 agreement between India and the USSR. Its first stage of upto 1 million tonnes of steel production was completed in 1961. Under a further agreement of September 12, 1959 its capacity was expanded to 2·5 million tonnes by 1967. Next, a June 3, 1972 agreement envisaged further expansion of its capacity to 4 million tonnes including the construction of a converter shop, and very modern metallurgical units of continuous steel casting machines and plate mill "3600". The details of construction were worked out by the Indian consultancy agency, MECON—which draws on years of experience in collaboration with Soviet counterparts—and the Soviet institute, Gipromez. It is estimated that 25,000 tonnes of equipment for mill "3600" will be provided by the USSR, while 38,000 tonnes of equipment will be made available by Indian sources, the bulk of which has been charged to the responsibility of the Soviet-assisted heavy machine-building plant in Ranchi. The latter, according to T. A. Pai, India's Minister for Industry and Civil Supplies, compares favourably with the best even in the USSR[30] and is capable of producing annually the entire range of equipments necessary for setting up a 1 million tonne-metallurgical enterprise.[31]

For the continuous steel casting machines, out of the requisite total of 13,500 tonnes of equipments, the USSR will deliver 5,500 tonnes, the rest to be provided locally. During the Brezhnev visit to India in November, 1973, it was agreed that the capacity of Bhilai was to be further raised to 7 million tonnes.[32] It is interesting to recall here that in both the cases of Bhilai and Bokaro, it was US unwillingness to help India build public sector steel plants that was put to good use by the USSR. Chester Bowles recalls how his efforts at interesting the US government under Eisenhower in this direction were given the brush off by the State Department which refused to credit the USSR with the ability to build modern metallurgical plants.[33]

Bokaro : After Bhilai, Bokaro became the symbol of Soviet steel—and stake—in India. Signed into existence in the mid-1960's, it is conceived to become the largest metallurgical enterprise in India. The fact that the USA declined to assist India in its construction and that the USSR stepped in to provide the assistance appears to be an indicator of the shape of things to come in India—those visualized and hoped for by the USSR. The USSR rendered technical assistance and extended credit of 200 million roubles for setting up Bokaro's first stage of 1.7 million tonnes. In 1970, an Indo-Soviet trade protocol laid down the agreement to raise its capacity to 4 million tonnes annually. Additional credits of 85 million roubles were granted for the second stage. The first stage was to be commissioned in 1975 while the second stage in 1977. Bokaro's twin 100-

tonnes oxygen-converter plants, commissioned in early February, 1974, are stated to incorporate advanced technology and represent an improvement upon the open-hearth process in Bhilai. Two additional converters have also been commissioned. The plate mill "1400" represents latest technology available in the USSR which enables the production of a wider spectrum of thin cold-rolled sheets, including automobile and corrugated sheets. The rolling mill "2000" is stated to be similar to the one recently commissioned at the Novolipetsk Iron and Steel Plant in the USSR. The rolling mill "1250" with the designed capacity of $1\frac{1}{2}$ million tonnes of steel is the biggest in India.

Bokaro produced its first pig iron in October, 1972, when blast furnace number one (capacity 2,000 cubic metres), India's largest, was put into operation. According to K. C. Khanna, Managing Director of the Bokaro Steel Ltd., Bokaro, has already made its way into the export markets of the USSR and Japan for its pig iron, earning thereby Rs. 11 crores in foreign exchange. It is also the biggest supplier of pig iron to the foundries in the country. Of the Fifth 5-Year Plan target of 17.5 million tonnes of ingot steel production, Bokaro is scheduled to provide 4 million tonnes. The biggest construction project in India, Bokaro is estimated to employ 60,000 people. According to a November 29, 1973 agreement between the USSR and India, its capacity is to be raised to 10 million tonnes annually. It is then expected to become the largest metallurgical enterprise in the whole of South and Southeast Asia.

India's own participation in the constructions at Bokaro would be on a large scale. While for Bhilai, established two decades earlier, 90% of the equipment came from the USSR, for Bokaro, two-thirds of all machinery and 90% of all structures are to be indigenously supplied, with the Soviet-assisted heavy machine-building plants in Ranchi and Durgapur playing a prominent role.[34]

The Soviet assistance to India has also extended to closely related spheres like raw material supplies to the steel mills : the Rajhara and Dalli iron ore mines, a number of coal pits and quarries as well as a large coal washery have been built with

Soviet aid.[35] The Soviet-assisted Nandini quarry provides Bhilai with limestone.[36]

According to a November 29, 1973 agreement, a copper concentration complex will be built in Malanjkhand with Soviet assistance.[37]

Further, a protocol on Soviet assistance to expand and modernize India's machine-tool industry was signed on September 23, 1974, by the head of a Soviet delegation of experts, V. K. Jouravla, Chief Engineer of the machine exporting organization, Stankozagran-postavka, and S. M. Ghosh, Joint Secretary, Ministry of Heavy Industry.[38] The Russians have already helped India build precision and mechanical instruments plants in Kota and Palghat.[39] A contract was signed in early 1974 in New Delhi between the Soviet heavy industry organization, Tiazhpromexport, and Kerala State Industrial Development Corporation for Soviet assistance in setting up a "highly specialized" refractory plant in Kerala with the annual capacity of 31,000 tonnes.[40]

The Korba Aluminium Project : The first of its kind in the public sector and the biggest in India, the Korba project consists of 2 complexes : the first designed to produce 200,000 tonnes of alumina with Hungarian cooperation was completed in April, 1973, and the second, smalter and fabrication unit, is to produce 100,000 tonnes of aluminium products with Soviet cooperation under a 1966 agreement and is scheduled for completion by 1975. Korba is expected to go into full production by 1976, thereby aiding significantly India's quest for self-sufficiency in aluminium, the demand for which is expected to be around 400,000 tonnes by 1978, and the world market price for which has shot up sharply. India has an abundant supply of bauxite, the key raw material needed for aluminium production.

India at present has the installed capacity of 210,000 tonnes of alumina and aluminium products. The Soviet aid for Korba is confined to highly sophisticated equipment comprising about 15% of the total equipment needed. The rest, as is lately the pattern, is being supplied by India's own concerns. Under the 1974 trade protocol, the USSR will buy 50,000 tonnes of alumina from Korba.⁴¹ Aluminium supply has become abundant recently which has led to the liberalization of its aluminium policy by the government in October, 1975. The latter is reportedly bracing up for exports of the commodity too.⁴²

Mention should be made of the projected 500,000 tonne-alumina plant in Sarguja, on which joint Indo-Soviet feasibility studies have been completed. This production unit is to be fed bauxite from deposits at Mandla, Sarguja and Balaghat districts. The USSR will provide the necessary machinery and buy up almost the entire output of the plant.⁴³

The MAMC : The Soviet-assisted mining and allied machinery plant in Durgapur is India's number one producer of coal-mining machinery. Soviet specialists are still cooperating with it, partly in order to modify Soviet-patented machinery to suit local requirements ; e.g., a smaller Indian model of the Soviet coal-cutting PL P-3 has been produced. 200 such machines, the basic tool for coal production, are to be produced in 2 years from 1974, saving, according to Soviet sources, Rs. 1 crore of foreign exchange.

However, A. C. Chatterjee, Managing Director of the Plant, laments the lack of orders for coal-mining equipment which has forced the plant to diversify its production. Absence of a steady market has resulted in the underutilization of its capacity, and to this is added the frequent inability to meet delivery schedules-problems which seem to be shared by many a public sector undertaking. The MAMC has supplied so far to the Bokaro steel plant conveyors and pumps worth Rs. 12-14 crores.⁴⁴ It will also play a significant role in India's efforts at raising coal output, as mentioned earlier.⁴⁵ Together with the heavy engineering plant in Ranchi, it manufactures blast-furnaces, steel-smelting, coke-oven equipments as well as structural steel for Bokaro.⁴⁶

Pharmaceuticals : The Indian Drugs and Pharmaceuticals complex comprises of the Surgical Instruments Plant in Madras, the Synthetic Drugs Plant in Hyderabad, and the Antibiotics Plant in Rishikesh. All three of them were built with Soviet technical and financial assistance, and Indian personnel needed to man them were trained at Soviet plants. The Hyderabad and the Rishikesh plants are scheduled for expansion with Soviet assistance during the Fifth 5-Year Plan period. When the expansion is completed, the IDPL will account for 50% of the production of bulk drugs and 20% of the medical industry.[47] Mention should be made of MECON, the Metallurgical and Engineering Consultants (India) Ltd., which evolved out of the years of Indo-Soviet collaboration in the construction of steel plants. It has been entrusted with the design and engineering aspects of Bokaro, and the engineering aspects of Bhilai and Korba. It will also prepare the detailed Project Report for the envisaged 2 million-tonne steel plant in Vijayanagar. MECON has been instrumental in saving foreign exchange by substituting the work of foreign designing and engineering concerns. Soviet specialists are reportedly helping MECON to train up indigenous personnel. Mr K. C. Mohan, its director, is quoted to have indicated its request for Soviet assistance for another 5 years in view of the massive tasks at hand in Bhilai and Bokaro.

MECON-designed plate mill "6300" in Bhilai will produce plates for ships and boilers for thermal plants, and its cold rolling mill "2000" in Bokaro will produce tin plates to meet the demands of the canning industry.[48]

Oil and Gas : The Soviet assistance to India in the sphere of prospecting and producing oil has been termed as "revolutionary" by a Western scholar.[49] The Soviet oil aid to India started from 1955 and became multifaceted.[50] India's former Minister for Petroleum and Chemicals, D. K. Barooah, stated in this connection :

> In fact, this industry (oil) in its entire range, from the exploration and extraction of oil to its refining and the training of personnel, has been built with the cooperation of the Soviet Union.[51]

And, according to Tansky, the US government economist, Soviet aid has "dominated" India's oil development in the public sector.[52]

At the turn of the 1960's Soviet assistance became instrumental in the discovery of oil and gas deposits in India—described by the Soviet Minister of Oil Industry, V. D. Shashin, as "promising"—at Ankleshwar, Cambay, Kalol, Rudrasagar, Lakwa, etc. Cooperation between India's Oil and Natural Gas Commission (ONGC) and corresponding Soviet organizations led to the identification of over 160 oil-bearing structures and 26 oil deposits in India. According to Shashin, India's oil and gas-bearing areas cover 1.6 million sq. km., which hold out a promising future for the country. By 1974, production from public sector oilfields in India reached 4.1 million tonnes annually. This was largely possible, it is stated, due to Soviet help.[53] For instance, off-shore exploration in India was conducted by the Soviet furnished ship, Akademic Arkhangelsky, which discovered during its surveys from 1964 through 1966 the promising oil-bearing structure, the Bombay High, in the Arabian Sea. The USSR also provided the design of the fixed platform for Aliabet and also helped fabricate and erect the platform at the site.[54]

During 1970-71, Indo-Soviet studies on the cost and the feasibility of oil production till 1980 were completed. The Indo-Soviet joint ventures in the field during the present decade are within the framework of those studies.

According to Shashin, the Soviet Oil Industry Minister, the Assam-Arakan and the Tripura sedimentary basings hold promise while large deposits of natural gas have already been discovered in Tripura.[55]

The ONGC is conducting oil explorations with Soviet assistance mainly in Gujarat and Assam. Soviet assistance is also extended to drilling in Jaisalmer, Tripura, in the Gulf basin of West Bengal, Kashmir and Himachal Pradesh. According to D. K. Barooah, the recently discovered Geliki oilfield in Assam, which has turned out to be the best so far, was intensively drilled upon the recommendation of Shashin.[56] About 12 out of every 100 workers of the 25,000-body ONGC are Soviet-trained. The amount of Soviet assisted drilling has topped the 2 million metres mark. As Shashin put it,

> In its relations with the Republic of India—its friend and business partner—the Soviet Union consistently follows the course of the consolidation of the state sector in India's oil industry.

He goes on to recommend the expansion of the capacity of the oil pipeline in the eastern region which has been built right upto the oil refinery in Barauni.[57]

In 1972, an Indo-Soviet team prepared an ambitious programme of oil exploration designed to prove a total reserve of 70 million tonnes of oil, including 5 million tonnes of off-shore oil.[58] The January 14, 1974 protocol, signed by the oil ministers of the two states, provided for "massive Soviet assistance" for India's oil industry. It was the result of the visit of Soviet oil experts to India led by Shashin himself. The Soviet side promised help in exploration and extraction of oil and gas in India, for which purpose five top Soviet experts were to be deputed to India for 2 years, while another five of them were to visit the country for shorter periods.

Among a variety of ways of producing better results, secondary recovery methods were slated for improvement. Since formation of paraffin deposits in tubings and flow-lines hamper recovery rates, the USSR promised to provide special enamel-coated tubings and even help India set up a manufacturing unit for such tubings.

Another agreement is expected to provide the services of 15 Soviet specialists to India, and on-the-job training of 28 Indian experts in the USSR. A variety of oil industry equipments, including 3 deep-drilling rigs and an automatic station to measure the flow of oil wells, will also be supplied.[59] It is interesting to note in this connection that the Heavy Machine Building Plant at Ranchi is stated for the production of deep-drilling rigs (3,000-5,000 m.).[60] There is currently a 5-year programme on in joint oil exploration in India.[61]

Shashin visited India again in January, 1975, following which talks were scheduled to be held in Moscow between him and his Indian counterpart, K. D. Malaviya, on how to make the ONGC more effective and on establishing an institute for "reserve engineering" (development of oilfields) at Baroda.[62]

Refineries : The spectacularity of the Soviet assistance to India in the realm of oil lies above all in the construction of refineries. In 1974, a delegation of the state sector Indian Oil Corporation—itself supplied with oil by the USSR to compete with the Western oil companies in India[63]—headed by its Chairman, C. R. Das Gupta, held talks in the USSR with the officials of V/O Neftekhimpromexport, the Soviet technical consultancy organization, regarding the construction of the oil refinery in Mathura. The 6-million tonnes refinery is to be the largest of its kind not only in India but in the entire South and Southeast Asian areas, and technically a most modern enterprise. Indian participation in its construction is scheduled to be far greater than in the case of the refineries in Barauni and Koyali, also built with Soviet assistance.[64] The latter two refineries reportedly account for 30% of India's oil refining capacity.[65] Another refinery was built with Rumanian assistance in Nunmati.[66] An agreement over the Mathura refinery was signed in Moscow on September 24, 1975. The value of the enterprise, which is expected to handle a wide variety of crude oil[67] is estimated at 20 million dollars. The USSR is scheduled to begin the supply of equipments in 1976, and the refinery is expected to become operational in 1979.[68]

The Soviet aid to India in exploiting her oil and gas deposits is not least significant in view of the fact that by 1973, the USSR moved to the position of the leading oil producing nation in the world outstripping the USA with a production of 429 million tonnes, West Siberia alone accounting for 88 million tonnes.[69] India seems keen on obtaining further know-how and assistance in this realm from the USSR.[70]

Coal : Coal as an alternate source of energy is held by the official Soviet position as worthy of the most active development in view of the growing oil crisis matching with the growing hunger for energy in the world. India has coal reserves estimated at 130,000 million tonnes, of which 26,000 million tonnes are coking coal.[71] India's target is to increase her coal production from 80 million tonnes in 1973-74 to 130-140 million tonnes by 1978-79.[72] The USSR assisted India in the late 1960's with the construction of 3 mines in Madhya Pradesh : the Manikpur open-cast mine, and the underground Banki and Surkachhar mines.[73] The Kathara coal washery, built with Soviet assistance, is one of the biggest in South and Southest Asia. The USSR has also facilitated India's efforts at augmenting production of coal by helping her build a coal-mining equipments plant in Durgapur and a heavy machine-building plant in Ranchi,[74] mentioned earlier. An electrical and mechanical workshop in Korba, set up with Soviet assistance, services and repairs mining machinery. Brezhnev's November, 1973-visit to India brought with it the prospect of Soviet assistance in building at Singrauli open-cast mines—a method favoured by the Russians for reasons of economy—and a mechanized underground mine in Raniganj.[75] According to J. G. Kumaramangalam, Chairman of the Coal Mines Authority, the Singrauli coalfield will enable a cut in transport costs for supplies to Punjab, Uttar Pradesh and Madhya Pradesh. The new mines at Singrauli and Raniganj are expected to yield 3 to 3.5 million tonnes of additional coal. It is further expected that Singrauli will eventually be able to produce upto 10 million tonnes annually. One of the largest coalfields in India, it will play a central role in feeding the new thermal power plants in Obra, Harduaganj, Badarpur, Faridabad, etc. Already in December, 1966 an agreement foresaw Indo-Soviet Cooperation in the construction of 5 coal mines with a total output of 6.5 million tonnes of coking coal per year to supply Bhilai and Bokaro.[76] In early 1974, a Soviet expert delegation headed by B. Bratchenko, Minister of Coal Industry, visited Indian mines. A protocol followed which provided for Soviet assistance in designing mines, supply of equipment and training of experts as well as cooperation in the production of coking coal in Kedlya, Pundil Teping (Bihar) and Ramgarh.[77] Shortly thereafter, in April, another team headed by N. A. Krylov, Chief Engineer of the Mine Designing Department of the USSR Ministry of Coal Industry, visited India. The Soviet experts favoured building of a large open-cast mine in Ramgarh with the capacity to produce 3.5 million tonnes of coking coal annually. This would be India's biggest open-cast mine. Further, they proposed the construction of an open-cast and an underground mine in the Kedlya area with a production capacity of 2-3 million tonnes of coking coal per year. The Russians also wanted to extend their assistance in setting up another coal washery in Ramgarh. The envisaged production of coking coal in Ramgarh would be able to feed Bokaro and other steel plants, and Soviet credits are available for its development.[78] Soviet advice will also be forthcoming regarding the increase of production of the existing mines in Raniganj.[79]

V. Pashkov, Deputy Counseller for Economic Affairs, USSR Embassy in India, mentions the possibility of Soviet assistance in developing coal deposits in Kusmunda near Korba. Coal from this area will enable better supplies to Maharashtra, Gujarat and Tamil Nadu.[80] Further, a Soviet designers' team helped the designing institute at Ranchi during April-October, 1974 to prepare a feasibility report on increasing coal output for power generation. According to Bratchenko, the Soviet Minister for Coal Industry, 9 large open-cast mines are planned for Singrauli, apart from the 2 already in operation. This, according to him, is a long-range plan for 25 years. For more immediate purposes, the Ramgarh mine is to be reconstructed with increased output. Of the 6 new open-cast mines to be started, Bina with 4.5 million tonnes of annual production has already been designed and is under construction.

For the Raniganj deposit, experts have recommended the construction of Janjra-1 and Janjra-2 mines with the total capacity of 5.3 million tonnes per year.[81] In her endeavour to raise coal output during the Fifth 5-Year Plan, India will take advantage of indigenously produced equipment, the bulk of which are to be supplied by the mining and allied machinery plant in Durgapur.[82] The Soviet assistance in the integrated development of India's coal in Madhya Pradesh, Uttar Pradesh and West Bengal, hence, will be the minimum necessary in terms of more sophisticated machinery which India does not yet produce.

As in the case of India's oil production, Soviet assistance in India's coal production takes on significance in the light of the fact that the USSR is a top producer of the commodity moving into the first position in the world in 1973 with 660 million tonnes.[83]

Energy : The Soviet aid to India's power-generating capacity has been extended in setting up 15 thermal-and hydro-power stations with the total capacity of 3 million kw., some of them being as follows : Neyveli thermal power station (600 mw),

Bhakra hydel power plant (450/600 mw), Patratu (440 mw), Obra (275 mw), and Harduaganj (110 mw).[84] The Soviet assisted Korba Thermal power plant provides Bhilai with power.[85]

In accordance with their policy of creating key structures in the state sector which would provide the basis for economic growth independent primarily of the West, the Russians have helped build the Heavy Electrical Equipments Plant in Hardwar, which, when it reaches its full capacity, is expected to ensure an annual increase of about 3 million kw in the installed power-generating capacity in India. The plant reportedly has mastered the production of 100,000 kw steam turbines, and tested a turbogenerator of 200,000 kw in the late 1973.[86]

India's Fifth 5-Year Plan target for power-generation has been fixed at 34 million kw,[87] which is conceivable to a significant degree due to a variety of Soviet assistance in this area, particularly in helping indigenous production of the necessary equipments. The Institute of High Temperatures of the USSR Academy of Sciences is also reportedly cooperating with Indian experts in designing and subsequently constructing magneto-hydrodynamic generators (MHD), which are stated to be able to contribute greatly to solving energy problems.[88]

SCIENCE AND TRAINING

Since a 1960 agreement between the USSR and India on cultural, scientific and technical cooperation, contacts between the scientific bodies of the two states have increased. A month after the 1971 Friendship Treaty, the joint Indo-Soviet Commission on Economic, Scientific and Technical Cooperation was created to tackle within its framework specific and technical problems. On October 2, 1972 a further agreement was signed in Moscow on cooperation in applied sciences and technology. It envisaged exchange of scientific delegations, research workers and specialists, trainees and lecturers, as well as of technical information, documents, and the introduction of the result of the researches in industry and agriculture. It also encompassed sale of patents and licenses and exchange of books and periodicals.

In February 1973, the first session of the joint Commission mentioned above took place in Delhi. The consequent programme drawn up for 1973-74 included cooperation in a number of branches of science and engineering, e.g., joint research on the manufacture of polybutylene rubber, which is an excellent substitute for natural rubber, programmed digital control machines, methods of using pre-stressed ferro-concrete structures and meteorological studies. In early 1974, a 2-year agreement on scientific and cultural exchange was signed in Moscow.[89]

Further, designing centres are to be set up in India based on the experience of the Soviet Institute of Industrial Designing and its branches. Cooperation between the Committee for Standards under the USSR Council of Ministers and the Indian Institute of Standards has been established for the purpose of standardization of products against the background of India's efforts at trade expansion.

A number of Soviet computers have been installed in key centres in India, e.g., the Bhava Atomic Research Centre uses the Soviet-made BESM-6 capable of performing a million operations per second ; the Indian Statistical Institute, Calcutta, uses the Urals ; the Soviet-assisted Institute of Technology in Bombay uses 2 Minsk-type computers and was reported to be acquiring the third generation ES-1030. The Thumba rocket launching centre also uses a Soviet computer.

In the sphere of scientific training, the faculty of geophysics at Osmania University, of metallurgy at the IIT Kanpur, and of aircraft construction at the IIT Bombay were established with Soviet assistance. These faculties train some 200 specialists anually for the public sector enterprises. The USSR has also assisted in organizing certain specialized secondary schools, viz., a metallurgical school at Bhilai, machine-building schools at Bhopal and Ranchi, an oil-and-gas industrial school at Baroda, an electrical engineering centre at Bhopal, and a radio training centre at Hyderabad.[90]

In adition, the Soviet-assisted industrial units in India also provide schooling in production techniques to thousands of technical employees. A centre is being set up in the Korba aluminium complex for training 100 specialists annually.[91]

About 2,300 Indian specialists received production-technical training directly in the USSR. For instance, a group of engineers from the Heavy Machine-Building Plant in Ranchi were training at 2 major centres of heavy machine building in the USSR in 1974 : Slaviansk (the Ukraine) and Orak (the Urals).[92] Further, under UNESCO projects, 50 Soviet experts worked in India between 1964 and 1973, training specialists in colleges at Warangal, Allahabad, Bhopal, Durgapur, Nagpur, Jamshedpur and Mangalore.[93] According to Prof. Nurul Hasan, India's Education Minister, 100 scholarships are being made available to Indian candidates for higher studies and research in the USSR.[94]

On February 18, 1975, a 5-year agreement on scientific and technological cooperation was signed between the USSR and India. Simultaneously, a 5-year programme of specific types of such cooperation was drawn up by the joint Indo-Soviet Committee of the USSR Academy of Sciences and the Indian National Science Academy. The agreement seeks to establish closer cooperation between the scientific bodies of the two states and to coordinate joint efforts at solving problems of common interest. Fields such as the geosciences, biology, mathematics, etc. have been covered. For instance, joint studies of the geo-magnetic and geo-electrical impulses in the Himalayan and the Deccan regions are to be conducted, such studies being also of interest for the discovery of mineral deposits, including oil. Studies of the different river basins of India are also to be conducted. Fundamental research in radiation and evolutionary history of extraterrestrial matter is also to be undertaken jointly.

In statistics, extensive cooperation has been envisaged involving the University of Poona and the ISI, New Delhi and Calcutta, on the one hand and the Staklov Institute of Mathematics, Moscow and Leningrad, on the other. A Soviet Science Information Centre has been planned for Delhi with the help of All-Union Institute of Scientific and Technical Information (VINITI) Moscow.[95]

Space

The Indo-Soviet collaboration in space technology was first mooted in 1970 by the late Dr Vikram Sarabhai and the then Soviet ambassador to India, N. M. Pegov, in Delhi. This was followed up in August 1971 by the visit of an Indian team to the USSR where it met Academicians Petrov and Kavtunenko. In February 1972, a Soviet delegation headed by Prof. Kavtunenko, by then director of the Soviet part of the joint Indo-Soviet cosmic project, came to India. This visit resulted on May 10 in an agreement in Moscow between the USSR Academy of Sciences and the Indian Space Research Organization (ISRO) regarding Soviet help in launching an Indian satellite, the 300 kg. Aryabhata with a diameter of 1·5 metres, which was launched successfully in early 1975 atop a Soviet rocket from a Soviet cosmodrome. In August, work on the satellite project was started in Bangalore, a centre of science and aviation, under the guidance of Prof. Dhawan, who took charge of ISRO. In early 1973, B. N. Petrov, President of the Council of Intercosmos, headed a 15-member team of cosmic experts to India to render technical assistance. Next on January 21, 1974 a 19-member team of "highly qualified" scientists and specialists in space technology, headed by Dr N. Novikov, Deputy Chairman of the Intercosmos Council, arrived in Delhi, whereupon they proceeded to Bangalore for a fortnight's stay to assist their Indian colleagues in their satellite programme.

In summer of the same year, a prototype was sent to the USSR for tests on a rocket. Okay came through by July. The USSR also helped construct the requisite ground station in Madras. While the Aryabhata project was the product largely of India's own efforts, Soviet technical aid was extended in building its spin-up system, tape recording system, power supply system, etc. On the other hand, Soviet sources stressed that the communication with the satellite would involve the Indian ground station only, although press reports in October, 1975 in India quoted Prof. U. R. Rao's reference to Aryabhata's communication also with a Moscow communication centre.[96]

Aside from the Aryabhata project, the Soviet technical assistance to India's space ventures has included meteorological research at Thumba—the latter itself built with Soviet assistance —where at least 52 Soviet M-100 rockets have been fired. The experience thus gained has enabled India to build her own Rohini rockets. Also, Indo-Soviet cooperation in satellite communication is a distinct possibility in the future. It is possible that India will participate in the Soviet Inter-Sputnik communication programme, which is on since November, 1971, just as she has participated in the US-sponsored SITE programme. Future joint Indo-Soviet work on planetary and other studies also falls within the realm of possibility as indicated by Nikolai Novikov, Vice-Chairman of the Intercosmos Council of the USSR Academy of Sciences.[97]

AGRICULTURE

The Soviet assistance to India in the field of agriculture has been far less spectacular than that in the realm of industrial enterprises. The Soviet role in providing food assistance to India, for instance, was dwarfed by the corresponding US sales of wheat, largely though not exclusively against rupee payment, to India during 1963-69 on a truly massive scale, accounting for 26 million tons, nearly three-fourths of the entire average annual US crop. It helped, according to Chester Bowles, the ex-US ambassador to India, 12% of the Indian population tide over food shortages.[98]

The Soviet assistance to India's agriculture began in 1955 when the USSR made a gift of Rs. 7·5 million worth of agricultural equipments exhibited in the World Agricultural Fair held in India. These included 70 tractors, 60 grain harvesters, trucks, bulldozers, a mobile workshop, etc. The Indian Government utilized these equipments in setting up the Suratgarh Central Mechanized Farm the following year, which became the biggest state farm in India. Three years later, additional equipments worth Rs. 400,000 were gifted by the USSR for setting up a repair shop for the farm. Other equipments for it were bought from the USSR. India opted for a second such farm at nearby Jetsar, for which the USSR provided trade credit of Rs. 2·53 million for the purchase of agricultural equipments.

Under a November 26, 1966 agreement, the USSR made further gifts of agricultural equipments to India worth Rs. 11 million for organizing 5 more state farms of 3,000-4,000 hectares each. These were set up during 1967-70 : Hissar (Haryana, August 1968), Ladhowal (Punjab, August 1965), Raichur (Mysore, October 1968), and Cannanore (Kerala, 1970). A State Farms Corporation was consequently created which now has under it 13 state farms while 4 more are to be organised during the Fifth 5-Year Plan in states like Madhya Pradesh, Bihar, Gujarat, etc. Suratgarh is to play the role of a training centre for drivers, mechanics and other skilled personnel for the state farms.

According to M. V. Mukhamedjanov, Counsellor for Agricultural Affairs, USSR Embassy in India, the State Farms Corporation has been promised 37,880 hectares of land by the Union Government. The Farm also plays a notable role in seed production, its production target at the end of the Fifth 5-Year Plan being 30,440 tonnes annually. The USSR sees the farm development programme as part of land reclamation and extension of cultivation to fallow lands in India. There are 20 million hectares of uncultivated land in India, according to Soviet estimates.

On June 18, 1971, an agreement was signed between India and the USSR on scientific and technical cooperation in agriculture and animal husbandry. This was followed up by an April 10, 1972 protocol which enabled greater exchange of delegations. The November 1973-visit of Brezhnev to India resulted in an agreement—among others—under which the USSR undertook to supply 1,000 Karakul and 3,000-4,000 Merino sheep and 200 Padamakaya goats for better breeding in India, assist research in fisheries, afforestation, sunflower and sugarbeet production, etc. On April 1, 1974, a protocol was signed on setting up 2 sheep-breeding farms, an experimental goat-breeding farm, and on sugarbeet cultivation in India with Soviet aid.[99] The latter is expected to help India utilize the idle capacity of her sugar mills and to boost production of sugar. Ramonskaya, a Soviet sugarbeet variety, has been adapted to Indian conditions.[100]

Cultivation of sunflower in the Soviet style is felt to be necessary for self-sufficiency in vegetable oil, and preliminary tests reportedly bear promise.[101] Further, the Soviet Institute of Rice Growing and the Indian Central Rice Research Institute are cooperating in developing and reproducing certain high-yield rice varieties and hybrids.[102] Cooperation is also taking place between the Central Arid Zone Research Institute in Jodhpur and the Institute of Unirrigated Agriculture in Samarkand (Uzbekistan). They are conducting research in agricultural development in arid and semi-arid areas and undertaking the introduction and development of drought-resistant varieties of plants.[103]

During the 1950's and the early 1960's the USSR supplied India with 35,000 tractors on a rupee-payment basis. The Soviet foreign trade organization Tractoexport has played a notable role in this providing with models like DT-14B, T-28, Byelorus, and T-25 (Vladimirets), At Loni in Uttar Pradesh, a private party under license from the Government has set up a tractor production unit with Soviet collaboration. Its peak production capacity is 10,000 tractors of 14-20 h.p. per year.[104] The Soviet foreign trade organization, V/0 Zapchastexport, now maintains a warehouse in Bombay port for spare parts of tractors deliverable to license-bearing Indian parties.[105]

Miscellaneous

Indo-Soviet cooperation has extended to shipping. India pays, according to one estimate, Rs. 170-180 crores in foreign exchange for freight charges to foreign shipping lines. India's consequent need of increasing her tonnage is partly being met by the USSR and her socialist allies who are to supply ships against rupee payment. India has placed orders for 7 ships, 4 cargo vessels and 3 tankers which are to be delivered in 1975. The 3 tankers of 16,300 DWT are being built in the Baltic shipyards.[106] The Soviet supply of ships to India is a new development and reflects the capacity of the USSR as a major ship-builder.[107]

A 1970 agreement between India and the USSR, which is aimed at facilitating mineral prospecting, provides for joint investigations of the structure of the depth of earth's crust and mantle in central India. Deep seismic sounding (DSS) technique has been applied there by specialists from the Geophysics Institute of the Academy of Sciences of the Ukraine. The USSR also supplied the necessary equipments. In December 1972 and November 1973, geological experiments were carried out. DSS-specialists have also been trained in India.[108]

Further, the Farakka Barrage Complex agreement was signed in 1965 in Calcutta, and the Soviet supply of a special construction equipment reportedly cut the cost of building the largest barrage in the world.[109]

In September, 1970, the Calcutta subway project was signed, the first of its kind in India. In December, 1972, after Soviet specialists had prepared the feasibility report, its foundation stone was laid by Mrs Indira Gandhi. On November 6, 1973, 2 contracts for Soviet assistance in deputation of 10 specialists to India and training of Indian personnel in the USSR in various aspects of subway construction were signed in New Delhi.

The subway is to connect Tollygung and Dum Dum; Indian engineers have visited the USSR for consultations while experts of the Lenmetroproyekt Institute, which is concerned with designing Soviet subways, visited Calcutta and studied geological and other problems. Work on the project began in 1973. On June 24, 1974, a protocol laid down that the USSR would supply two 5.5 metre tunnel shields and five muckers (loaders for them), 12,500 tonnes of steel sheet piles, and 12 diesel hammers for driving the piles. The tunnel shields will be supplied with the full complex of machines. It also provided for training more Indian personnel and deputing Soviet consultants to India.

The length of the subway will be 17.5 km. with 17 stations designed for an 8-coach formation (platform length : 170 metres). The estimated cost will be Rs. 140 crores with a foreign exchange element of Rs. 23.7 crores. The subway is expected to be commissioned in 1979. Over 300 trains will carry 1.32 million passengers daily.[110] Following Calcutta, it is possible that other metropolitan centres of India will also go for subway construction.

In rounding up the preceding survey of Soviet aid to India

TRADE ECONOMIC AID AND COLLABORATION WITH INDIA

in the economic sphere, it should be mentioned that about 70 industrial and other Soviet-assisted projects have been or are being built in India, 51 of them having been commissioned by 1973. According to Soviet sources, the USSR's assistance accounts for 80% of India's oil extraction, 30% of oil refining capacity, 85% of heavy engineering goods, 60% of electrical equipments, 30% of steel and 20% of electricity.[111]

SOVIET MILITARY ASSISTANCE TO INDIA

This is nearly the only aspect of aid which enjoys no Soviet advertisement. The Soviet military aid to India followed economic aid, the reverse of the pattern in Egypt. In October, 1960, came the first agreement of India's purchase of various types of Soviet aircraft. It was followed by further orders in 1961 and 1962. In August, 1962, on the eve of the Sino-Indian border clash, a major agreement was concluded on the construction of a plant in India for the production of MIG-21s. This may have been the first licensing for building Soviet aircraft outside the USSR, including the Soviet bloc. A missile complex and training school was established with Soviet assistance in 1963 and the purchase of advanced fighter-bombers and other modern weapons proceeded over the years.

According to Howard Wriggins, some 200 million dollars worth of Soviet military equipments are transferred annually to India. Their total value till the end of 1969 was put by him at 650 million dollars. By the end of 1971, according to Charles B. McLane, the value of Soviet military aid to India probably exceeded 1 billion dollars.[112]

The USSR has come to occupy the position of the leading arms supplier to India. On the eve of the Indo-Pakistani war of 1971, India was estimated to have more than 300 MIG-21s and 140 SU-7 bombers, and more aircraft were stated to be en route to India. At the turn of this decade, it was further estimated that India had in her possession 450 Russian tanks, 50 SAM-2 (Guideline) missiles, and 4 Soviet-built submarines, as well as an assorted number of styxmissile firing patrol boats, artillery of different types, small arms, etc.

McLane ably sums up the leitmotif behind the Soviet aid programmes, including military ones, as follows :

> The emergence of the Soviet Union as the principal supplier of arms to India in the 1960's was, of course, an important factor in international developments in South Asia, but so far as Moscow's policies in India are concerned, this new undertaking must be seen in the context of a continuing Soviet activity there. Russian objectives in India had from the start been to decrease New Delhi's dependence on the Western powers especially the United States, and to increase its obligations to the USSR. The sale of arms to India—at least before the Friendship Treaty of 1971—was merely another way of accomplishing this end, along with trade, economic aid, cultural cooperation and diplomatic exchanges.[113]

NOTES AND REFERENCES

1. Charles B. McLane, *Soviet-Asian Relations*, vol. II of *Soviet-Third World Relations*, London, Central Asian Research Centre, 1973, p. 59.
2. McLane, *op. cit.*, p. 59.
3. Shankar Narain, "Significant Provisions of 1974 Indo-Soviet Trade Protocol", *Soviet Review* (henceforth *SR*), Information bulletin of the Soviet Embassy, New Delhi, No. 5, vol. XI. Jan. 21, 1974, pp. 28-29, and Ivan Grishin (Deputy Foreign Trade Minister of the USSR), "Soviet-Indian Trade Poised for Further Advance", *SR*, No. 7, vol. XL Feb. 14, 1974, pp. 53-55.
4. Grishin, *op. cit.*, and A. Petrov, "Growing Soviet-Indian Trade" *SR*, No. 28, vol. XI, June 20, 1974, pp. 31-32.
5. R. K. Sharma, "Indo-Soviet Economic Cooperation : New, Higher Phase", *SR*. Nos. 36-37, vol. XI, Aug. 8, 1974, pp. 34- 38.
6. V. I. Smirnov (Counsellor and Trade Representative of the USSR in India), "Achievements of Soviet-Indian Trade", *SR*, No. 4, vol. XII, Jan. 23, 1975, pp. 37-40.
7. Sankar Narain and M. P. Saxena, "Expanding Soviet Market for India's Traditional Export Commodities", *SR*, No. 30, vol. XI, June 27, 1974, p.p. 47-51.
8. Attar Chand, "Indo-Soviet Cooperation in Agriculture", *SR*, No. 44, Vol. XI, Sept. 26, 1974, pp. 33-38.

9. "Friendship and Cooperation", *SR*, No. 8. Vol. XII, Feb. 20, 1975, p. 33.

10. Smirnov. *op. cit.*

11. Balraj Kumar (Managing Director, York Hosiery Mills, Ludhiana), "Knitwear Industry of India and Soviet Role in Its Development", *SR*, No. 17. vol. XII, April 10, 1975, pp. 27-29.

12. *Amrita Bazar Patrika* (henceforth *Patrika*) Calcutta, October 17, 1975.

13. *Patrika, op. cit.*, August 14, 1975.

14. *Patrika, op. cit.*, Sept. 25, 1975.

15. Grishin, *op. cit.*, and V. Klochek (of the Ministry of Foreign Trade of USSR), "Foreign Trade of USSR in 1973", *SR*, No. 27, vol. XI. June 13, 1974, pp. 39-40.

16. Klochek, *op. cit.*, and I. Kapranov (Chief of the Planning and Economic Department, the State Committee of the Council of Ministers for Foreign Economic Relations), "Example of Soviet Cooperation with Developing Countries", *Moscow News*, No. 34 (1285) Saturday, Aug. 23, 1975, p. 6.

17. Sharma, *op. cit.*,

18. D. P. Chattopadhyaya (Minister of Commerce), "Soviet-Indian Trade Blazing a New Trail", (interview), *SR*, No. 37, vol. XII, Aug. 14, 1975, p. 24.

19. Leo Tansky, *US and USSR Aid to Developing Countries. A Comparative Study of India, Turkey, and the UAR.* Praeger, New York, 1967. pp. 18-27.

20. Tansky, *op. cit.*, p. 28.

21. Tansky, *op. cit.*, pp. 28-29.

22. McLane, *op. cit.*, p. 58.

23. Tansky, *op. cit.*, p. 34.

24. Tansky. *op. cit.*, pp. 18-19.

25. Tansky, *op. cit.*, p. 17.

26. Tansky, *op. cit.*, p. 169.

27. McLane, *op. cit.*, p, 59.

28. L. Klochkovsky, "Peking and Indo-Soviet Cooperation", *SR*, No. 5. vol. XI, Jan. 31, 1974, pp. 39-40, and Klochek, *op. cit.*, pp. 39-40.

29. Adapted from Tansky, p. 108 and McLane, pp. 62-75, *op. cit.*

30. "Indo-Soviet Cooperation : An Inspring Example", (interview with T. A. Pai, Minister for Industry and Civil Supplies), *SR*, No. 44, Vol. XII, Sept. 25, 1975, p. 53.

31. "Chronicle of Soviet-Indian Friendship", *SR*, No. 3, vol. XII, Jan. 16, 1975. pp. 28-29.

32. Shankar Narain, "Progress of Bhilai and Bokaro", *SR*, vol. XI June, 13, 1974. pp. 48-50.

33. Chester Bowles, *Promises to Keep*, Harper & Row. New York, 1971, p. 542.

34. Shankar Narain, n. 32, Klochkovsky, *op. cit.*, K. C. Khanna

(Managing Director, Bokaro Steel Ltd.,) "Bokaro : Story of Progress", *SR*, No. 1, vol. XII, Jan. 2, 1975, pp. 29-32 Klochek, *op. cit.*, "Chronicle..." *op. cit.*, and A. Garetovsky, "Sound Basis for India's Metallurgical Industry", *SR*, No. 4, vol. XII, Jan. 23, 1975, pp. 50-52.

35. Garetovsky, *op. cit.*
36. Kapranov, *op. cit.*
37. Garetovsky, *op. cit.*
38. "Chronicle of Soviet-Indian Friendship and Cooperation", *SR*, No. 46, vol. XI, Oct. 3, 1974, pp. 20-21.
39. T. A. Pai, "Vital Role of Soviet Assistance in India's Industrialization", (interview), *SR*, No. 4, vol. XII, Jan. 23, 1975, pp. 17-19 and McLane, p. 59.
40. "Diary of Soviet-Indian Friendship, 1974", *SR*, No. 6, vol. XII, Feb. 6, 1975, pp. 4-72.
41. Shankar Narain, "Progress of Korba Aluminium Project", *SR*, No. 22, Vol. XI, May 9, 1974, pp. 47-48.
42. *Patrika, op. cit.*, October 17, 1975.
43. Shankar Narain, "Korba Aluminium Plant : Second Phase of Development", *SR*, No. 34, vol. XII, July 24, 1975, pp. 36 37.
44. "New Vistas Before MAMC" (interview with A. C. Chatterjee, Managing Director of the Durgapur Mining and Allied Machinery plant), *SR*, Nos. 36-37, vol. XI, Aug. 8, 1974, pp. 48-49.
45. Pai, n. 30.
46. Klochek, *op. cit.*
47. Shankar Narain, "IDPL—A Wise Insurance that Paid", *SR*, No. 33, vol. XI, July 18, 1974, pp. 49-50.
48. I. Shvarts, "MECON Makes Giant Strides Forward," *SR*, Nos. 36-37, Vol. XI, Aug. 8. 1974, pp. 46-47.
49. Dietmar Rothermund, *Indian und die Sowjetunion*, Arbeits-Gemeinschaft fuer Osteuropaforschung, Boehlau Verlag, Tuebingen, 1968, pp. 79-81.
50. "Massive Soviet Assistance to India's Oil Industry", (interview with K. D. Malaviya, Minister for Petroleum and Chemicals), *SR*, No. 4, vol. XII, Jan. 23, 1975, pp. 20-22.
51. "India's Oil Industry : "Bright Prospects of Development", (interview with D. K. Barooah, former Minister for Petroleum and Chemicals), *SR*, No. 38, Vol. XI, Aug. 15, 1974, pp. 17-18.
52. Tansky, *op. cit.*, p. 18.
53. V. D. Shashin (USSR Minister of Oil Industry), "Expanding Cooperation Between Soviet and Indian Oil Industries", *SR*, No. 12, Vol. XII, March 13, 1975, pp. 21-22.
54. Malaviya, *op. cit.*
55. V. D. Shashin; "Prospects of Oil Industry in India", *SR*, No. 57, Vol, XI, Dec. 12, 1974, pp. 29-31.
56. Barooah, *op. cit.*

57. V. D. Shashin, "Soviet-Indian Cooperation in Oil Industry", *SR*, No. 38, vol. XI, Aug. 15, 1974, pp. 11-13.
58. Malaviya, *op. cit.*
59. "Further Soviet Assistance for India's Oil Industry", *SR*, No. 5. vol. XI, Jan. 31, 1974, pp. 30-31.
60. L. I. Eiranov (Head, Southest Asia Department, State Committee for Foreign Economic Relations) "Soviet Assistance for India's Economic Development", *SR* No. 43, vol. XI, Sept. 19, 1974, pp. 25-26.
61. Barooah, *op. cit.*
62. *Patrika*, *op. cit.*, Aug. 11, 1975.
63. Rothermund, *op. cit.*, pp. 79-81.
64. "Mathura Refinery—Indicative of India's Industrial Advance" *SR*, No. 26, vol. XI, June 3, 1974, pp. 42-43.
65. Eiranov, *op. cit.*
66. Tansky, *op. cit.*, p, 107.
67. Malaviya, *op. cit.*
68. *Patrika*, *op. cit.*, Sept. 25, 1975.
69. Shashin, n. 56, *op. cit.*
70. "India Seeks New Oil Technology from USSR", *SR*, No. 41, vol. XII, Sept. 4, 1975, pp. 44-45.
71. B. Bratchenko (USSR Minister of Coal Industry), "Cooperation Between Miners of the USSR and India", *SR*, No. 13, vol. XII, March 20, 1975, pp. 13-14.
72. "India Fully Equipped to Meet Coal Target", *SR*, No. 5, vol. XI, Jan. 31, 1974, pp. 32-33.
73. V. Gordopolov (Counsellor for Economic Affairs, USSR Embassy in India), "Soviet-Indian Cooperation in Coal Industry", *SR*, No. 15, vol. XI, March 28, 1974, pp. 20-21.
74. See n. 72.
75. Gordopolov, *op. cit.*
76. Bratchenko, *op. cit.*
77. Gordopolov, *op. cit.*, and "Growth of Soviet-Indian Cooperation in Coal-Mining" (interview with Boris Bratchenko, USSR Minister of Coal Industry,) *SR*, Nos. 36-37, vol. XI, Aug. 8, 1974, p. 16.
78. "Soviet-Indian Cooperation in the Development of Coal Production", *SR*, No. 26, vol. XI, June 3, 1974. pp. 44-45.
79. "Soviet Assistance for Coal Development in India", (interview with J. G. Kumaramangalam, Chairman of the Coal Mines Authority), *SR*, No. 32, vol. XI. July 11; 1974 pp. 51-53.
80. V. Pashkov (Deputy Counsellor for Economic Affairs, USSR Embassy in India), "Growth of Soviet-Indian Economic and Technical Cooperation", *SR*; No. 32, vol. XI, July 11, 1974, pp. 39-43.
81. Bratchenko, n. 71, *op. cit.*
82. Pai, n. 30, *op. cit.*,
83. Gordopolov, op. cit.

84. Eiranov, *op. cit.*, and Khanna, *op. cit.*
85. Kapranov, *op. cit.*
86. Eiranov, *op. cit.*
87. "Importance of Indo-Soviet Protocol Stressed", (interview with the late D. P. Dhar, then Minister of Planning), *SR*, No. 46, vol. XI, Oct. 3, 1974, p. 7.
88. V. Tkachenko, "Soviet-Indian Cooperation in Science and Technology" *SR*, No. 43. vol. XII, Sept. 18, 1975. p. 39.
89. "Diary...", *op. cit.*
90. V. P. Yelutin (USSR Minister of Higher and Specialized Secondary Education), "Soviet-Indian Cooperation in Education", *SR*, no. 38 vol. XI, Aug. 15, 1974, pp. 14-16.
91. Narain, n. 41, *op, cit.*
92. "Indian Design Engineers in USSR", *SR*, No. 38, vol. XI, August 15, 1974, pp. 30-31.
93. Yelutin, *op. cit.*
94. "Unlimited Scope of Soviet-Indian Cooperation", (interview with Prof. Nurul Hassan, Minister of Education), *SR*, No. 28, vol. XI, June 20, 1974, p. 29.
95. Shankar Narain, "Significant Advance in Indo-Soviet Scientific Cooperation", *SR*, Nos. 10-11, vol. XII, March 6, 1975, pp. 53-54.
96. *Patrika*, October 20, 1975.
97. "Soviet Specialists on the Indian Sputnik", *SR*, No. 16, vol. X, March 31, 1973, pp. 37-41. E, Ivanov, "Soviet-Indian Cooperation in Complex Space Research", *SR*, No. 16, vol. XI, April 4, 1974, pp. 62-63, T. N. Srivastava, "Indo-Soviet Cooperation in Science and Technology", *SR*, No. 33, vol. XI, July 18, 1974, pp. 39-48, Prof. U. R. Rao (Project Director, Indian Scientific Satellite Project), "Soviet-Indian Collaboration in Space Studies", *SR*, No. 57, vol. XI, Dec. 12, 1974, pp. 34-35, and "Diary...", *op. cit.*
98. Bowles, *op. cit.* p. 534.
99. "Diary...", *op. cit.*
100. M. V. Mukhamedjanov (Counsellor for Agricultural Affairs, USSR Embassy in India), "Soviet-Indian Agricultural Cooperation", *SR*, No. 11, vol. XI, March 7, 1974, pp. 27-29, Srivastava, *op. cit.*, and Chand, *op. cit.*
101. Srivastava, *op. cit.*
102. Chand, *op. cit.*
103. Chand, *op. cit.*
104. Chand, *op. cit.*
105. Shankar Narain, "Spare Parts for Soviet Tractors in India", *SR*, No. 18, vol. XII, April 17, 1975, pp. 39-40.
106. "Diary...", *op. cit.*
107. Shankar Narain, "Soviet Assistance for India's Shipping Development", *SR*, No. 28, vol. XI, June 20, 1974, pp. 33-34.

108. S. Petrov, "Soviet Assistance for Mineral Prospecting in Central India", *SR*, Nos. 36-37, vol. XI, Aug. 8, 1974, pp. 44-45.

109. Debes Mookherjee (Consultant, CMDA), "Growing Indo-Soviet Cooperation", *Patrika*, Aug. 9, 1975.

110. Pritam Lal, "Soviet Cooperation in Calcutta Metro Project", *SR*, No. 43, vol. XI, Sept. 19, 1974, pp. 27-28.

111. Klochkovsky, *op. cit.*, and P. Timofeyev, "An Important Form of Soviet Assistance to the Developing Countries", *SR*, No. 27, vol. XI, June 13, 1974, pp. 45-47.

112. W. Howard Wriggins, "The Presence in Southern Asia of Outside Powers", in James C. Charlesworth (ed.), *A New American Posture Toward Asia*, *The Annals* of the American Academy of Political and Social Sciences, vol. 390, Philadelphia, July 1970, p. 53, and McLane, *op. cit.*, p. 59.

113. McLane, *op. cit.*, p. 59.

Chapter VII

CONCLUSION: THE UNDERLYING ISSUES

It has been the endeavour of this dissertation to develop a theoretical framework covering Soviet Weltanschauung and global policy and to examine the data on Soviet ideology and policy towards India in the context of that framework. Chapter I has argued the need for such a framework in terms of theory-building in International Relations, and has offered a basic two-component structure explaining post-Stalin Soviet global policy. Chapter II has explained the concept of the "central dynamics" of Soviet foreign policy and has illustrated it with a historical case-study of India. Thereupon, it has moved on to study three important variables (viz., the US and Chinese policies, and Soviet economic problems) affecting its operation in India (and elsewhere). Chapter III has attempted to bring out the leitmotives behind both theoretical and operative Soviet military policy; the evidence in favour of the second component of the framework of this dissertation, the "nodal restraint", has seemed to be strong. A consideration of the implications of the "central dynamics" and the variables affecting its operation in terms of the theoretical framework has then followed. The latter has seemed to have had little difficulty in accommodating these variables.

Having thus created the overall pattern of Soviet world-view and strategy in the post-Stalin era, the focus has narrowed down to the Indian context. Chapter IV has concentrated on a major Soviet tenet today, viz., the "non-capitalist path". It has sought to capture the latter's significance for the Indian context by tracking it back over time and placing it in the broader context of the overall pattern of Soviet foreign policy developed earlier. Chapter V takes up an analysis of the implications of Soviet views on the role of the state in India. Chapter VI surveys a whole range of idiographic information on the flow of Soviet economic and military aid to India. It throws

CONCLUSION : THE UNDERLYING ISSUES

empirical light on Soviet thinking on India depicted in Chapters IV and V.

Once the longer-range and more enduring issues underlying post-Stalin Soviet foreign policy are grasped, the organic linkage of the latter with the overall Soviet conceptualization of India becomes evident. Seen in that broader context, such conceptualization throws up a number of complex but interesting issues. The latter in their turn indicate that some of the ideological tenets are themselves undergoing transformation in order to adjust to the rapidly shifting reality in the third world (e.g., the unconventional praise for the theoretical role of the state in India, the upgrading of cultural-institutional factors as key to economic progress, etc.). All these considerations form the content of the concluding Chapter. Awareness of such problems and issues against the background of the broader context precludes one from explaining away Soviet policy of cultivating friendship with India in simplistic terms. One author has attributed such friendship to alleged Soviet apprehensions about the risk of a communist India gravitating towards China. Because of this fear, he concludes from his study of Indo-Soviet relations, post-Stalin USSR has not encouraged the CPI to stage a political take-over.[1] But this "de-eschatology of Soviet policy"[2] involves more complexities than that, as this book has sought to demonstrate.

As far as the first part of this dissertation is concerned, which deals with uncovering the leitmotives of the Soviet foreign policy, the image that emerges is one of a cautious and defence-oriented USSR which aims at transforming the third world by generally restrained means. The unmistakable message, as seen in class and foreign policy analyses on India, is that of keeping moves well below the nuclear threshold. Such an image finds varying degrees of favour with Rober C. Tucker, Denna F. Fleming, Michael P. Gehlen, Louis Halle, Frederick Schuman, Trisks and Finley, and others. Indeed, the "mixed" image of the Soviet foreign policy has been gaining ground in recent years as much as the "ultra-hard" image held sway in American academia at the the turn of the 1960's.[3] Even Stalin's foreign policy may not have been as high in risk-taking as often made out to be. As Ulam comments, Stalin and his socialist allies did not march into Yugoslavia after Tito's defection in 1948 despite the unlikelihood at the time of Western intervention in an inter-socialist dispute. "The blockade of Berlin", Ulam continues, "could be lifted momentarily at the first sign that it might lead to a shooting war. ...The dictator's irrational quirks, so pronounced during his last phase, did not preclude a degree of calculation and caution when it came to foreign affairs".[4]

Given the basic postulate of moderated Soviet foreign policy, it is little wonder that the latter has taken to the gradualistic track of changing the third world by means of supporting the expansion of the state sector. It is paradoxical to find in this connection that Soviet commentators cheerfully assert that "characteristically, progressive changes of the non-capitalist type begin first in the superstructure."[5] This echo of Myrdal's "institutional approach" clearly relegates the classical importance of the economic substructure in Marxism to a secondary position. The Soviet conceptualization of India and the third world today is flexible enough to acknowledge the fact of overwhelming cultural-institutional predomination which acts as a drag on efficient economic organization, innovation and production. The classic apophthegm of Marx : "It is not the consciousness of the people that determines their being but rather their social being which determines their consciousness"[6] is stood on its head.

Nonetheless, in other matters affecting India the Soviet ideology is headed, in the opinion of this author, in the right direction. The Russians have put their stakes on the right horse, namely, the state sector in the developing societies. That sector in India, like in a number of other backward countries, remains for historical reasons the chief entrepreneur and organiser of economic life. This clear fact has not been as universally recognized as it may seem at first sight. The Chinese would like to negate the existing framework of political and economic institutions in toto. The USA still bemoans the ubiquitious presence of the state sector. It goes to the credit of the Soviet ideology that it encourages the growth of the latter in India

CONCLUSION : THE UNDERLYING ISSUES   167

most activiely, as has been seen. It seems that the Soviet policy is to encourage at the same time all manifestations of moderate leftism in political and economic directions. Ultimately, in some distant future, genuine socialism would emerge—so seems to run the main line of Soviet thinking. The Soviet ideology of India's "formative sector" has to confront practical problems and dilemmas. They have been well stated by the US economist, Dr Gustav Papanek, who has had considerable direct experience in Asian problems :

> A private enterprise strategy can provide incentives to increase production, but it also tends to make income distribution less equal. So some Governments use public enterprise strategy : They nationalize industry and other economic activities. They then have a very difficult time managing the economy efficiently, because it is hard to provide appropriate economic incentives to managers of public enterprises.[7]

Most of India's public sector enterprises suffer from underutilized capacity and inefficient management. Only recently, a drive has been undertaken to raise capacity utilization of public sector manufacturing units between 50% and 80%. By the end of 1975-76, the sum of Rs. 5,000 crores would constitute effective capital in the public manufacturing sector, and the latter has been prodded hard to show a minimum profit of Rs. 500 crores (10%). All enterprises have been asked to take a hard look at their production costs, materials management and inventories control.[8]

Thus while Soviet ideology panegyrizes the principle of state sector expansion in countries like India, the Russians are too experienced in the field themselves not to take a good look at its problems and actual performance. India is torn asunder between the Scylla of allotting top priority to the economic growth philosophy and the Charybdis of assigning equitable distribution of wealth the first place. She has through her plans professed to incline towards the latter. She, therefore, suffers from attendant problems of inadequate economic growth. According to a recent World Bank study, the growth of India's Gross

Domestic Product for the 1970's is not expected to exceed 3%. It was 1·3% during 1970-74. Per capita consumption is expected to "stagnate" during 1970-80.[9] Soviet ideological literature adequately reflects these problems but are unable to offer any hard solutions.

It is in this context that consideration should be given to the Soviet characterization of the present stage of history and its future prospects, especially as they bear on India and the third world generally. It seems that radicalization of politics is the trend in the third world,[10] and Soviet ideology says as much. As problems keep multiplying thereby frustrating rising expectations and choking off the few available escalators of upward mobility, political power tends to slip into the hands of more radical forces like the army or pro-communist elements. The case of Indochina states in recent times is a correct indicator. India herself has been moving away from the general euphoria of a Western-type democracy. If the tendency towards a system collapse is to be arrested, drastic socio-economic reorganization would become necessary. Such changes constituting a step-function can be initiated only by tough organizing forces mentioned before. It seems to suit the Soviet way of thinking so long as this function is carried out in the desired direction to the desired leftist degree. When the official Soviet line proclaims that this is an age of "transition to socialism", it must be some of these considerations that prompt it. The multidimensional problems of the third world coupled with the latter's phenomenal population growth need such drastic solutions that no moderate and liberal government acting through time-consuming democratic processes can ever hope to cope with them. Moreover, the general tendency around the world is for the state to increase its areas of function and responsibility. The welfare state concept has seen to that. Given these factors, the USSR is perhaps not too wide of the mark in asserting that free private enterprise and capitalism would never hold sway in the third world.

Predictably, therefore, the 1975 amendments to the constitution of India, the emergency measures, the 20-point economic programme and the like instituted by Indira Gandhi have

CONCLUSION : THE UNDERLYING ISSUES

evoked sympathy and understanding in the USSR. The deprivation of judicial power as reflected in the 39th and 40th amendments seemed to the latter as a step in the direction of long-needed tough reforms. Consequently, a warm message of felicitations on the Indo-Soviet Treaty to the President and the Prime Minister of India from the Soviet triumvirate was published in August 1975 on the front pages of Moscow's chief newspapers. The practice over the past two years had been to address such felicitations to non-official bodies like the ISCUS.[11]

Indira Gandhi's explanation that she was determined to put an end to the "functioning anarchy" that was India must have fallen on willing ears in the USSR, even though not on every occasion has she seen eye to eye with the latter. She stated that "suddenly we had a vision of this country going towards anarchy".[12] In the light of the foregoing discussion on the trend towards the radicalization of politics in the third world this statement would hardly sound novel. It did not to the Soviet ears either.

As one Soviet commentator, personally acquainted with the Indian scene, puts it :

> Recent events in India—the state of emergency, the ban on pro-fascist, extreme left and pro-Maoist parties and groups and the arrest of their leaders, the 20 point economic programme and the other measures the Indian Government has taken, show that Indira Gandhi, with the support of the trade unions, the vast majority of Congress, the Indian Communist Party and the masses is fighting the right-wing and reactionary elements, and the imperialists, colonialists and Maoists who support them from outside.[13]

By 1975, the Indian Government was even using patently communist terms as "neo-imperialism" and "fascism" in depicting threats posed by them. In the international conference against fascism held in Lalit Narayan Nagar in Bihar in December, the Congress President, D. K. Barooah, stated that "The dark forces of neo-imperialism and eastern racial arrogance are combining in a sinister attempt to snuff out the light of democracy in this part of the world", but that the backbone of the anti-national, fascist and reactionary forces had been broken. He urged the delegates to watch out for "fascism", "imperialism" and "reaction".[14] His choice of such terms and concepts must have been music to Soviet ears, not to mention their pleasure at the conference itself. Indeed, Soviet commentaries on Indira Gandhi's recent domestic measures verge on unconcealed enthusiasm. As a recent Soviet article notes:

> The advancement along the road of progress of a vast country like India with her diverse and complex problems poses that country with numerous difficulties. The more so that in a situation where new India remains a target of attacks by the outside forces which to this day cannot reconcile themselves with the independent and progressive course pursued by this great state. This is precisely why the actions taken by the Indian Government against the internal and external reactionaries were responded to with full understanding in the Soviet Union.[15]

A similar chord is struck in another assessment which notes "fierce resistance" of "reactionaries" to "democratic transformations carried out by the government with the backing of the progressive forces." It goes on to state that such opponents of India's progress made an attempt to paralyze the state administration and to seize power by spreading chaos and terror in the country and added:

> In that difficult moment Prime Minister Mrs Indira Gandhi did not yield to the pressure of reaction. A state of emergency was declared in the country and the activities of anti-government element were resolutely curbed. After introducing the state of emergency the government launched a 20-point programme aimed at improving the people's living conditions and the working of the economy. The first successes have already been achieved in the implementation of this programme.[16]

A prominent scholar characterizes with satisfaction recent socio-economic steps taken by India as "promising". He then observes :

> This has brought [the progressive elements] under heavy pressure from the reactionaries both at home and abroad, but they are not retreating. On the contrary, they are continuing to give effect to the progressive course proclaimed by the Indira Gandhi Government.[17]

V. Kudryavtsev, who had headed a Soviet delegation to India in 1971, asserts that "India became the most crucial target of imperialist reaction" because "it objectively plays a very important role both in Asia and throughout the world... ...India is an important link in the chain of progressive forces throughout the world...". Because of this, notes the *Izvestia* commentator, "all progressive forces of the world followed with anxiety the struggle of India's progressive forces which rallied behind Indira Gandhi's government against attack of internal reaction and imperialism. ...Therefore. the Soviet Union, other socialist countries and the peace-loving forces took the side of Indira Gandhi's government and backed her resolute measures against reaction that had become active."[18]

Commenting on the Soviet press reaction to Indira Gandhi's recent domestic policies, APN Political Analyst S. Beglov states that :

> The Soviet press invariably expressed understanding and solidarity with all the measures, including the comprehensive socio-economic programme, initiated by India's leaders with the support of the progressive and genuinely patriotic forces of the country.[19]

The most authoritative assessment of India in 1976 came from Brezhnev in the course of his Central Committee Report to the 25th CPSU Congress delivered on February 24, 1976. He opened his reference to India by directly coming to the point :

> We attach special importance to friendship with that great country.

He went on :

> In the past five years Soviet-Indian relations have risen to a new level. Our countries have concluded a Treaty of Peace, Friendship and Cooperation. And even this short period has clearly shown its tremendous significance for our bilateral tie......
> Close political and economic cooperation with the Republic of India is our constant policy.

Tracing the contours of official Soviet perception of recent socio-political developments in India, Brezhnev categorically stated :

> The Soviet people appreciate and, more, are in solidarity with India's peace-loving foreign policy and the courageous efforts of her progressive forces to solve her difficult socio-economic problems. We wish the people and government of India complete success in these efforts.[20]

India's problems, the moves made by Indira Gandhi to tackle them, and the Soviet support throw up the vintage controversy over liberty versus equality as they stand in a zero-sum relationship in the third world. Liberty, fundamental rights and freedom of belief and expression were enshrined in India's constitution after the example of western democratic societies. Although noble in themselves they have had little relevance to the needs and problems of India's masses, a substantial body of which is illiterate.[21] The result has been typical : the elite classes have tended to protect their privileges and the status quo under their cover. Grosss inequality of every sort is the stark reality of most developing societies. But there can be no way of narrowing the gap without cutting down some of the cover mentioned above. As Finance Minister C. Subramaniam explained, India's recent amendments to the constitution were made to ensure that the judiciary did not in future interfere with action against economic offences.[22]

To be sure, in practice efforts in such directions may be quite counterproductive, given mammoth bureaucracy and general governmental inefficiency. Nevertheless, in principle this seems to be the only way out so long as the role of the state in political, social and economic organization is held supreme.

CONCLUSION : THE UNDERLYING ISSUES

It is not part of the task of this dissertation to assess the true motivation behind Indira Gandhi's "garibi hatao" policies. It is sufficient to note for the present purposes that these policies are at least made to appear left-oriented. This left-orientation of state power is what the Soviet ideology hopes for and acclaims, for reasons discussed elsewhere.

In foreign policy matters, the USSR's position has been partly vindicated by the reduced military presence of the USA in Asia. The USSR seems to be interested now in an Asian collective security arrangement which would automatically keep out the West and restrain China. But the Asian collective security concept as propounded by Moscow remains vague; the Asian states generally have accorded it a cool reception.

The third world today is in a state of continuous adjustment to a rapidly evolving reality, both externally and internally. It is difficult to predict, therefore, anything with certainty. However, the Soviet ideological concepts and tenets that have been discussed are flexible and wide in scope. They will probably remain, therefore, for a long time to come reflecting the general course of the Soviet foreign policy. The latter will also move along fairly established tracks, particularly in relation to India and this is already in evidence with the preliminary talks held between Gromyko and the Janata External Affairs Minister in April 1977. The substantial Soviet economic collaboration with India will continue being designed to bolster industrialization and the state sector. All these activities will persist because the Soviet foreign policy today is geared to fight world capitalism right at the microlevel of individual countries.

NOTES AND REFERENCES

1. Hemen Ray, *Indo-Soviet Relations* 1955-1971, Jaico, Bombay, 1973, p. 295.
2. Term used by Donaldson, *op cit*, pp. 260-261.
3. For an analysis of the works of the scholars mentioned as well as for an interesting classification, see William Welch, *American Images of Soviet Foreign Policy*, New Haven & London, Yale Univ. Press, 1970.

4. Adam B. Ulam, *Expansion and Coexistence*, Secker & Warburg, London, 1968, p. 439.

5. *The Newly Independent States*, *op. cit.*, p. 111.

6. Karl Marx, "Zur Kritik der Politischen Oekonomie", Marx & Engels, *Ausgewaehlte Werke*, Moscow, *op cit.*, p. 188 (author's translation).

7. Interview of Gustav Papanek, *Span*, USIS, New Delhi, Dec. 1975, p. 9. For more detailed discussion of growth problems in the third world, see R. Nurske, *Problems of Capital Formation in Underdeveloped Areas*, New York, Oxford University Press, 1953.

8. *The Statesman*, Oct. 6, 1975.

9. *Amrita Bazar Patrika*, Aug. 11, 1975.

10. See, for example, Rupert Emerson, *From Empire to Nation*. Scientific Book Agency, Calcutta, 1970 (Indian ed.), Chapter XV. A similar point is developed by John H. Kautsky in his *The Political Conference of Modernization*, John Wiley and Sons. Inc., New York, 1972, where he denies that the political development for those countries which experienced modernization from within would be similar to that of others which had modernization from without. The latter may not develop into democracies but into authoritarian societies.

11. *The Sunday Amrita Bazar Patrika*, Aug. 10, 1975.

12. *The Statesman*, Aug 15, 1975.

13. M. Menshikov, "My Years in India", *Moscow News*, Moscow, No. 47 (1298), Nov. 22, 1975, p. 6.

14. *Amrita Bazar Patrika*, Dec. 5, 1975.

15. Y. Tsaplin, "The Sound Foundations of Soviet-Indian Ties", *International Affairs*, Moscow, No. 8, August 1976, p. 73.

16. V. Skosyrev, "India : Following the Course of Independence and Progress", *SR*, No. 4, vol. XIII, Jan 26, 1976, p. 20.

17. R, Ulyanovsky, "The Developing Countries : Aspects of Political Scene", *SR*, No. 47-48, vol. XIII, Oct. 21, 1976, p. 37.

18. V. Kudryavtsev, "Some Views on India", *SR*, No. 24, vol. XIII, May 27, 1976, pp. 4-5.

19. Spartak Beglov, "Common Objectives of Soviet and Indian Peoples", *SR*, vol. XIII, No. 24, May 27, 1976, p. 9.

20. 25th CPSU Congress. Report of the Central Committee of the Communist Party of the Soviet Union and the Party's Immediate Objectives in Home and Foreign Policy, delivered by Brezhnev, *SR*, No. 10-11, vol. XIII, March 4, 1976, p. 13.

21. See, for instance, Myrdal, *op cit.*, vol, II.

22. *Amrita Bazar Patrika*, July 26, 1975.

BIBLIOGRAPHY

1. *Communist Sources*
A. Books

Afanasyev, V., *Marxist Philosophy*, Progress, Moscow, 1965.
" , *Socialism and Communism*, Progress, Moscow, 1972.
Balabushevich, V., *Some Problems of History of India*, Moscow, 1963.
" , and Prasad, Bimal (eds.), *India and the Soviet Union*, Delhi, 1969.
Diakov, A. M., *New Stages in India's Liberation Struggle*. Bombay, People's Publishing House, 1950.
" , *The Crisis of the Colonial System*, Foreign Languages Publishing House, Moscow, 1949.
Fundamentals of Marxism-Leninism, Foreign Languages Publishing House, Moscow, 1963.
Geschichte der Kommunistischen Partei der Sowietunion, Institut fuer Marxismus-Leninismus beim ZK der KPdSU, Progress, Moscow. (Three volumes appeared till 1972 out of the projected total of six).
Kemp, K. M., *Bharat-Rus*, ISCUS, Delhi, 1948.
Kondrat' ev. U.A., and Fituni, L.A., *Indiva, Ekonomicheskoe Razvitie i Sotrudnichestvo SSSR*, Nauka, Moscow, 1965.
Krasin, Yuri, *Sociology of Revolution. A Marxist View*, Progress, Moscow, 1972.
Lenin, V. I., *Selected Works*. (3 vols.), Progress, Moscow, 1970.
" *Collected Works*, (vols. I and II used), Foreign Languages Publishing House, Moscow, 1960.
" *The Development of Capitalism in Russia*, Progress, Moscow, 1967.
Marx and Engels, *Ausgewaehlte Werke*, (Single vol.), Progress, Moscow, 1972.
" *Werke*, Dietz, Berlin, 1962 (vol. XIX used).
" *Ausgewachlte Schriften*, (2 vols.), Dietz, Berlin, 1972.

Marx, Karl, *Capital*, (3 vols.), Vol. I published by Foreign Languages Publishing House, Moscow (no date), Vols. II and III by Progress, Moscow (1967 and 1966, respectively).

Marxism-Leninism : *On War and Army*, Progress, Moscow, 1972. (authors unknown).

Oriental Countries Today, (vol. I), Statistical Publishing Society (Indian Statistical Institute in collaboration with the Academy of Sciences of the USSR), Calcutta, 1975 (further volumes were awaiting publication at the time of preparing this bibliography).

Pavlov, V. *India* : *Economic Freedom V. Imperialism*. New Delhi, People's Publishing House, 1963.

Pavlov, V., Rastyannikov, V., and Shirokov, G., *India* : *Social And Economic Development*, Progress, Moscow, 1975.

Plekhanov, G. (N. Beltov), *The Development of the Monist View of History*, Progress, Moscow, 1972.

Problems of War and Peace, Progress, Moscow, 1972 (authors unknown).

Roy, M. N., *Revolution and Counter-Revolution in China*, Renaissance Publishers, Calcutta, 1945.

„ *Russian Revolution*, Renaissance Publishers, Calcutta, 1949.

„ *Memoirs*, Allied Publishers, Bombay, 1964.

Shirokov, G. K., *Industrialization of India*, Progress, Moscow, 1973.

Sladkovsky, M. I., Kovalyov, Y. F., and Sidikhmenov, V. Y., (eds.), *Leninism and Modern China's Problems*, Moscow, 1972.

Solodovnikov, V., and Bogoslovsky, V., *Non-Capitalist Development. An Historical Outline*, Progress, Moscow, 1975.

Trotsky, Leon, *The History of the Russian Revolution*, Sphere, London, 1967 (3 vols.).

Ulyanovsky. R., and Pavlov. V., *Asian Dilemma* : *A Soviet View and Myrdal's Concept*, Progress, Moscow, 1973.

B. **Monographs, Collections, Reports, Speeches, Documents, etc.**

Agreement on Economic and Trade Cooperation, *Soviet Review*, vol. X, No. 58, Dec. 6, 1973, New Delhi.

Agreement on Cooperation in Planning, *Soviet Review*, vol. X, No. 58, Dec. 6, 1973, New Delhi.

Ajubei, A., et al., *Face to Face with America*, Foreign Languages Publishing House, Moscow, 1960.

Alexandrov, I., *The Preaching and Practice of the Chinese Leaders*, Novosti, Moscow, 1971.

Bavrin, E., *Mongolia's Road to Socialism*, Novosti, Moscow, 1973.

Brezhnev, L., Report of the Central Committee of the Communist Party of the Soviet Union to the 23rd. Congress of the CPSU (March 29, 1966) *23rd. Congress of the CPSU*, 1966, Novosti, Moscow (no date).

„ Report of the Central Committee of the Communist Party of the Soviet Union to the 24th. Congress of the CPSU (March 30, 1971), *Information Bulletin*, No. 7-8 (188-189), vol. 9 (Special Issue), Peace and Socialism Publishers, Prague, 1971.

„ Speech at the 15th. Trade Union Congress of the USSR (March 24, 1972), *Neue Zeit*, Moscow, No. 14, April 1972.

„ *The Fiftieth Anniversary of the USSR. Report*, (Dec. 21, 1972), Novosti, Moscow, 1972.

„ *Our Course : Peace and Socialism*, Novosti, Moscow, 1973 (speeches).

„ *Following Lenin's Course*, Progress, Moscow, 1972 (speeches).

„ Speeches delivered in India, 1973 : on Nov. 26, 27, 28, 29, 30. *Soviet Review*, New Delhi, No. 58, vol. X, Dec. 6, 1973.

„ Report of CPSU Central Committee, 25th. CPSU Congress, February, 1976. *Soviet Review*, New Delhi, No. 10-11, Vol. XIII, March 4, 1976.

Bulganin, N.A. and Khruschev, N. S., *Speeches during*

Sojourn in India, Burma and Afganistan, Tass, New Delhi, 1956.

Chatterjee, A. C., New Vistas Before MAMC, (interview), *Soviet Review* (Information Bulletin of the USSR Embassy in India), New Delhi. Nos. 36-37, vol. XI. Aug. 8, 1974.

Chattopadhyaya, D. P., Soviet-Indian Trade Blazing a New Trail, (interview), *Soviet Review,* No. 37, vol. XII, Aug. 14, 1975.

Chronicle of Soviet-Indian Friendship and Cooperation, *Soviet Review,* No. 46, vol. XI, Oct. 3, 1974.

Chronicle of Soviet-Indian Friendship, *Soviet Review,* No. 3, vol. XII, Jan. 16, 1975.

Comintern, Fifth Congress. Abridged Report of Meetings held in Moscow, June 17th. to July 18th. 1924, CPGB (no date), London.

Comintern and National Colonial Questions, Documents of Congresses, CPI Publication, no. 9, March 1973 (C86), New Delhi.

Current Digest of the Soviet Press, Columbus, Ohio.

Degras, Jane (ed.), *The Communist International. Documents 1919-1943,* (3 vols.). Oxford University Press. London. 1956-1965.

Diary of Soviet-Indian Friendship, 1974, *Soviet Review,* No. 6, vol. XII, Feb. 6, 1975.

Dhar, D. P., Importance of Indo-Soviet Protocol Stressed, (interview). *Soviet Review,* vol. XI, Oct. 3, 1974.

Engels, F., Letter to N. F. Danielson, in Marx and Engels, *Ausgewaehlte Schriften* (2 vols), Dietz, Berlin, 1972, vol. II.

„ Letter to K. Kautsky, in Marx and Engels, *On Colonialism.* Foreign Languages Publishing House. Moscow, Second Impression (no date).

Ghosh, Litto, and Singh, Kartar (eds.), *Unity in Diversity. 50 Glorious Years of Soviet Socialist Republics,* ISCUS, New Delhi (no date).

(The) Great Debate, People's Publishing House, New Delhi, 1963 (documents on Sino-Soviet conflict).

Gromyko, A., *Policy of Realism* (speech at the 23rd. CPSU Congress, April 2, 1966), Novosti, (no date).

Hassan, Nurul, Unlimited Scope of Soviet-Indian Cooperation, (interview), *Soviet Review*, No. 28, vol. XI, June 20, 1974.

Joint Soviet Indian Declaration, *Soviet Review*, vol, X, No. 58, Dec. 6, 1973, New Delhi.

Khruschev, N. S. *On the Programme of the Communist Party of the Soviet Union.* Report delivered to the 22nd. Congress of the CPSU. October 18, 1961, Supplement to Soviet Land, New Delhi, No. 24, Dec. 1961.

„ *International Situation and Soviet Foreign Policy,* Soviet Land, USSR Embassy Publication, New Delhi, 1959.

„ *The Present International Situation and the Soviet Foreign Policy,* Soviet Land, USSR Embassy Publication, New Delhi, 1962.

„ *Speeches and Interviews on World Problems*, 1957, Foreign Languages Publishing House, Moscow, 1958.

„ *For Victory in Peaceful Competition with Capitalism*, Hutchinson & Co., London, 1960 (Speeches and interviews).

Kosygin, A., Report on the Directives for the Five-Year Economic Development Plan of the USSR for 1966-1970 (April 5, 1966), *23rd. Congress of the CPSU. 1966*, Novosti, Moscow, (no date).

„ Directives of the 24th. Congress of CPSU for the Five-Year Economic Development Plan of the USSR for 1971-1975. Report (April 6, 1971), *Information Bulletin*, No. 7-8 (188-189), vol. 9 (Special Issue), Peace and Socialism Publishers, Prague, 1971.

Kumaramangalam, J. G., Soviet Assistance for Coal Development in India, (interview), *Soviet Review*, No. 32, vol. XI, July 11, 1974.

Lenin, V. I., *Speeches at Congresses of the Communist International*, Progress, Moscow, 1972.

Lenin, *National Liberation Movement in the East*, Foreign Languages Publishing House, Moscow, 1957.

Leninist Line—International Solidarity, (a Soviet press review), Novosti, Moscow, 1972.

Malaviya, K. D., Massive Soviet Assistance to India's Oil Industry, (interview), *Soviet Review*, No. 4, vol. XIII, Jan. 23, 1975.

Marx, K., Draft replies to Vera Zasulich, in Marx and Engels, *Werke*, Dietz, Berlin, 1962, vol. XIX.

„ Brief an die Redaktion der 'Otetschestwennyje Sapiski', in Marx and Engels, *Werke*, Dietz, Berlin, 1962, vol. XIX.

„ Brief an V. I. Sassulitsch, in Marx and Engels, *Werke*, Dietz, Berlin, 1972 Vol. XIX.

„ and Engels, *Manifest der Kommunistischen Partei*, Dietz, Berlin, 1967.

„ *Notes on Indian History*, Foreign Languages Publishing House, Moscow, (no date).

„ and Engels, *On Colonialism*, (letters and articles), Foreign Languages Publishing House, Moscow (no date).

„ and Engels, Vorrede zur zweiten russischen Ausgabe des Manifests der Kommunistischen Partei, *Werke*, Dietz, Berlin, 1962. Vol. XIX.

Milestones of Soviet Foreign Policy, 1917-1967, Progress, Moscow, 1967 (treaty documents).

Mission of Friendship, Soviet Land Booklets, New Delhi 1973.

National Liberation Movement. Current Problems, Novosti, Moscow (*no date*).

Neue Zeit (weekly), Moscow.

The Newly Independent States : Problems of Development, Novosti, Moscow, 1972 (authors unknown).

Novoe Vremya, (weekly), Moscow.

Pai, T. A., Indo-Soviet Cooperation : An Inspiring Example, (interview), *Soviet Review*, No. 44, Vol. XII, Sept. 25, 1975.

„ Vital Role of Soviet Assistance in India's Industrialization, (interview), *Soviet Review*, No. 4, vol. XII, Jan. 23, 1975.

Popov, Y., *Marxist Political Economy as Applied to the African Scene*, Novosti, Moscow, 1973.

Simoniya, N., *Peking v. National Liberation*, Novosti, Moscow, 1970.

Soviet Military Review, Krasnaya Zvezda, Moscow.

Stalin, J. V., *Economic Problems of Socialism in the USSR*, Foreign Languages Press, Peking, 1972.

„ *Marxism and National Colonial Question*, Lawrence and Wishart, London, 1947.

„ *The Foundations of Leninism and Concerning Questions of Leninism*, National Book Agency, Calcutta, 1967 (Indian ed.)

C. Articles

Astafyev, G. V., and Fomichova, M. V., "The Maoist Distortion of Lenin's Theory of National Liberation Movement", in Sladkovsky, Kovalyov and Sidikhmenov (eds.), *Leninism and Modern China's Problems*, Progress, Moscow, 1972.

Balabushevich, V., and Dyakov. A., "Some Problems of the Contemporary History of India in Soviet Idoelogical Studies", in Litto Ghosh and K. Singh (eds.), *Unity in Diversity. 50 Glorious Years of Union of Soviet Socialist Republics*. ISCUS. New Delhi (no date).

Barooah, D. K., "India's Oil Industry : Bright Prospects of Development". *Soviet Review*, vol. XI, Aug. 15, 1974.

Bratchenko, B., "Cooperation Between Miners of the USSR and India", *Soviet Review*, No. 13, vol. XII, March 20, 1975.

Chand, Attar, "Indo-Soviet Cooperation in Agriculture", *Soviet Review*, No. 44, vol. XI, Sept. 26, 1974.

Derzhavin, A., "The Soviet Union and India : Cooperation for Peace", *International Affairs*, Moscow, No. 1, 1974.

Diakov, A. M. "Natsionalnoe Dvizhenie na Iuge Indii posle Vtoroi Mirovoi Voiny". *Uchenve Zaniski Instituta Vostokovedenin.* Part I. Nauka, Moscow, 1950.

Eiranov, L. I., "Soviet Assistance for India's Economic Development", *Soviet Review*, No. 43, vol. XI, Sept. 19, 1974.

Engels, F., "Soziales aus Russland", in Marx and Engels, *Ausgewachlte Schriften* (2 vols.), Dietz, Berlin, 1972, vol. II.

"Friendship and Cooperation'" *Soviet Review*, No. 8, vol. XII, Feb. 20, 1975 (author unknown).

"Further Soviet Assistance for India's Oil Industry", *Soviet Review*, No. 5, vol. XI, Jan. 31, 1974 (author unknown).

Gordopolov. V., "Soviet-Indian Cooperation in Coal Industry". *Soviet Review*, No. 15, vol. XI, March 28, 1974.

Grishin, I., "Soviet-Indian Trade Poised for Further Advance", *Soviet Review*, No. 7, vol. XI, Feb. 14, 1974.

„ and Petrov, A., "Growing Soviet-Indian Trade", *Soviet Review*, No, 28. vol. XI, June 20, 1974.

„ and Klochek, V., "Foreign Trade of USSR in 1973", *Soviet Review*, No. 27, vol. XI, June 13,1974.

Gryaznov, E., "India : Main Tendencies of Socio-Economic Development", *International Affairs*, Moscow, No. 12, 1971.

"India Seeks New Oil Technology from USSR", *Soviet Review*, No. 41, vol. XII, Sept. 4, 1975.

"India Fully Equipped to Meet Coal Target" *Soviet Review*, No. 5, Vol. XI, Jan. 31, 1974.

"Indian Design Engineers in USSR", *Soviet Review*, No. 38, vol. XI, Aug. 15, 1974.

Ivanov, E., "Soviet-Indian Cooperation in Complex Space Research", *Soviet Review*, No. 16, vol. XI, April 4, 1974.

Kapranov, I., "Example of Soviet Cooperation with Deve-

„ loping Countries", *Moscow News*, No. 34 (1285). Saturday, Aug. 23, 1975.

Kim, G. F., and Kaufman, A. S., "Certain Problems of National Llberation Revolutions in the Light of Lenin's Ideas", *Narody Azii i Afriki*, Moscow, No. 2, 1972.

Klochkovsky, L., "Peking and Indo-Soviet Cooperation", S*oviet Review*, No. 5, vol. XI. Jan. 31. 1974.

Kollontai, V., "Problems of Planning in the Third World", *National Liberation Movement* : *Current Problems*, Novosti, Moscow (no date).

Kotovsky, G. G., "The Implementation of Progressive Socio-Economic Transformations in the Developing Countries" in Ghosh, L., and Singh, K. (eds.), *Unity in Diversity. 50 Glorious Years of Union of Soviet Socialist Republics*, ISCUS, New Delhi, (no date).

Kumar, Balraj, "Knitwear Industry of India and Soviet Role in Its Development", *Soviet Review*, No. 17, vol. XII, April 10, 1975.

Lal, Pritam, "Soviet Cooperation in Calcutta Metro Project", *Soviet Review*, No. 43, vol. XI, Sept. 19, 1974.

Lenin, V. I., "What the 'Friends of the People' Are and How They Fight the Social-Democrats", *Collected Works*, Foreign Languages Publishing House, Moscow, 1960, vol. I.

„ "Two Tactics of Social-Democratic Revolution", *Selected Works*, Progress, Moscow, 1970, vol. I.

Leonidov, S , "Maoists in Asia", *Unity*, Monthly Review of the Soviet Press, APN, Moscow, No. 9, 1972.

Levkovsky, A., "Social Aspects of the Development of the State Sector in Newly-Independent Countries", *Soviet Review*, No. 27, vol. XI, June 13, 1974.

Li. Vi, "Social Movements in Developing Countries", *International Affairs*, Moscow, No. 6, 1974.

Manchkha, P., "In the Vanguard of Anti-Colonial Struggle," *Unity*. Monthly Review of the Soviet Press, APN, Moscow, No. 9, 1972.

Marx. K., "Zur Kritik der Politischen Oekonomie." in Marx and Engels, *Ausgewaehlte Werke*. Progress, Moscow, 1972.

"Mathura Refinery—Indicative of India's Industrial Advance." *Soviet Review*. No. 26, vol. XI, June 3, 1974 (author unknown).

Mayevsky, Victor, "Son of India", *Current Digest of the Soviet Press*. Columbus, Ohio, vol. XXI, No. 46, p. 15 (reprinted from *Pravda* Nov. 14, 1969).

Menshikov, M., "My Years in India," *Moscow News*. Moscow, No. 47 (1298), Nov. 22, 1975.

Mukhamedjanov, M. V., "Soviet-Indian Agricultural Cooperation", *Soviet Review*, No. 11, vol. XI, March 7, 1974.

Narain, Shankar, "Significant Provisions of 1974 Indo-Soviet Trade Protocol", *Soviet Review*. Nov. 5, vol. XI, Jan. 21, 1974.

„ "Progress of Bhilai and Bokaro," *Soviet Review*, No. 28, vol. XI, June 13, 1974.

„ "Progress of Korba Aluminium Project," *Soviet Review*, No. 22, vol. XI, May 9, 1974.

„ "Korba Aluminium Plant : A Second Phase of Development," *Soviet Review*, No. 34, vol. XII, July 24, 1975.

„ "IDPL—A Wise Insurance that paid," *Soviet Review*, No. 33, vol. XI, July 18, 1974.

„ "Significant Advance in Indo-Soviet Scientific Cooperation," *Soviet Review*, Nos. 10-11, vol. XII, March 6, 1975.

„ "Spare Parts for Soviet Tractors in India", *Soviet Review*, No. 18, vol. XII, April 17, 1975.

„ "Soviet Assistance for India's Shipping Development," *Soviet Review*, No. 28, vol. XI, June 20, 1974.

Pavlov, V. I., "Theory and Practice of Planning in Third-World Countries," *Soviet Review*, No. 14, vol. XII, March 27, 1975.

Pegov, N. M., "In the Interests of Peace and Progress," in J. Bibhakar (ed.), *A Model Relationship—25 Years of Indo-Soviet Diplomatic Ties*. Punjabi Publishers, New Delhi, 1972.

Petrov. S., "Soviet Assistance for Mineral Prospecting in Central India, "*Soviet Review*, Nos. 36-37, vol. XI, Aug. 8, 1974.

Popov, V., "Soviet Planning Experience and Third World Countries", *Soviet Review*, No. 4, vol. XII, Jan. 23, 1975.

Powik, Gerhard, "Objective and Subjective Factors in the Current World Revolutionary Process (II)," *German Foreign Policy*, Institute of International Relations, Berlin, vol. X, No. 4, 1971.

Rao, U. R., "Soviet-Indian Collaboration in Space Studies," *Soviet Review*, No. 57, vol. XI, Dec. 12, 1974.

Sanakoyev, S., "A New Phase in Soviet-Indian Relations," *International Affairs*, Moscow, No. 2, 1974.

Savinov, V., "Der Neunte Fuenfjahrplan der UdSSR," *Neue Zeit*, Moscow, No. 49, Dec. 1971.

Sharma, R. K., "Indo-Soviet Economic Cooperation : New, Higher Phase," *Soviet Review*, Nos. 36-37, vol. XI, Aug. 8, 1974.

Shashin, V. D., "Soviet-Indian Cooperation in Oil Industry", *Soviet Review*, No. 38, vol. XI, Aug. 15, 1974.

,, "Expanding Cooperation Between Soviet and Indian Oil Industries", *Soviet Review*, No. 12, vol. XII, March 13, 1975.

,, "Prospects of Oil Industry in India," *Soviet Review*, No. 57, vo. XI, Dec. 12, 1974.

Shumsky, V., and Kachanov, V., "Social Democracy at the International Cross-roads," *International Affairs*, Moscow, No. 12, Dec. 1971.

Shvarts, I., "MECON Makes Giant Strides Forward," *Soviet Review*, Nos. 36-37, vol. XI, Aug. 8, 1974.

Skachkov, Semyon, "Economic Cooperation of the USSR with the Developing Countries", *Socialism, Theory and Practice*, Novosti, Moscow, No. 2, Feb., 1974.

"Soviet-Indian Cooperation in the Development of Coal Production", *Soviet Review*, No. 26, vol. XI, June 3, 1974 (author unknown).

"Soviet Specialists on the Indian Sputnik", *Soviet Review*, No. 16, vol. X, March 31, 1973 (author unknown).

Srivastava, T. N., "Indo-Soviet Cooperation in Science and Technology", *Soviet Review*, No. 33, vol. XI, July 18, 1974.

Timofeyev, P., "An Important Form of Soviet Assistance to the Developing Countries," *Soviet Review*, No. 27 vol. XI, June 13, 1974.

Tiulpanov, S. I., and Weiz, G. M., "Problems of India's State Enterprises", *Narody Azii i Afriki*, Moscow No. 3, 1970.

Tkachenko, V., "Soviet-Indian Cooperation in Science and Technology", *Soviet Review*, No. 43, vol. XII. Sept. 18, 1975.

Trubnikov, V., "Non-Capitalist Path: From Theory to Practice", *Soviet Review*, No. 43, vol. XI, Sept. 19, 1974.

Tyagunenko, V., "World Socialism and National Liberation Revolutions", *Soviet Military Review*, Krasnaya Zvezda, Moscow, No. 10, Oct. 1973.

Ulyanovsky, R., "Socio-Economic Problems of the Newly Free Countries", *Unity*, Monthly Review of the Soviet Press, APN, Moscow, No. 9, 1972.

Volkov, M., "Contemporary Productive Forces and Peculiarities of Capitalism in the Third World", *Soviet Review*, No. 57, vol. XI, Dec. 12, 1974.

Yelutin, V. P. "Soviet-Indian Cooperation in Education", *Soviet Review*, No. 38, vol. XI, Aug. 15, 1974.

Zevin, I. Z., "Socialist Economic Integration and Cooperation with Third World Countries," *Narody Azii i Afriki*, Moscow, No. 2, 1972.

II. Non-Communist Sources

A. Books

Aspaturian, Vernon V., *Process and Power in Soviet Foreign Policy*, Boston, Little, Brown, 1971.

Bandyopadhyaya, J., *Indian Nationalism versus International Communism*, Firma K. L. Mukhopadhyay, Calcutta, 1966.

Barnds, W. J., *India, Pakistan and the Great Powers*, Praeger, New York, 1972.

Beloff, Max, *The Foreign Policy of Saviet Russia, 1929-1941*, London. vol. I (1947), vol. II, (1949).

Bhattacharya, D., *India's Five-Year Plans, 1951-61*, Udayan Granthagar, Calcutta, 1968.

Bibhakar, Jagdish, *A Model Relationship, 25 Years of Indo-Soviet Diplomatic Ties*, Punjabi Publishers, New Delhi, 1972.

Birke, Ernst, and Neumann, Rudolf (eds.), *Die Sowietisieurung Ost-Mitteleuropas*, Alfred Metzner Verlag, Frankfurt/M., Berlin, 1959.

Bowles, Chester, *Promises to Keep*, Harper and Row, New York, 1971.

Brecher, Michael, *The New States of Asia : A Political Analysis*, Oxford University Press, London, 1963.

Brown, W. N., *The US and India and Pakistan*, Cambridge, Harvard University Press, 1963.

Brzezinski, Z. K., *Ideology and Power in Soviet Politics*, Praeger, New York, 1962.

„ and Friedrich, Carl J., *Totalitarian Dictatorship and Autocracy*, The Times of India Press, Bombay, 1969 (Indian ed.).

„ and Huntington, Samuel P., *Political Power : USA, USSR*, New York, Viking, 1964.

Bunge, Mario, *Scientific Research,* (vol. II), Springer Verlag, New York 1967.

Carr, E. H., *History of Soviet Russia,* of which those volumes perused are as follows :

„ *The Bolshevik Revolution 1917-23*, vols. I, II and III Pelican, Harmondsworth, 1966 ;

„ *The Interregnum 1923-24*, Pelican, Harmondsworth, 1969 ;

„ *Socialism in One Country, 1924-1926*, Pelican, Harmondsworth, vols. I and II (1970), vol. III (1972).

Chakravarti, P. C., *India's China Policy*, Bloomington, Indiana University Press, 1962.

Charlesworth, James C., (ed.), *Contemporary Political Analysis*, The Free Press, New York, 1967.

Chopra, Pran. *Before and After the Indo-Soviet Treaty*, S. Chand & Co., New Delhi (no date).

Dallin, David J., *Soviet Foreign Policy After Stalin*, J. B. Lippincott Co., Philadelphia, 1961.

Davids, Jules, *America and the World of Our Time. United States Diplomacy in the Twentieth Century*, Random House, New York, 1970.

Deutscher, Issac, *Stalin*, Penguin, Harmondsworth, 1968.
   The Prophet Armed, Trotsky, 1879-1921 vol. I.
,,   *The Prophet Unarmed, Trotsky : 1921-1929*, vol. II.
,,   *The Prophet Outcast, Trotsky : 1929-1940*, vol. III, Vintage, New York, 1965.

Dickson, Paul, *Think Tanks*, New York, Atheneum, 1972.

Donaldson, Robert H., *Soviet Policy Toward India : Ideology and Strategy*, Harvard University Press, Cambridge, Massachusetts, 1974.

Drieberg, Trevor, Malik, H., and Joshi, D. K., *Towards Close Indo-Soviet Cooperation*, Vikas, Delhi, 1974.

Druhe, David N., *Soviet Russia and Indian Communism*, Bookman Associates, New York, 1959.

Edwardes, Michael, *Nehru. A Political Biography*, Praeger, New York, 1971.

Edwards, H. Sutherland, *Russian Projects against India. From the Czar Peter to General Skobeleff*, Remington & Co. Publishers, London 1885.

Emerson, Rupert, *From Empire to Nation*, Scientific Book Agency, Calcutta, 1970 (Indian ed.).

Farrell, R. Barry (ed.), *Approaches to Comparative and International Politics*. Northwestern University Press, Evanston, 1966.

Fischer, Louis. *The Soviets in World Affairs. 1917-1929*. (2 vols.), Princeton, N. J., Princeton University Press. 1951.

Fleron, Frederic J., Jr. (ed.), *Communist Studies and the*

,,   *Social Sciences* : *Essays on Methodology and Empirical Theory.* Rand McNally, Chicago, 1969.

,,   and Hoffmann, Erik P. (eds.), *The Conduct of Soviet Foreign Policy,* Aldine, Chicago, 1971.

Gelman, H., *Communist Strategies in Asia.* Praeger, New York, 1962.

Garthoff, Raymond L., *Soviet Military Policy* : *A Historical Analysis.* Praeger, New York, 1966.

Halperin, Morton H., *Defense Strategies for the Seventies,* Little, Brown & Co., Boston, 1971.

Haxthausen, von. *The Russian Empire* : *Its People, Institutions and Resources.* (trans.), Chapman & Hall London, 1856, vol. I.

Hoffmann, Stanley H., *Contemporary Theory in International Relations.* Prentice-Hall of India, New Delhi, 1964 (Indian ed.).

Imam, Zafar, *Colonialism in East-West Relations. A Study of Soviet Policy Towards India and Anglo-Soviet Relations 1917-1947.* Eastman Publication, New Delhi, 1969.

Jacobson, Harold K. (ed.), *America's Foreign Policy,* Random House, New York, 1965.

Jain, J. P., *Soviet Policy Towards Pakistan and Bangla Desh,* Radiant Publishers, New Delhi, 1974.

Kanet, Roger E. (ed.), *The Behavioural Revolution and Communist Studies,* The Free Press, New York, 1971.

Kaplan, Morton, *System and Process in International Politics,* John Wiley and Sons, Inc., New York, 1957.

,,   *Macropolitics,* Aldine, Chicago, 1969.

Kapur, Harish, *The Soviet Union and the Emerging Nations. A Case Study of Soviet Policy Towards India,* Michael Joseph Ltd., London, 1972.

,,   *The Embattled Triangle. Moscow-Peking-New Delhi,* Abhinav Publications, New Delhi, 1973.

Kaushik, D., *Soviet Relations with India and Pakistan,* Vikas, Delhi, 1971.

Kautsky, John H., *The Political Consequences of Modernization,* John Wiley & Sons, Inc., New York, 1972.

,, *Moscow and the CPI* : *A Study in the Postwar Evolution of International Communist Strategy*, New York, Wiley & Sons, 1956.

Keizer, Willem, *The Soviet Quest for Economic Rationality, 1953-1968*, Rotterdam University Press, Rotterdam, 1971.

Kennedy, Malcolm, *A History of Communism in East Asia*, Praeger, New York, 1957.

Kintner, W. R., and Pfaltzgraff, R. L. (eds.), *SALT* : *Implications far Arms Control in the 1970's*, Pittsburgh, University of Pittsburgh Press, 1973.

Kissinger, Henry A((ed.), *Problems of National Strategy* : *A Book of Readings*. Praeger, New York, 1965.

,, *American Foreign Policy*, A. H. Wheeler & Co., Allahabad, 1971 (Indian ed.).

Knorr, Klaus, and Rosenau, James N. (eds.), *Contending Approaches to International Politics*, Princeton, N. J., Princeton University Press, 1969.

Kulkarni, Maya, *Indo-Soviet Political Relations (Since the Bandung Conference of 1955)*. Vora & Co., Bombay, 1968.

Leonhard, W., *Child of the Revolution*, Gateway, Chicago, 1967.

Littauer, R., and Uphoff, N. (eds.), *The Air War in Indo-China*, Beacon Press, Boston, 1972.

Lowenthal, R. (ed.), *Issues in the Future of Asia* : *Communist and non-Communist Alternatives*, New York, Praeger, 1969.

Marcuse, Herbert, *Soviet Marxism. A Critical Analysis*, Pelican, London, 1971.

McKenzie, K. E., *Comintern and World Revolution. 1928-1943*. Columbia University Press, New York, 1964.

McLane, Charles B., *Soviet-Asian Relations*, London, Central Asian Research Centre, 1973.

Menon, K. P. S., *The Indo-Soviet Treaty. Setting and Sequel*, Vikas, Delhi, 1971.

,, *The Flying Troika*, Oxford University Press, London, 1973.

,, *India and the Cold War*, Bhavan's Book University, Bombay, 1966.

Moore, Barrington Jr., *Soviet Politics—The Dilemma of Power*, Harvard University Press, Cambridge, Massachusetts, 1950.

Morgenthau, Hans J., *Politics among Nations*. Scientific Book Agency, Calcutta, 1966 (Indian ed.).

Myrdal, Gunnar, *Asian Drama* : *An Inquiry into the Poverty of Nations*. Pelican, 1968 (3 vols.).

Naik, J. A., *Soviet Policy Towards India. From Stalin to Brezhnev*, Vikas, Delhi, 1970.

,, *India, Russia, China and Bangla Desh*, S. Chand & Co., New Delhi, 1972.

Newhouse, John, *Cold Dawn. The Story of Salt*, Holt, Rinehart & Winston, New York, 1973.

Nollau, Gunther, *International Communism and World Revolution*, London, Hollis & Carter, 1961.

Nurske, Ragnar, *Problems of Capital Formation in Underdeveloped Areas*, New York. Oxford University Press, 1953.

Osgood, Robert E., et al., *Retreat From Empire*, Johns Hopkins University Press, Baltimore and London, 1973.

Overstreet, Gene D., and Windmiller, Marshall, *Communism in India*, University of California Press. Berkeley and Los Angeles, 1959.

Owen Henry (ed.), *The Next Phase in Foreign Policy*, The Brookings Institution, Washington, D. C., 1973.

Palmer, Norman D., *South Asia and US Policy*, Boston, Houghton Mifflin, 1966.

Parsons, Talcott, *The Social System*, Amerind Publishing Co., New Delhi, 1972 (Indian ed.).

Ploss, Sidney I. (ed.), *The Soviet Political Process. Aims, Techniques and Examples of Analysis*, Gim & Co., Massachusetts, 1971.

Ray, Hemen, *Indo-Soviet Relations. 1955-1971*, Jaico, Bombay, 1973.

Rosenau, James N., *Linkage Politics*, The Free Press, New York, 1969.

(Ed.), *International Politics and Foreign Policy*. The Free Press, New York, 1969 (revised ed.).

Rothermund, Dietmar, *Indian und die Sowietunion*. Arbeitsgemeinschaft fuer Osteuropaforschung, Boehlau Verlag, Tuebingen, 1968.

Roy, Ajit, *Planning in India : Achievements and Problems*, National, Calcutta, 1965.

Sager, P., *Moscow's Hand in India*, Bombay, Lalvani Publishing House, 1967.

Sardesai, S. G., *India and the Russian Revolution*, New Age, New Delhi, 1967.

Sawyer, C. A., *Communist Trade with Developing Countries. 1955-65*, Praeger, New York, 1966.

Scalapino, Robert A. (ed.), *The Communist Revolution in Asia*, Englewood Cliffs, N. J., Prentice-Hall, 1969.

Sen Gupta, B., *The Fulcrum of Asia*, Pegasus, New York, 1970.

Sharma, Dev, *Tashkent. A Study in Foreign Relations with Documents*, Gandhian Institute of Studies, Varanasi, and Central Book Depot, Allahabad (Joint Publishers), 1966.

Shulman, Marshall D., *Beyond the Cold War*, Yale University Press, New Haven and London, 1966.

Smith III, Mark E., and Johns Jr., Claude (eds.), *American Defense Policy*, Johns Hopkins, Baltimore. 1968.

Stein, Arthur, *India and the Soviet Union, The Nehru Era*, University of Chicago Press, Chicago and London, 1969.

Tansky, Leo, *US and USSR Aid to Developing Countries. A Comparative Study of India, Turkey, and the UAR*, Praeger, New York, 1967.

Tanter, Raymond, and Ullman, Richard H., *Theory and Policy in International Relations*, Princeton, N. J., Princeton University Press, 1972.

Tarschys, Daniel, *Beyond the State*. The Swedish Institute of International Affairs, Stockholm, 1971.

Thornton, T, P. (ed.), *The Third World in Soviet Perspective*, Princeton, N. J., Princeton University Press, 1964.

Treadgold, Donald W. (ed.), *Soviet and Chinese Communism*, University of Washington, Washington, 1967.
Triska, Jan F., and Finley, David D., *Soviet Foreign Policy*, Macmillan, Toronto, 1969.
Ulam, Adam B., *Expansion and Coexistence*, Secker & Warburg, London, 1968.
Wasby, Stephen L., *Political Science. The Discipline and its Dimensions*. Scientific Book Agency, Calcutta, 1970. (Indian ed.).
Welch, William, *American Images of Soviet Foreign Policy*, New Haven and London, Yale University Press, 1970.
Wilber, Charles K., *The Soviet Model and Underdeveloped Countries*. The University of North Carolina Press, Chapel Hill, 1969.
Wolfe, Thomas W., *Soviet Strategy at the Crossroads*, Rand Corporation, Cambridge, Massachusetts, 1964.
Zagoria, Donald S., *The Sino-Soviet Conflict. 1956-1961*, Princeton, N. J., Princeton University Press, 1962.
Zimmerman, William, *Soviet Perspectives on International Relations, 1956-1967*, Princeton, N. J., Princeton University Press, 1969.

B. Articles, Reports and Periodicals

Aspaturian, Vernon V., "Moscow's Options in a Changing World", *Problems of Communism*, vol. 21, July-August 1972.

,, "Internal Politics and Foreign Policy in the Soviet System", in R. Barry Farrell (ed.), *Approaches to Comparative and International Politics*, Northwestern University Press, Evanston, 1966.

Badgley, John H., "The American Territorial Presence in Asia", in James C. Charlesworth (ed.), *A New American Posture Toward Asia. The Annals* of the American Academy of Political and Social Science, Philadelphia, vol. 390, July 1970.

Baritz Joseph J., "The Soviet Strategy of Flexible Res-

,, ponse", *Bulletin*, Institut zur Erforschung der UdSSR, Munich, vol. 16, No. 4, April 1969.

Barnds, William J., "Moscow and South Asia", *Problems of Communism*, USIA, Washington, D. C., vol. 21, May-June 1972.

Barnett, A. Doak, "The New Multipolar Balance in East Asia : Implications for United States Policy", in J. Charlesworth (ed). *A New American Posture Toward Asia. The Annals* of the American Academy of Political and Social Science, Philadelphia, vol. 390, July 1970.

Bergson, Abram, "Toward a new Growth Model", *Problems of Communism*, March-April 1973, vol. XXII, No. 2.

Bonavia, David, "The Soviet Economy", *Statesman*, May 29, 1972, Calcutta (reprinted from the Times, London).

Brzezinski, Z. K., "The Politics of Underdevelopment", in Harold K. Jocobson (ed.), *America's Foreign Policy*, Random House, New York, 1965.

,, "US-Soviet Relations", in Henry Owen (ed.), *The Next Phase* in Foreign Policy. The Brookings Institution, Washington, D. C., 1973.

Campbell, John C., "The Communist Powers and the Middle East : Moscow's Purposes", *Problems of Communism*, No. 5, vol. 21, Sept.-October 1972.

Charlesworth, James C. (ed.), *A New American Posture Toward Asia. The Annals of the American of Political and Social Science*, Philadelphia, vol. 390, July 1970.

Cimbala, Stephen J., "New Myths and Old Realities : Defense and Its Critics", *World Politics*, Princeton, N. J., vol. XXIV, No. 1, October 1971.

Clough, Ralph N., "East Asia", in Henry Owen (ed.), *The Next Phase in Foreign Policy*, The Brookings Institution, Washington, D. C., 1973.

Coffey, J. I., "Soviet ABM Policy : The Implications for the West", *International Affairs*, Chatham House, London, vol. 45, No. 2, April 1969.

Congress, U. S., Joint Economic Committee, *Hearings together with Compilations of Studies on Dimensions of Soviet Economic Power*, 87th. Congress, 2nd. Session, December 1962, Washington, D. C., U. S. Government Printing Office (U.S : G.P.O.) 1966.

„ *New Directions in the Soviet Economy*, 89th. Congress, 2nd. Session, U.S.G.P.O., 1966.

Daniels, Robert V., "Doctrine and Foreign Policy", in Hoffmann and Fleron, Jr., (ed.), *The Conduct of Soviet Foreign Policy*, Aldine, Chicago, 1971.

Farrell, R. Barry, "Foreign Policies of Open and Closed Political Societies", *Approaches to Comparative and International Politics*, (edited by himself), Northwestern, Evanston, 1966.

Fleron, Frederic J., Jr., "Soviet Area Studies and the Social Sciences : Some Methodological Problems in Communist Studies", in *Communist Studies and the Social Sciences : Essays on Methodology aud Empirical Theory*, (edited by himself), Rand McNally, Chicago, 1969.

Galtung, Johan, "The Social Sciences. An Essay on Polarization and Integration", in Knorr, Klaus and Rosenau, James (eds.), *Contending Approaches to International Politics*, Princeton, N. J., Princeton University Press, 1969.

Gasteyger, Curt, "Moscow and the Mediterranean", *Foreign Affairs*, New York, vol. 46, No. 4, July 1968.

Gati, Charles, "History, Social Science, and the Study of Foreign Policy", in Hoffmann and Fleron, Jr. (eds.), *The Conduct of Soviet Foreign Policy*, Aldine, Chicago, 1971.

Ghatate, N. M. (ed.), *Indo-Soviet Treaty, Reactions and Reflections*, Deendayal Research Institute, New Delhi, 1972.

Gupta, K., "Indo-Soviet Relations in Retrospect". *Afro-Asian and World Affairs*, New Delhi, vol. 2, No, 3, 1965.

Gupta, Sisir, "India and the Soviet Union", *Current History*, Philadelphia, March 1963.

Halperin, Morton, H., "The Role of Force in the Nuclear Age", in Mark E. Smith III and Claude Johns, Jr., (eds.), *American Defense Policy*, Johns Hopkins, Baltimore, 1968.

Heren, Louis, "Russia Reaps the harvest of Marxist Mistakes", *Statesman*, December 17, 1972 (reprinted from *The Times*, London).

Howe, Russell Warren, "Moves on Rhodesia", *Statesman*, July 16, 1973.

Hudson, G. F., Lowenthal and Macfarquhar, *The Sino-Soviet Dispute*, London, The Eastern Press, 1961 (documents).

Hunt, R. N. Carew, "Importance of Doctrine", in Hoffmann and Fleron, Jr. (eds.), *The Conduct of Soviet Foreign Policy*, Aldine, Chicago, 1971.

India's Trade with East Europe—A Study by the Indian Institute of Foreign Trade, Directorate of Commercial Publicity, Ministry of Commerce, New Delhi, 1966.

Jervis, Robert, "The Costs of the Quantitative Study of International Relations", in Knorr and Rosenau (eds.), *Contending Approaches to International Politics*, Princeton, N. J., Princeton University Press, 1969.

Kahn, Hermann, "Alternative National Strategies", in Mark E. Smith III and Claude Johns, Jr. (eds), *American Defense Policy*, Johns Hopkins, Baltimore, 1968.

Kiva, A., views discussed, *USSR and the Third World*. London. vol. I, No. 3, 15 Feb-21 March 1971.

Laird, Melvin, report to the Senate on Soviet military activities, *Statesman*, 16 Feb., 1972.

Lambeth, Benjamin S., "Moscow and the Missile Race", *Current History*, vol. 61, No. 362, Oct. 1971.

Lowenthal, Richard, "The Logic of One-Party Rule" and "A Difference in Kind", in Hoffmann and Fleron, Jr., (eds.), *The Conduct of Soviet Foreign Policy*, Aldine, Chicago, 1971.

Mackintosh, Malcolm, "Soviet Strategic Policy", *The World Today*, London, vol. 26, No. 7, July 1970.

Meyers, J. B., "Soviet Airmobility", *US Army Aviation Digest*, Sept. 1971.

(The) Military Balance, 1971-72 and 1972-73, International Institute for Strategic Studies, London.

Morison, David, "USSR and Third World" (first instalment), *Mizan*, London, vol. XII, No. 1.

Morris, Sam W., "The Soviet-US Grain Deal—Its Global Impact", *The American Reporter*, New Delhi, Nov. 1, 1972, vol. XXII, No. 22.

Nixon, R., "State of the Union", *Statesman*, Calcutta, 21 January, 1972.

Osgood, Robert E., "The Theory of Limited War", in Mark E. Smith III and Claude Johns, Jr. (eds.), *American Defense Policy*, Johns Hopkins, Baltimore, 1968.

Papanek, Gustav, interview, *Span*, USIS, New Delhi, December 1975.

Prasad, Bimal, *Indo-Soviet Relations. 1947-1972. A Documentary Study*. Allied, Bombay, 1973.

Robinson, Thomas W., "Soviet Policy in East Asia", *Problems of Communism*, Nov-Dec. 1973, vol. 23, No. 6.

Readers' Digest, Public sector supplement, Sept. 1974, Bombay.

Scalapino, Robert A., "Patterns of Asian Communism", *Problems of Communism*, Jan-April 1971, vol. XX, Nos. 1-2 (Special issue with focus on Asia)

Schwelien, Joachim "ABM Accord in Moscow and ULMS Program in the USA", *Aussenpolitik*, vol. 23, 3/72, Hamburg (English ed.).

Senate, U. S., 93rd. Congress, 1st. Session, *Hearings* before the Committee on Foreign Relations, Washington, D. C., U S Govt. Printing Office, 1973, Part I.

Sen Gupta, B., "Moscow and Bangladesh", *Problems of Communism*, March-April 1975, vol. XXIV, No. 2.

Sharp, Samuel S., "National Interest : Key to Soviet Politics", in Hoffmann and Fleron, Jr., (eds.) *The Conduct of Soviet Foreign Policy*, Aldine, Chicago, 1971·

,, "The Soviet Economy", *Statesman*, Aug. 6, 1973 (reprinted from *The Economist*, London).

(The) Strategic Survey, 1971, IISS, London.

Talbot, Phillips, "The American Posture Toward India and Pakistan", in Charlesworth (ed.), *A New American Posture Toward Asia, The Annals* of the American Academy of Political and Social Science, Philadelphia, vol. 390, July 1970.

"UAR and USSR : The Dialogue on Socialism", *Mizan*, London, vol. X, No. 1, Jan-Feb 1968 (author unknown).

Ulam, Adam B., "Soviet Ideology and Soviet Foreign Policy", in Hoffmann and Fleron, Jr. (eds.), *The Conduct of Soviet Foreign Policy*, Aldine, Chicago, 1971.

UNCTAD, *Problems Arising in Trade Relations between Countries having Different Economic and Social Systems : A Case Study Prepared by UNCTAD Secretariat on Trade and Economic Relations between India and the Socialist Countries of Eastern Europe*, Geneva, July 1967.

Unna, Warren W., "The U. S. Military—A Steady Growth of Elitism", *Statesman*, Oct. 15, 1972.

Vaidyanath, R., "Recent Trends in Soviet Policies Towards India and Pakistan", *International Studies*, Bombay, vol. VII, No. 3, January 1966.

Wall, Patrick, "A Threat to Europe's Supply Routes" *Statesman*, 19 Feb. 1973.

Welch, William, and Triska, Jan F. "Soviet Foreign Policy Studies and Foreign Policy Models", *World Politics*, vol. 23, No. 4, July 1971.

Wolfe, Thomas W., "Shifts in Soviet Strategic Thought", *Foreign Affairs*, New York, vol. 42, No. 3, April 1964.

,, "The Soviet Military Since Khruschev", Current History, vol. 57, No. 338, Oct. 1969.

World Bank study, 1975, *Amrita Bazar Patrika*, Calcutta, Aug. 11, 1975.

Wriggins, W. Howard, "*The Presence in Southern Asia of*

„ *Outside Powers*", in Charlesworth (ed.). *A New American Posture Towards Asia. The Annals* of the American Academy of Political and Social Science, vol. 390, July 1970.

Wright, A. W., "Systemic Ills in Soviet Agriculture", *Problems of Communism*, Jan-Feb 1975, vol. XXIV, No. 1.

Young, Oran R., "The Perils of Odysseus : On Constructing Theories of International Relations", in R. Tanter and R. Ullman (eds.), *Theory and Policy in International Relations*. Princeton, N. J., Princeton University Press, 1972.

Zagoria, Donald S., "Russia, China, and the New States", in Donald W. Treadgold (ed.), *Soviet and Chinese Communism*, University of Washington, 1967.

Zodpo, Ciro, "Soviet Ships in the Mediterranean and the US-Soviet Confrontation in the Middle East", *Orbis*. Philadelphia, Spring, 1970, vol. 14, No. 1.

INDEX

Agriculture 153-55
Balabushevich, V. V., 30, 112 fn.
Barooah, D. K. 143-44, 161 fn., 169
Bhilai 138-39
Bokaro 139-41
Bratchenko, B. 147, 161 fn.
Brezhnev, Leonid I., 46-48, 90 fn., 84, 109, 128, 171
Brzezinski, Zbigniew K., 3-5, 16, 18, 32, 39, 86
Central Dynamics, 8-54, 75-86, 93, 107, 164
—and India, 19-32
—and US response, 33-39
Chattopadhyaya, D. P., 135
China
—national liberation, 39-45, 68, 72, 73, 75-80
—Soviet differences with, 39-45
Cominform, 30
Comintern
—Second Congress, 22
—Third Congress, 22
—Fourth Congress, 23
—Fifth Congress, 24
—Sixth Congress, 26
—Seventh Congress, 28
—identity with Soviet policy, 19-20
Deoli Thesis, 29
Dyakov, A.. 30, 112 fn.
Eiranov, L. I. 161 fn.
Energy, 148-49
Expretation, 11
Farakka 156
Feedback, 75-80
Galtung, Johann, 7-8
Grishin, Ivan, 132, 159 fn.
Gromyko, A., 75
Gryaznov, E., 112 fn., 129 fn.

Hassan, Nurul 151
Haxthausen, Baron von, 93-94
Indian authors, 6
Indira Gandhi's government, see *Soviet*
Indo-Soviet trade figures, 135
Khan, Hermann, 67, 68
Khrushchev, Nikita S., 41, 45, 55, 56, 67, 75, 76, 78, 80, 83, 84 99, 111 fn.
Kissinger, Henry A., 15, 19, 66, 74
Klochkovsky, L , 156. fn., 163 fn.
Kollontai V., 130 fn.
Korba (aluminium project), 141-42
Krasin, Yuri, 69-71
Kun, Bela, 71
Kuusinen, Otto, 26, 27
Lenin, V. I, 17, 19, 20, 22, 40, 70, 97, 98, 101
Levkovsky, A., 118, 129 fn,
Malaviya, K. D., 160 fn., 161 fn.
Malenkov, G. 40, 75
MAMC (mining and allied machinery), 142
Marx, Karl, and Engels, F.
—on non-capitalist path, 93-7
—on India, 20-21, 166
Mayevsky, V., 113 fn.
Menshihov, M., 174 fn.
Mikhailovsky letter, 94-96
Ming, Wang, 28
Morgenthau, Hans J., 3, 10, 11, 58
Myrdal, Gunnar, 123
Narodniks, 94, 96
National Democracy, 92, **100**,105
Nodal Restraint 9-11, 55-86, 93, 107
Oil (and gas), 143
Pai, T. A., 160 fn . 161 fn.
Papanek, Gustav, 167
Pavlov, V. see *Ulyanovsky*, and,130 fn.

INDEX

Pegov, N. M., 107
Pharmaceuticals, 142-43
Piao, Lin, 42
Plekhanov, G., 97
Popov, V., 130 fn.
Rao. U. R., 162 fn.
Refineries, 145-46
Roy, M. N., 22, 23, 25, 26, 40, 81, 86 101
Science, 149-51
Shashin, V. D., 143-44, 161 fn.
Shirokov, G.K., 112 fn., 114, 126, 129 fn., 130 fn.
Skachkov, Semyon, 112 fn.
Space, 152-53
Stalin, J. V., 17, 19, 20, 24, 25, 31, 40, 73, 80, 81, 99
—ideology 2-6, 26, 27, 30, 31, 41-42, 80-82, 101, 167
—strategic doctrine, 65-75
—economy, 45-48
—strategic arms, 55-59
—conventional navy, 59-65
—The Mediterranean, 60 62
—The Indian Ocean, 62-65
—military aid to India, 157-58
—production collaboration with India, 127-28
Soviet Views On

—Indira Gandhi's government, 45, 102-04, 108-10, 168-71
—Third World Socialism, 105 06, 118-19
—national liberation war, 71-73, 86
—protectionism, 120-21
—nationalization of foreign capital, 121-22
—planning in Third World, 122-23
—(for Soviet aid to India, see under sectoral headings)
Tyagunenko, V., 112 fn.
Troyanovsky, K. M., 21
Trubnikov, V., 102
Ulyanovsky, R., 102, 117-19, 129 fn., 130 fn., 174 fn.
USA
—policy towards Asia, 33-39
—leadership, 37
—military power, 55-65
Volkov, M., 129 fn.
Welch, William, 173 fn.
Yelutin, V.P., 162 fn.
Zagoria, Donald S., 35, 72, 78, 79 111 fn.
Zasulich, Vera, 95
Zevin, I. Z, 130 fn.
Zhdanov, A., 30
Zinoviev, G., 22, 23

Augsburg College
George Sverdrup Library
Minneapolis, Minnesota 55454